D1649377

THE ROUTLEDGE ATLAS OF
THE FIRST WORLD WAR

"Every map, with its accompanying notes, is almost a chapter of history in itself"
Michael Thomas, *Times Educational Supplement*
"...presents a mass of familiar and far less familiar information simply and tellingly"
Economist

From its origins to its terrible legacy, the tortuous and bloody course of the Great War is vividly set out in a series of 164 fascinating maps. Together the maps form a comprehensive and compelling picture of the war that shattered Europe, and illustrates its military, social, political and economic aspects. Beginning with the tensions that already existed, the atlas covers:

- **The Early Months of the War** – from the fall of Belgium to the fierce fighting at Ypres and Tannenberg
- **The Developing War in Europe** – from Gallipoli to the horrors of the Somme and Verdun
- **Life at the Front** – from living underground, the trench system and the mud of Passchendaele to the war graves
- **War in the Air and at Sea** – from the Zeppelin raids to the battles in the North Sea, shipping losses and the Atlantic convoys
- **War, Economics and Industry** – from gold gains and losses to food supplies and munitions production
- **Technology and the New Horrors** – from phosgene gas attacks to submarines, tanks and mines
- **The Home Fronts** – from German food riots to the air defence of Britain, the Russian Revolution and the collapse of Austria-Hungary
- **Diplomacy and Strategy** – from the conflicting aims of all the powers to the Versailles Treaty and reparations
- **The Aftermath** – from war debts and war deaths to the new map of Europe

Sir Martin Gilbert is one of the leading historians of his generation. An Honorary Fellow of Merton College, Oxford, he is the official biographer of Churchill as well as the author of *The First World War* UK (HarperCollins); USA (Henry Holt) and *The Second World War* UK (Weidenfeld); USA (Holt). http://www.martingilbert.com

BOOKS BY MARTIN GILBERT

The Routledge Atlas of American History
The Routledge Atlas of the Arab–Israeli Conflict
The Routledge Atlas of British History
The Routledge Atlas of the First World War
The Routledge Atlas of the Holocaust
The Routledge Atlas of Jewish History
The Routledge Atlas of Russian History

Recent History Atlas, 1860–1960
Jerusalem Illustrated History Atlas
Children's Illustrated Bible Atlas
The Appeasers (*with Richard Gott*)
The European Powers, 1900–1945
The Roots of Appeasement
Sir Horace Rumbold, Portrait of a Diplomat
Churchill, A Photographic Portrait
Jerusalem, Rebirth of a City
Exile and Return, The Struggle for Jewish
    Statehood
Auschwitz and the Allies
Shcharansky, Hero of our Time

The Jews of Hope, The Plight of Soviet
    Jewry Today
The Holocaust, The Jewish Tragedy
First World War
Second World War
In Search of Churchill
History of the Twentieth Century (in three
    volumes)
From the Ends of the Earth: The Jews in the
    Twentieth Century
Letters to Auntie Fori: The 5000-Year History of
    the Jewish People and Their Faith

THE CHURCHILL BIOGRAPHY IS COMPLETE IN EIGHT VOLUMES:

Volume I. Youth, 1874–1900 *by Randolph S. Churchill*
    Volume I. Companion (in two parts)
Volume II. Young Statesman, 1900–1914 *by Randolph S. Churchill*
    Volume II. Companion (in three parts)
Volume III. 1914–1916 *by Martin Gilbert*
    Volume III. Companion (in two parts)
Volume IV. 1917–1922 *by Martin Gilbert*
    Volume IV. Companion (in three parts)
Volume V. 1922–1939 *by Martin Gilbert*
    Volume V. Companion 'The Exchequer Years' 1922–1929
    Volume V. Companion 'The Wilderness Years' 1929–1935
    Volume V. Companion 'The Coming of War' 1936–1939
Volume VI. 1939–1941, 'Finest Hour' *by Martin Gilbert*
    The Churchill War Papers: Volume I 'At the Admiralty'
    The Churchill War Papers: Volume II 'New Surrender', May–December
    The Churchill War Papers: Volume III '1941, The Ever-Widening War'
Volume VII. 1941–1945, 'Road to Victory' *by Martin Gilbert*
Volume VIII. 1945–1965, 'Never Despair' *by Martin Gilbert*

Churchill – A Life *by Martin Gilbert*

Editions of documents
Britain and Germany Between the Wars
Plough My Own Furrow, The Life of Lord Allen of Hurtwood
Servant of India, Diaries of the Viceroy's Private Secretary, 1905–1910

THE ROUTLEDGE ATLAS OF
THE FIRST WORLD WAR

Martin Gilbert

Routledge
Taylor & Francis Group

LONDON AND NEW YORK

First published 1970 as *The Atlas of the First World War*
by Weidenfeld & Nicolson

Then published 1985 as *The Dent Atlas of the First World War*
By J. M. Dent Ltd.

Second edition first published 1994
by Routledge
11 New Fetter Lane, London EC4P 4EE

Simultaneously published in the USA and Canada
by Routledge
29 West 35th Street, New York, NY 10001

Reprinted (twice) 2003

This edition first published 2002

Routledge is an imprint of the Taylor & Francis Group

Printed and bound in Great Britain by
Bell & Bain Ltd, Glasgow

British Library Cataloguing in Publication Data
A catalogue record for this book is available from the British Library

ISBN 0–415–28507–0 (Hbk)
ISBN 0–415–28508–9 (Pbk)

Table of Contents

Introduction to the First Edition
Field-Marshal The Viscount Montgomery of Alamein,
KG, GCB, DSO

The idea of teaching history by a series of maps was new to me until Martin Gilbert's historical atlas of British history had come my way. I was at once intensely interested and later studied those of other countries and nations which he published. Such visual pictures of historical facts cannot fail to be of real value to students in schools and universities; they would look through a window, as it were, at the subject before getting down to a detailed study—which is, of course, essential.

My own study of history has proved to me, a soldier, that the verdict of war has been, time and again, a deciding factor in the process of historical change—though, of course, not the only one. But it has always been the arbiter when other methods of reaching agreement have failed.

This atlas of the 1914–18 war is therefore of particular interest to me, since I led my platoon of some 30 men into battle against the German army in August 1914, and remained on the western front in Europe until the war ended. It was an honour when my friend Martin Gilbert asked me to write an introduction to this atlas.

I look forward eagerly to his atlas of the 1939–45 war in which I fought on the battlefields of Africa and Europe—but by then being somewhat more senior in rank than in 1914.

MONTGOMERY OF ALAMEIN FM

Preface

This Atlas is intended as an introductory guide to as many aspects of the First World War as can reasonably be put in map form: the military, the naval, the aerial, the diplomatic, the technical, the economic, and pervading all, the human. The principal books upon which I have drawn for both facts and ideas are listed in the bibliography at the end of the volume. Two of the maps are constructed entirely from material in the British Government archives at the Public Record Office in London: *A Plan for the Middle East 1915* (map 34) from a Cabinet paper entitled "The Spoils" written in March 1915 by the Colonial Secretary, Lewis Harcourt, which contained the first formal proposals for the post-war future of Palestine; and *British Defences Against a Possible German Invasion 1915* (map 44) from the facts given to the members of the War Council at the beginning of January 1915. I have tried to build up each map by a detailed study of the available evidence, some of it extremely well known, some obscure, and some, as with the two maps above, previously unpublished.

Many of the subjects mapped here, although written about elsewhere, have not been put in map form before. But it is my hope that the visual aspect of a map such as *German War Aims in the West 1914–1918* (map 124), or *British Supplies to the Allies 1914–1918* (map 140) can be as useful, and as revealing, as the printed form; and that the putting together of normally scattered and diverse facts such as *Food Riots in Germany 1916* (map 77), *British Labour Corps 1914–1918* (map 136) or *Gold Gains 1914–1918* (map 143) can give an unexpected interest to problems which, because of their unfamiliarity, do not always find a place in general histories of the war.

During the four years in which I compiled these maps and prepared the drafts, I was fortunate in the advice given by colleagues and friends. The Imperial War Museum, and in particular Dr Christopher Dowling and Mr Vernon Rigby, gave me the benefit of their wide knowledge and critical skills. Dr Immanuel Geiss gave me the advantage of his careful study of German war aims and policy; Mr Michael Glenny gave the Russian maps the benefit of his unique blend of scholarship and zeal; Mr and Mrs Tsvi Hercberg accompanied me to several battlefields on the western front and encouraged me with their enthusiasm and suggestions; Madame Taillandier gave me a vivid insight into the effect of the war on a French village cruelly thrust into the front line. The Commonwealth (formerly Imperial) War Graves Commission provided me with excellent detailed maps of the western front on which over two thousand British graveyards mark the savage progress and preserve a sombre echo of the fighting of over fifty years ago. Mr Norman Pemberton, the Commonwealth War Graves representative at Çanakkale, kindly took me to the cemeteries which he guarded with such care upon the Gallipoli Peninsula; Mr A. G. Major accompanied me to the summit of Sari Bair from where, gazing down at the Aegean Sea across the whole Anzac area, we felt almost in the living presence of the aspirations, the folly, the suffering and the heroism of mankind. The Mayor of Eceabat (the town of Maidos on maps 35 and 38), Mr Vedat Okay, and the Governor of Çanakkale, Mr Celâlettin Tüfekçi, gave me every help while I was at the Dardanelles, and Mr Okay not only put a jeep at my disposal, but gave up his own time to ensure that my visit to the battlefields was as comprehensive as it could be. My visit there was made possible by the generosity of the Turkish Government which invited me to Turkey in connection with my work on the Official Biography of Sir Winston Churchill, and enabled me to pursue simultaneously my researches both as a historian and as a historical geographer.

Mr Arthur Banks supervised with his usual skill the activities of his team of cartographers, of whom the late Mr Terry Bicknell deserves a special mention for his high standard of cartography. Jane Cousins supervised the final cartographic corrections. Mr Joseph Robinson C.B.E. examined the maps with the thorough professional eye of a former member of the diplomatic service. Mrs Jean Kelly again gave the maps the advantage of her geographic expertise; and Sarah Graham, as well as typing all the preparatory matter, the bibliography and the index, subjected the maps to a further critical scrutiny. I am deeply grateful to all those who have helped to eliminate errors and ambiguities, but for those which remain I bear the sole responsibility.

I should welcome suggestions for future maps, and for corrections or additions to the existing ones.

Thirty-four years have passed since Mr A. J. P. Taylor gave me my last undergraduate tutorial in his room overlooking the Deer Park at Magdalen. Until his death I never ceased to benefit by his extraordinary enthusiasm for history and by his advice. It is he, for example, who, by urging me to include graphs in this Atlas, led me to prepare *Casualties and Prisoners on the British Front 1918* (map 119) and *British Merchant Shipping Losses 1917–1918* (map 85), as well as for the graph which appears on *Allied Losses Off North America 1917* (map 86). Likewise, it was his railway enthusiasm which made me look more closely at the rail and transport problems of the First World War and to draw *The Berlin–Bagdad Railway by 1914* (map 4), *Communications at Ypres by 1918* (map 22) and *Railway Communications of the Central Powers 1916* (map 61).

I wish above all to thank my late father, Mr Peter Gilbert, for his constant interest and true enthusiasm. By his questionings he led me to many searches which I might otherwise have neglected. Twice during my work on the Atlas he came with me to the Ypres Salient and together we would listen to the Last Post as it was sounded every night under the Menin Gate. He also tramped with me over

Flanders' fields in search of the mine craters of *Messines: The Mines* (map 90) and in order to find the precise location of the farms and fortifications of *Churchill in Flanders 1916* (map 58). It is therefore with a sense of gratitude for this as for so many other things that I dedicate this volume to his memory.

Nine years have passed since the third printing of this atlas; for this new edition I have drawn five new maps, including *British Court-Martial Executions, 1914–1918* (map 162) and two maps showing United States' preparations for the unfought campaign of 1919 (maps 160 and 161).

MARTIN GILBERT
Merton College
Oxford
17 January 1994

List of Maps

Section One

PRELUDE TO WAR

It is a painful and terrible thing to think how easy
it is to stir up a nation to war . . . and you will find
that wars are always supported by a class of arguments
which, after the war is over, the people find were
arguments they should not have listened to.

JOHN BRIGHT
House of Commons
31 March 1854

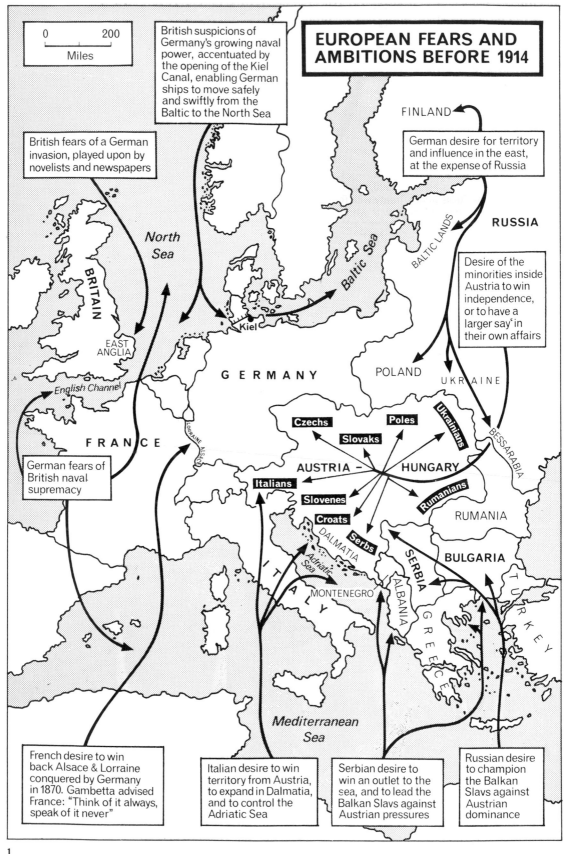

EUROPEAN FEARS AND AMBITIONS BEFORE 1914

0 — 200
Miles

British suspicions of Germany's growing naval power, accentuated by the opening of the Kiel Canal, enabling German ships to move safely and swiftly from the Baltic to the North Sea

British fears of a German invasion, played upon by novelists and newspapers

FINLAND

German desire for territory and influence in the east, at the expense of Russia

RUSSIA

BALTIC LANDS

Desire of the minorities inside Austria to win independence, or to have a larger say in their own affairs

North Sea

Baltic Sea

Kiel

BRITAIN

EAST ANGLIA

English Channel

GERMANY

POLAND

UKRAINE

BESSARABIA

FRANCE

LORRAINE ALSACE

German fears of British naval supremacy

Czechs

Poles

Ukrainians

Slovaks

AUSTRIA – HUNGARY

Italians

Slovenes

Rumanians

RUMANIA

Croats

DALMATIA

Serbs

SERBIA

BULGARIA

ITALY

Adriatic Sea

MONTENEGRO

ALBANIA

GREECE

TURKEY

Mediterranean Sea

French desire to win back Alsace & Lorraine conquered by Germany in 1870. Gambetta advised France: "Think of it always, speak of it never"

Italian desire to win territory from Austria, to expand in Dalmatia, and to control the Adriatic Sea

Serbian desire to win an outlet to the sea, and to lead the Balkan Slavs against Austrian pressures

Russian desire to champion the Balkan Slavs against Austrian dominance

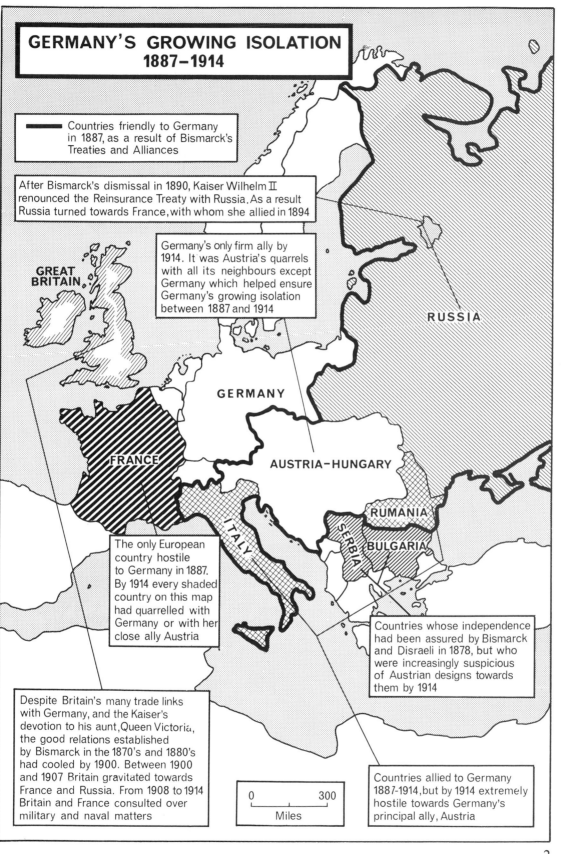

GERMANY'S GROWING ISOLATION 1887–1914

━━━ Countries friendly to Germany in 1887, as a result of Bismarck's Treaties and Alliances

After Bismarck's dismissal in 1890, Kaiser Wilhelm II renounced the Reinsurance Treaty with Russia. As a result Russia turned towards France, with whom she allied in 1894

Germany's only firm ally by 1914. It was Austria's quarrels with all its neighbours except Germany which helped ensure Germany's growing isolation between 1887 and 1914

GREAT BRITAIN

RUSSIA

GERMANY

FRANCE

AUSTRIA-HUNGARY

ITALY

RUMANIA

SERBIA

BULGARIA

The only European country hostile to Germany in 1887. By 1914 every shaded country on this map had quarrelled with Germany or with her close ally Austria

Countries whose independence had been assured by Bismarck and Disraeli in 1878, but who were increasingly suspicious of Austrian designs towards them by 1914

Despite Britain's many trade links with Germany, and the Kaiser's devotion to his aunt, Queen Victoria, the good relations established by Bismarck in the 1870's and 1880's had cooled by 1900. Between 1900 and 1907 Britain gravitated towards France and Russia. From 1908 to 1914 Britain and France consulted over military and naval matters

Countries allied to Germany 1887–1914, but by 1914 extremely hostile towards Germany's principal ally, Austria

0   300

Miles

THE MINORITIES OF THE CENTRAL POWERS IN 1914

FRANCE

Belgians

Danes

Baltic Sea

GERMANY

Metz
Strassburg
French

Posen

Prague

Czechs

Poles

RUSSIA

Italians

ITALY

Slovenes

Trieste

Pressburg

Ukrainians

AUSTRIA-HUNGARY

Croats

Slovaks

Serbs

Adriatic Sea

Sarajevo

The three central Empires each contained large minority groups who wished for eventual independence. Many of these groups hoped that an Allied victory might lead to their liberation. The Allies encouraged such hopes, and offered to support the minorities if they turned against their imperial masters

SERBIA

RUMANIA

Rumanians

GREECE

Black Sea

Aegean Sea

Constantinople

RUSSIA

Greeks

TURKEY

Russians

Kars

Mediterranean Sea

Armenians

Arabs

Kurds

Arabs & Jews

Jerusalem

Arabs

0 — 100
Miles

3

THE BERLIN-BAGDAD RAILWAY BY 1914

Germany hoped to gain important trade and political influence in Turkey and Persia by the construction of the Berlin-Bagdad railway. With the exception of 175 miles in Serbia, its 1,875 miles ran through countries sympathetic to Germany. But British traders could make as much use of it as they wished, and French investors had a strong financial interest. The railway was in no sense a cause of war, although British public opinion saw it as evidence of German and Austrian expansionist tendencies

0   200
Miles

━━━ The Berlin-Bagdad railway. The Adana-Aleppo and Mardin-Mosul sections were not completed on the outbreak of war in 1914

■   Serbia: the only country on the Berlin-Bagdad railway not associated with Germany, and also hostile to Austria-Hungary

┼┼┼ Branch line completed by 1914

- - - Branch line proposed to the Persian oilfields

Directors of the railway in 1914

German	11
French	8
Turkish	4
Swiss	2
Austrian	1

Russian sphere of influence

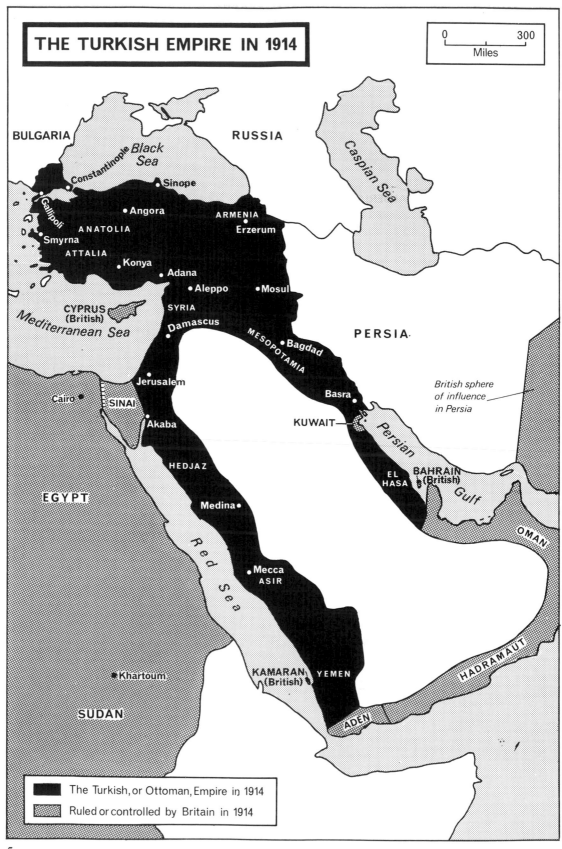

THE TURKISH EMPIRE IN 1914

0 — 300
Miles

BULGARIA

RUSSIA

Black Sea

Constantinople

Sinope

Gallipoli

Angora

ARMENIA

Erzerum

ANATOLIA

Smyrna

ATTALIA

Konya

Adana

Aleppo

Mosul

CYPRUS (British)

SYRIA

Mediterranean Sea

Damascus

MESOPOTAMIA

Bagdad

PERSIA

Caspian Sea

British sphere of influence in Persia

Jerusalem

Cairo

SINAI

Basra

KUWAIT

Akaba

HEDJAZ

EGYPT

Medina

EL HASA

BAHRAIN (British)

Persian

Gulf

OMAN

Red Sea

Mecca

ASIR

Khartoum

KAMARAN (British)

YEMEN

HADRAMAUT

SUDAN

ADEN

	The Turkish, or Ottoman, Empire in 1914
	Ruled or controlled by Britain in 1914

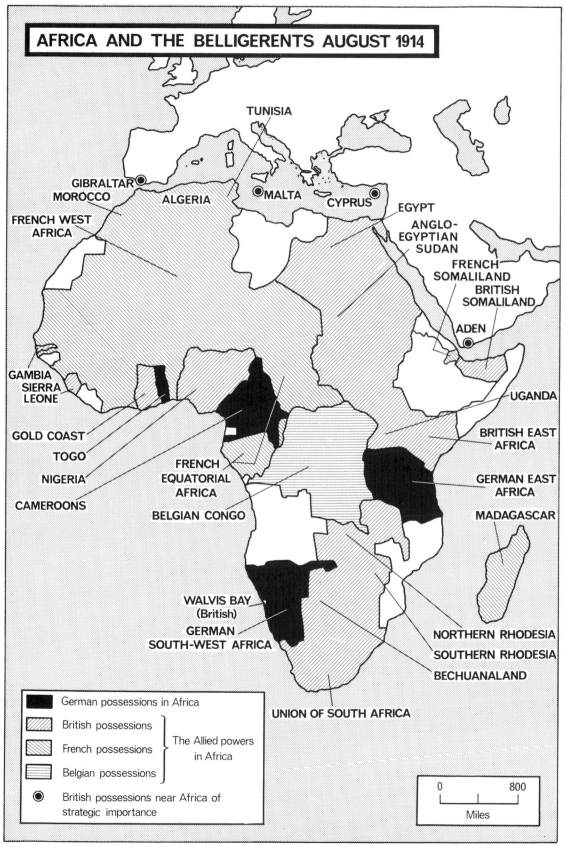

AFRICA AND THE BELLIGERENTS AUGUST 1914

TUNISIA

GIBRALTAR
MOROCCO
ALGERIA
MALTA
CYPRUS
EGYPT
ANGLO-
EGYPTIAN
SUDAN
FRENCH WEST
AFRICA
FRENCH
SOMALILAND
BRITISH
SOMALILAND
ADEN

GAMBIA
SIERRA
LEONE

UGANDA

GOLD COAST
BRITISH EAST
AFRICA
TOGO
NIGERIA
FRENCH
EQUATORIAL
AFRICA
GERMAN EAST
AFRICA
CAMEROONS
MADAGASCAR
BELGIAN CONGO

WALVIS BAY
(British)
GERMAN
SOUTH-WEST AFRICA
NORTHERN RHODESIA
SOUTHERN RHODESIA
BECHUANALAND

UNION OF SOUTH AFRICA

German possessions in Africa

British possessions

French possessions ⎱ The Allied powers
                    ⎰ in Africa

Belgian possessions

⊙ British possessions near Africa of
  strategic importance

0   800

Miles

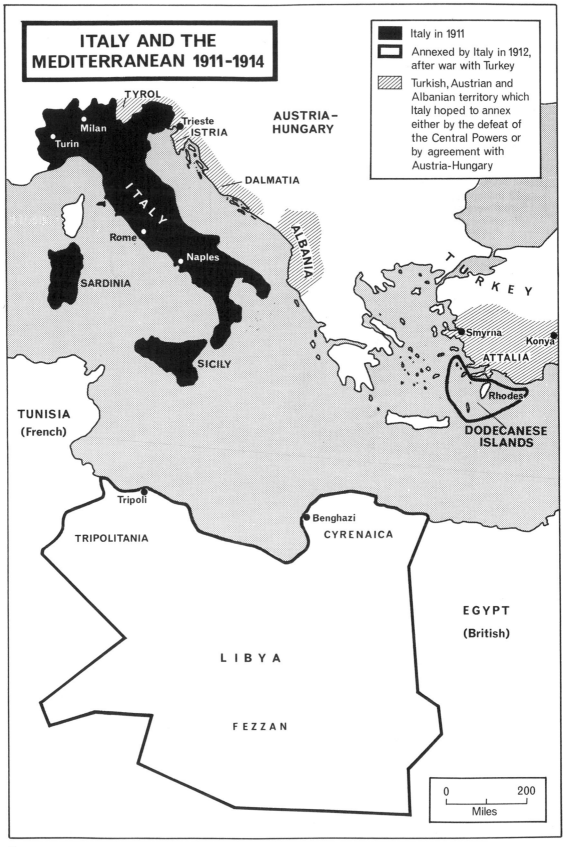

ITALY AND THE MEDITERRANEAN 1911-1914

Italy in 1911

Annexed by Italy in 1912, after war with Turkey

Turkish, Austrian and Albanian territory which Italy hoped to annex either by the defeat of the Central Powers or by agreement with Austria-Hungary

TYROL

Milan

Turin

Trieste
ISTRIA

AUSTRIA–
HUNGARY

ITALY

DALMATIA

Rome

ALBANIA

Naples

TURKEY

SARDINIA

Smyrna

Konya

ATTALIA

SICILY

Rhodes

DODECANESE
ISLANDS

TUNISIA
(French)

Tripoli

Benghazi
CYRENAICA

EGYPT
(British)

TRIPOLITANIA

LIBYA

FEZZAN

0   200
Miles

SERBIA AND ITS NEIGHBOURS 1878 – 1914

0 ————— 100
Miles

2 The Serbs of Bosnia looked to Serbia for their future, as Austrian rule was oppressive

11 Austria feared unrest among its 23 million subject Slavs if Serbia were allowed to build up its power and prestige

10 Serbia's only active ally among the Great Powers. Russia disliked Austria's growing influence in the Balkans. The Balkan Slavs looked to Russia as their champion

1 Independent from Turkey, 1878, after nearly 500 years of Turkish rule

3 Austria ruled Dalmatia, a Serb outlet to the sea, including the ports of Spalato and Cattaro

MONTENEGRO
4 Serbia's only Balkan ally, a mountainous country with no easy access to the sea, and only one port

5 Created from Turkish territory as a result of Austrian pressure in 1912, deliberately cutting Serbia off from the sea

8 Bulgaria, anxious to annex Serbian Macedonia

6 Conquered from Turkey by Greece during the Balkan war 1912-1913. Serbia had hoped to expand to Salonika and the sea

9 Novibazar and Macedonia, conquered by Serbia from Turkey 1912-1913

7 Conquered from Turkey by Bulgaria 1912-1913, again frustrating Serb ambitions seaward

■ Serbia in 1878
□ Conquered by Serbia in 1913
▨ Serbia's allies

RUSSIA
Odessa
RUMANIA
Bucharest
AUSTRIA – HUNGARY
DALMATIA
Spalato
BOSNIA
Sarajevo
Belgrade
SERBIA
Nish
MONTENEGRO
Cattaro
NOVIBAZAR
Dulcigno
Skopje
MACEDONIA
Ochrid
Durazzo
ALBANIA
Valona
Salonika
Kavalla
Dedeagatch
Constantinople
TURKEY
BULGARIA
Sofia
Black Sea
Adriatic Sea
GREECE
Prevesa
Aegean Sea
Athens
Mediterranean Sea

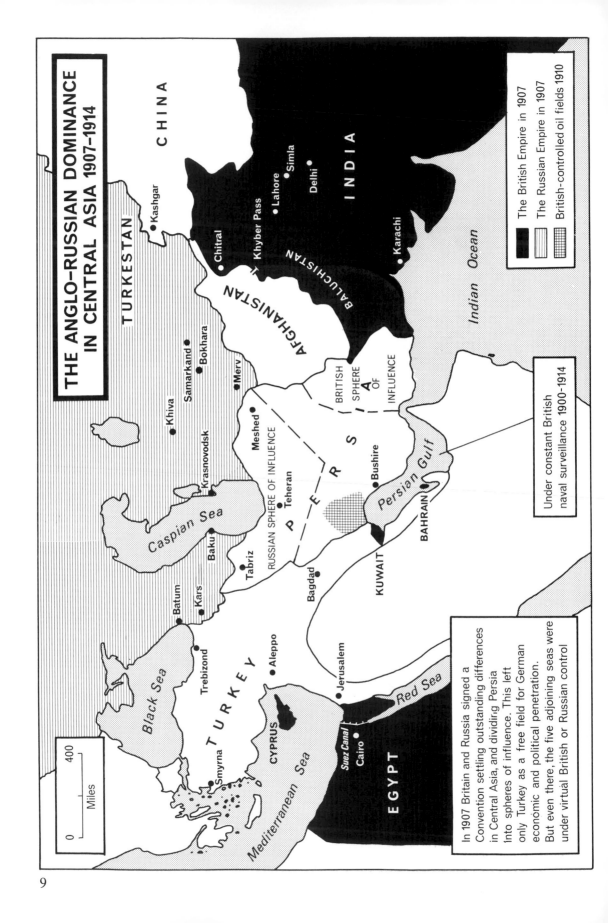

THE ANGLO-RUSSIAN DOMINANCE IN CENTRAL ASIA 1907-1914

The British Empire in 1907
The Russian Empire in 1907
British-controlled oil fields 1910

CHINA

TURKESTAN

INDIA

Kashgar

Simla
Lahore
Delhi

Chitral
Khyber Pass

AFGHANISTAN

BALUCHISTAN

Karachi

Indian Ocean

Samarkand
Bokhara

Merv

Khiva

Krasnovodsk

Meshed

Caspian Sea

RUSSIAN SPHERE OF INFLUENCE

P   E   R   S   I   A

BRITISH
SPHERE
OF
INFLUENCE

Teheran

Baku

Bushire

Persian Gulf

BAHRAIN

Tabriz

Kars

KUWAIT

Batum

Bagdad

Under constant British
naval surveillance 1900-1914

Black Sea

Trebizond

Aleppo

Jerusalem

T U R K E Y

CYPRUS

Smyrna

Mediterranean Sea

Red Sea

Suez Canal
Cairo

E G Y P T

0   400

Miles

In 1907 Britain and Russia signed a
Convention settling outstanding differences
in Central Asia, and dividing Persia
into spheres of influence. This left
only Turkey as a free field for German
economic and political penetration.
But even there, the five adjoining seas were
under virtual British or Russian control

9

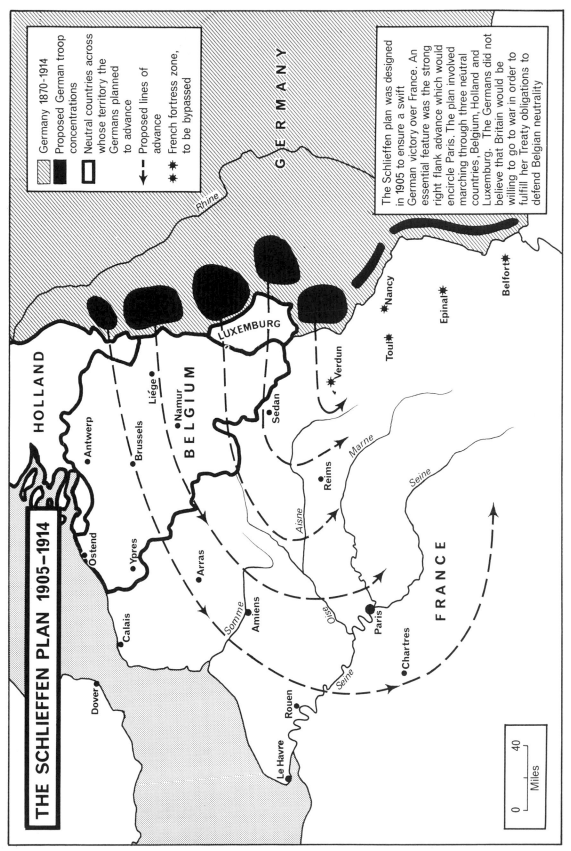

THE SCHLIEFFEN PLAN 1905–1914

Legend:
- Germany 1870–1914
- Proposed German troop concentrations
- Neutral countries across whose territory the Germans planned to advance
- Proposed lines of advance
- French fortress zone, to be bypassed

The Schlieffen plan was designed in 1905 to ensure a swift German victory over France. An essential feature was the strong right flank advance which would encircle Paris. The plan involved marching through three neutral countries, Belgium, Holland and Luxemburg. The Germans did not believe that Britain would be willing to go to war in order to fulfill her Treaty obligations to defend Belgian neutrality

GERMANY

HOLLAND

BELGIUM

LUXEMBURG

FRANCE

Rhine

Antwerp

Brussels

Liége

•Namur

Sedan

Verdun

•Nancy

Toul

Reims

Marne

Aisne

Seine

Epinal

Belfort

Ostend

Ypres

Arras

Somme

Amiens

Oise

Paris

Seine

•Chartres

Calais

Dover

Le Havre

Rouen

0   40
Miles

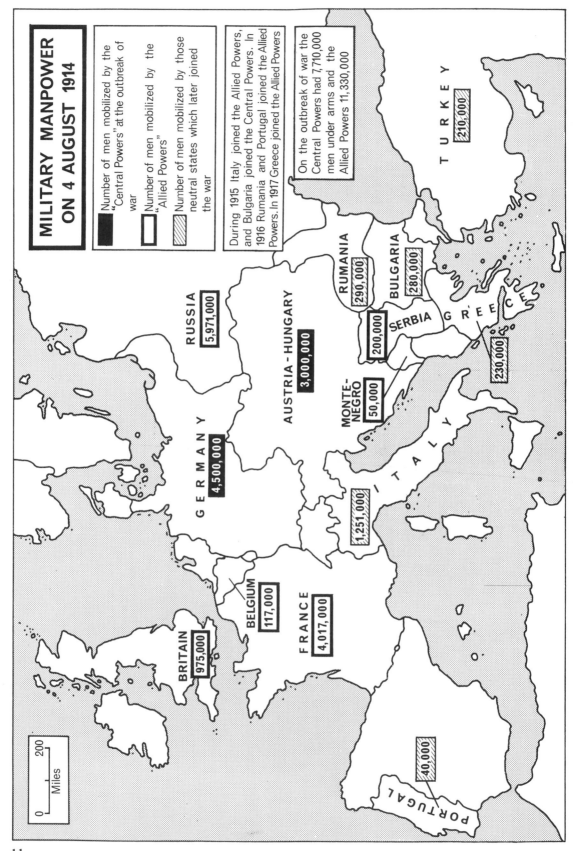

MILITARY MANPOWER ON 4 AUGUST 1914

- ■ Number of men mobilized by the "Central Powers" at the outbreak of war
- ☐ Number of men mobilized by the "Allied Powers"
- ▨ Number of men mobilized by those neutral states which later joined the war

During 1915 Italy joined the Allied Powers, and Bulgaria joined the Central Powers. In 1916 Rumania and Portugal joined the Allied Powers. In 1917 Greece joined the Allied Powers

On the outbreak of war the Central Powers had 7,710,000 men under arms and the Allied Powers 11,330,000

TURKEY 210,000

RUSSIA 5,971,000

AUSTRIA-HUNGARY 3,000,000

RUMANIA 290,000

BULGARIA 280,000

SERBIA 200,000

GREECE 230,000

MONTE-NEGRO 50,000

GERMANY 4,500,000

ITALY 1,251,000

BELGIUM 117,000

FRANCE 4,017,000

BRITAIN 975,000

PORTUGAL 40,000

200

0 Miles

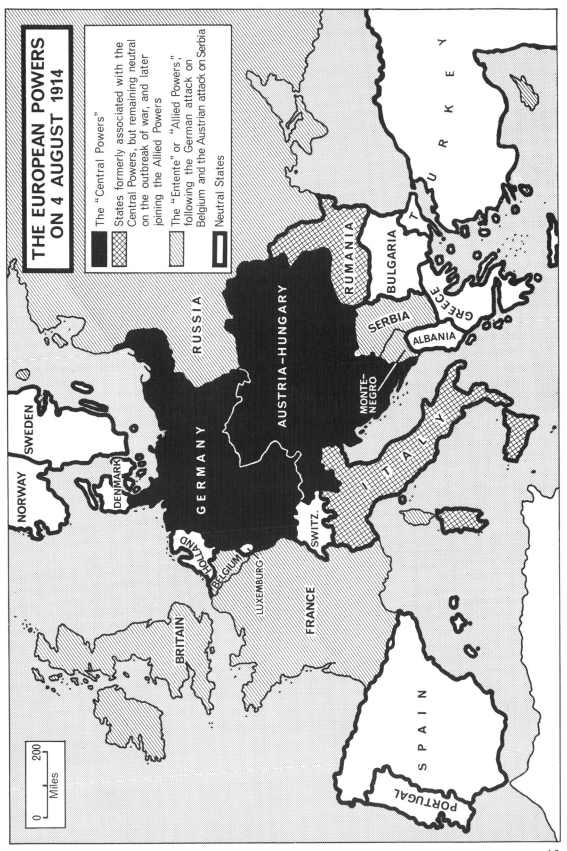

THE EUROPEAN POWERS
ON 4 AUGUST 1914

The "Central Powers"

States formerly associated with the
Central Powers, but remaining neutral
on the outbreak of war, and later
joining the Allied Powers

The "Entente" or "Allied Powers",
following the German attack on
Belgium and the Austrian attack on Serbia

Neutral States

NORWAY

SWEDEN

DENMARK

RUSSIA

GERMANY

HOLLAND

BELGIUM

LUXEMBURG

FRANCE

SWITZ.

AUSTRIA–HUNGARY

ITALY

MONTE-
NEGRO

RUMANIA

SERBIA

BULGARIA

ALBANIA

GREECE

TURKEY

SPAIN

PORTUGAL

200

0

Miles

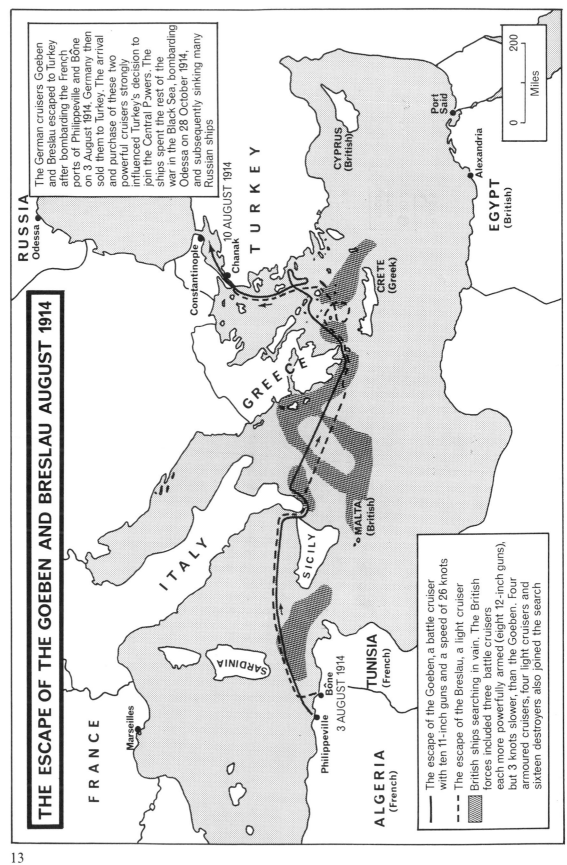

THE ESCAPE OF THE GOEBEN AND BRESLAU AUGUST 1914

The German cruisers Goeben and Breslau escaped to Turkey after bombarding the French ports of Philippeville and Bône on 3 August 1914. Germany then sold them to Turkey. The arrival and purchase of these two powerful cruisers strongly influenced Turkey's decision to join the Central Powers. The ships spent the rest of the war in the Black Sea, bombarding Odessa on 28 October 1914, and subsequently sinking many Russian ships

RUSSIA
Odessa

TURKEY

Constantinople
Chanak
10 AUGUST 1914

CYPRUS
(British)

CRETE
(Greek)

GREECE

Alexandria

Port Said

EGYPT
(British)

0   200
Miles

ITALY

SARDINIA

SICILY

MALTA
(British)

FRANCE

Marseilles

Bône
Philippeville
3 AUGUST 1914

TUNISIA
(French)

ALGERIA
(French)

—— The escape of the Goeben, a battle cruiser with ten 11-inch guns and a speed of 26 knots

--- The escape of the Breslau, a light cruiser

British ships searching in vain. The British forces included three battle cruisers each more powerfully armed (eight 12-inch guns), but 3 knots slower, than the Goeben. Four armoured cruisers, four light cruisers and sixteen destroyers also joined the search

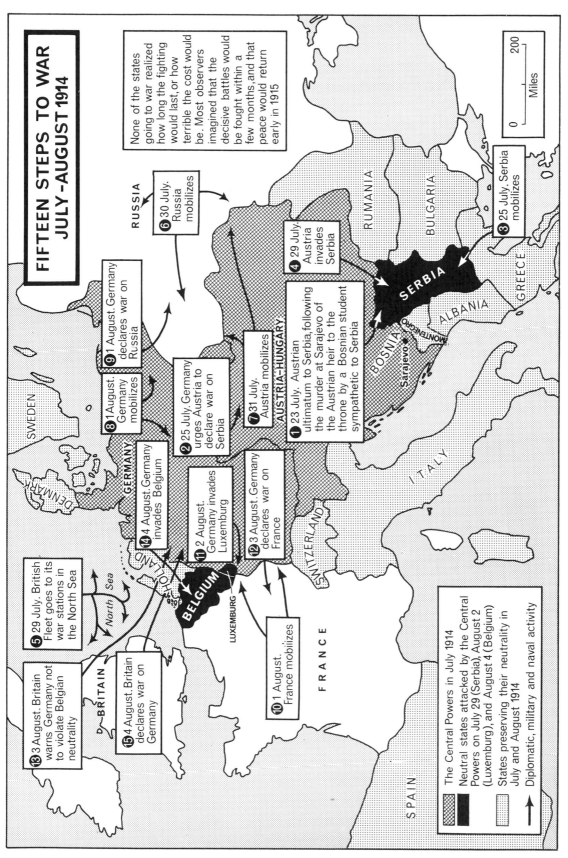

FIFTEEN STEPS TO WAR
JULY–AUGUST 1914

None of the states going to war realized how long the fighting would last, or how terrible the cost would be. Most observers imagined that the decisive battles would be fought within a few months, and that peace would return early in 1915

⑥ 30 July. Russia mobilizes

④ 29 July. Austria invades Serbia

③ 25 July. Serbia mobilizes

① 23 July. Austrian ultimatum to Serbia, following the murder at Sarajevo of the Austrian heir to the throne by a Bosnian student sympathetic to Serbia

② 25 July. Germany urges Austria to declare war on Serbia

⑦ 31 July. Austria mobilizes

⑨ 1 August. Germany declares war on Russia

⑧ 1August. Germany mobilizes

⑭ 4 August. Germany invades Belgium

⑪ 2 August. Germany invades Luxemburg

⑫ 3 August. Germany declares war on France

⑤ 29 July. British Fleet goes to its war stations in the North Sea

⑬ 3 August. Britain warns Germany not to violate Belgian neutrality

⑮ 4 August. Britain declares war on Germany

⑩ 1 August. France mobilizes

0   200
Miles

RUSSIA

SWEDEN

DENMARK

GERMANY

HOLLAND

BELGIUM

LUXEMBURG

BRITAIN

North Sea

FRANCE

SWITZERLAND

SPAIN

ITALY

AUSTRIA–HUNGARY

BOSNIA
Sarajevo

MONTENEGRO

SERBIA

ALBANIA

GREECE

BULGARIA

RUMANIA

The Central Powers in July 1914

Neutral states attacked by the Central Powers on July 29 (Serbia), August 2 (Luxemburg), and August 4 (Belgium)

States preserving their neutrality in July and August 1914

Diplomatic, military and naval activity

14

Section Two

1914

Now, God be thanked Who has matched us with His hour,
  And caught our youth, and wakened us from sleeping,
With hand made sure, clear eye, and sharpened power,
  To turn, as swimmers into cleanness leaping,
Glad from a world grown old and cold and weary,
  Leave the sick hearts that honour could not move,
And half-men, and their dirty songs and dreary,
  And all the little emptiness of love! . . .

RUPERT BROOKE
"1914"

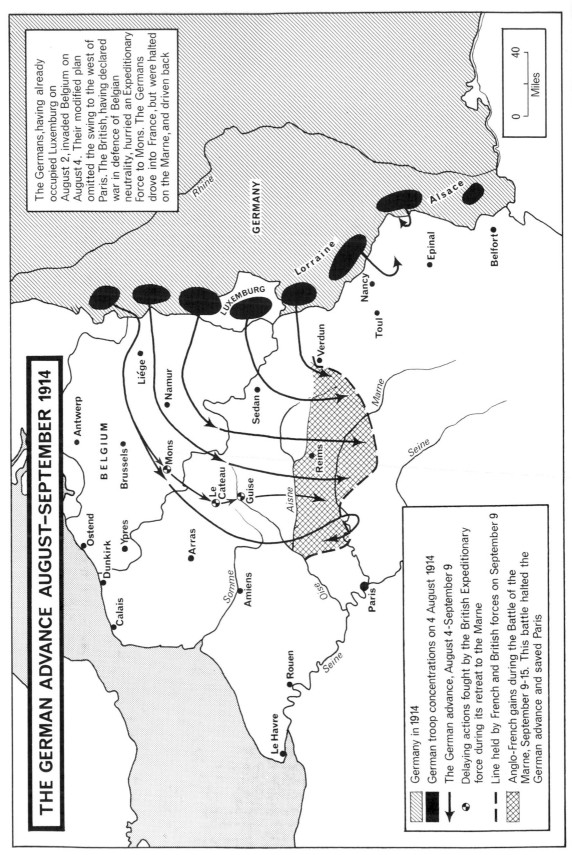

THE GERMAN ADVANCE AUGUST–SEPTEMBER 1914

The Germans, having already occupied Luxemburg on August 2, invaded Belgium on August 4. Their modified plan omitted the swing to the west of Paris. The British, having declared war in defence of Belgian neutrality, hurried an Expeditionary Force to Mons. The Germans drove into France, but were halted on the Marne, and driven back

GERMANY

Rhine

Alsace

Lorraine

LUXEMBURG

Nancy

Toul

Epinal

Belfort

Verdun

Liége

Namur

Sedan

Reims

Antwerp

BELGIUM

Brussels

Mons

Le Cateau

Guise

Aisne

Marne

Seine

Ostend

Ypres

Dunkirk

Arras

Somme

Amiens

Oise

Paris

Calais

Seine

Rouen

Le Havre

Germany in 1914

German troop concentrations on 4 August 1914

The German advance, August 4–September 9

Delaying actions fought by the British Expeditionary force during its retreat to the Marne

Line held by French and British forces on September 9

Anglo-French gains during the Battle of the Marne, September 9–15. This battle halted the German advance and saved Paris

0   40

Miles

15

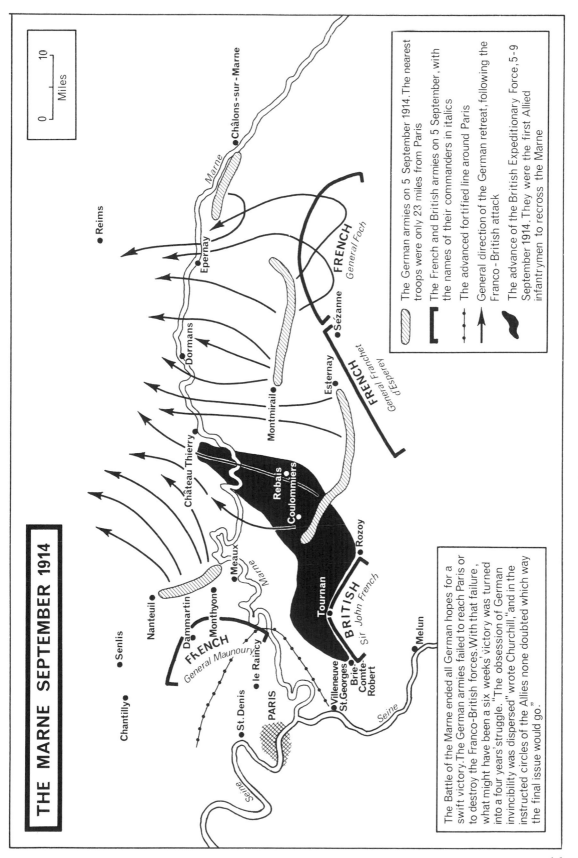

THE MARNE SEPTEMBER 1914

The Battle of the Marne ended all German hopes for a swift victory. The German armies failed to reach Paris or to destroy the Franco-British forces. With that failure, what might have been a six weeks' victory was turned into a four years' struggle. "The obsession of German invincibility was dispersed" wrote Churchill, "and in the instructed circles of the Allies none doubted which way the final issue would go."

The German armies on 5 September 1914. The nearest troops were only 23 miles from Paris

The French and British armies on 5 September, with the names of their commanders in italics

The advanced fortified line around Paris

General direction of the German retreat, following the Franco-British attack

The advance of the British Expeditionary Force, 5-9 September 1914. They were the first Allied infantrymen to recross the Marne

FRENCH *General Foch*

FRENCH *General Franchet d'Esperey*

FRENCH *General Maunoury*

BRITISH *Sir John French*

Reims
Châlons-sur-Marne
Épernay
Dormans
Sézanne
Esternay
Montmirail
Château Thierry
Rebais
Coulommiers
Rozoy
Tournan
Meaux
Nanteuil
Senlis
Chantilly
Dammartin
Monthyon
le Raincy
St. Denis
Villeneuve St. Georges
Brie Comte Robert
Melun
PARIS

Marne
Seine

0   10
Miles

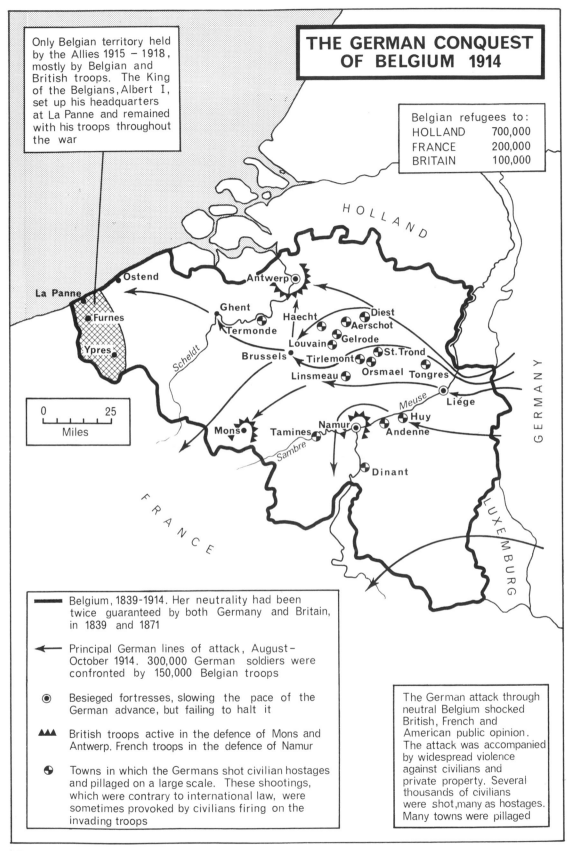

THE GERMAN CONQUEST OF BELGIUM 1914

Only Belgian territory held by the Allies 1915 – 1918, mostly by Belgian and British troops. The King of the Belgians, Albert I, set up his headquarters at La Panne and remained with his troops throughout the war

Belgian refugees to:
HOLLAND 700,000
FRANCE 200,000
BRITAIN 100,000

HOLLAND

GERMANY

LUXEMBURG

FRANCE

Ostend
La Panne
Furnes
Ypres
Ghent
Antwerp
Haecht
Termonde
Diest
Aerschot
Gelrode
Louvain
St. Trond
Brussels
Tirlemont
Linsmeau
Orsmael
Tongres
Liége
Huy
Mons
Tamines
Namur
Andenne
Dinant

Scheldt
Sambre
Meuse

0   25
Miles

Belgium, 1839-1914. Her neutrality had been twice guaranteed by both Germany and Britain, in 1839 and 1871

Principal German lines of attack, August–October 1914. 300,000 German soldiers were confronted by 150,000 Belgian troops

⊙ Besieged fortresses, slowing the pace of the German advance, but failing to halt it

▲▲▲ British troops active in the defence of Mons and Antwerp. French troops in the defence of Namur

◕ Towns in which the Germans shot civilian hostages and pillaged on a large scale. These shootings, which were contrary to international law, were sometimes provoked by civilians firing on the invading troops

The German attack through neutral Belgium shocked British, French and American public opinion. The attack was accompanied by widespread violence against civilians and private property. Several thousands of civilians were shot, many as hostages. Many towns were pillaged

17

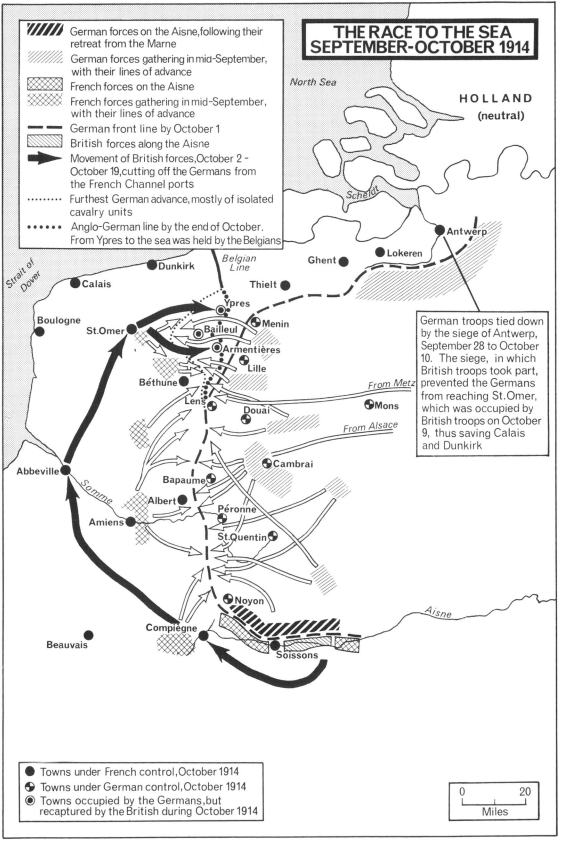

THE RACE TO THE SEA
SEPTEMBER-OCTOBER 1914

German forces on the Aisne, following their retreat from the Marne

German forces gathering in mid-September, with their lines of advance

French forces on the Aisne

French forces gathering in mid-September, with their lines of advance

German front line by October 1

British forces along the Aisne

Movement of British forces, October 2 - October 19, cutting off the Germans from the French Channel ports

Furthest German advance, mostly of isolated cavalry units

Anglo-German line by the end of October. From Ypres to the sea was held by the Belgians

North Sea

HOLLAND
(neutral)

Scheldt

Strait of Dover

Belgian Line

Dunkirk

Calais

Thielt

Ghent

Lokeren

Antwerp

Ypres

Boulogne

St.Omer

Bailleul

Menin

Armentières

Lille

Béthune

From Metz

Lens

Douai

Mons

From Alsace

Abbeville

Somme

Cambrai

Bapaume

Albert

Péronne

Amiens

St.Quentin

German troops tied down by the siege of Antwerp, September 28 to October 10. The siege, in which British troops took part, prevented the Germans from reaching St.Omer, which was occupied by British troops on October 9, thus saving Calais and Dunkirk

Noyon

Compiègne

Beauvais

Soissons

Aisne

● Towns under French control, October 1914

✚ Towns under German control, October 1914

◉ Towns occupied by the Germans, but recaptured by the British during October 1914

0   20
Miles

18

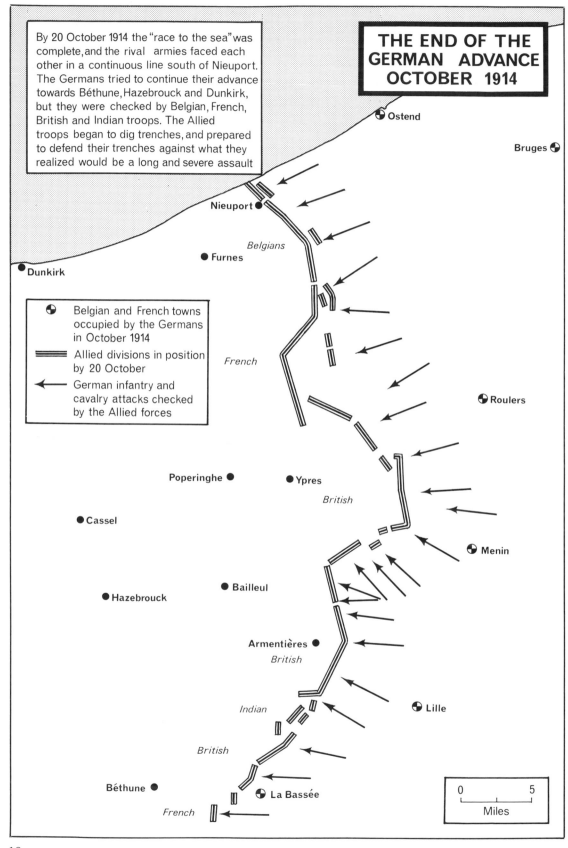

By 20 October 1914 the "race to the sea" was complete, and the rival armies faced each other in a continuous line south of Nieuport. The Germans tried to continue their advance towards Béthune, Hazebrouck and Dunkirk, but they were checked by Belgian, French, British and Indian troops. The Allied troops began to dig trenches, and prepared to defend their trenches against what they realized would be a long and severe assault

THE END OF THE GERMAN ADVANCE OCTOBER 1914

Ostend

Bruges

Nieuport

Belgians

Furnes

Dunkirk

Belgian and French towns occupied by the Germans in October 1914

Allied divisions in position by 20 October

German infantry and cavalry attacks checked by the Allied forces

French

Roulers

Poperinghe

Ypres

British

Cassel

Menin

Bailleul

Hazebrouck

Armentières

British

Lille

Indian

British

Béthune

La Bassée

French

0   5
Miles

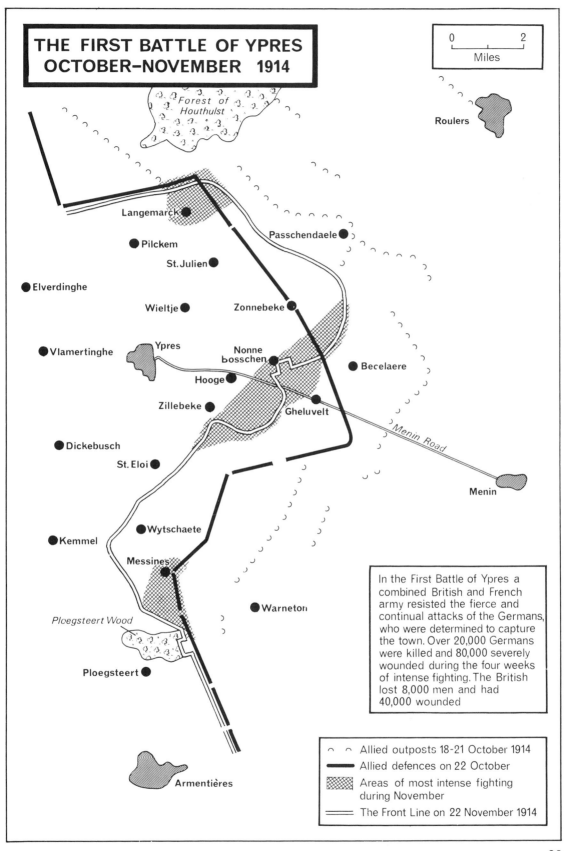

THE FIRST BATTLE OF YPRES OCTOBER–NOVEMBER 1914

0   2
Miles

Forest of Houthulst

Roulers

Langemarck

Pilckem

Passchendaele

St. Julien

Elverdinghe

Wieltje

Zonnebeke

Ypres

Nonne bosschen

Vlamertinghe

Hooge

Becelaere

Zillebeke

Gheluvelt

Dickebusch

Menin Road

St. Eloi

Menin

Wytschaete

Kemmel

Messines

Warneton

Ploegsteert Wood

Ploegsteert

In the First Battle of Ypres a combined British and French army resisted the fierce and continual attacks of the Germans, who were determined to capture the town. Over 20,000 Germans were killed and 80,000 severely wounded during the four weeks of intense fighting. The British lost 8,000 men and had 40,000 wounded

Armentières

⌒ ⌒ Allied outposts 18-21 October 1914

▬▬ Allied defences on 22 October

▨ Areas of most intense fighting during November

═══ The Front Line on 22 November 1914

20

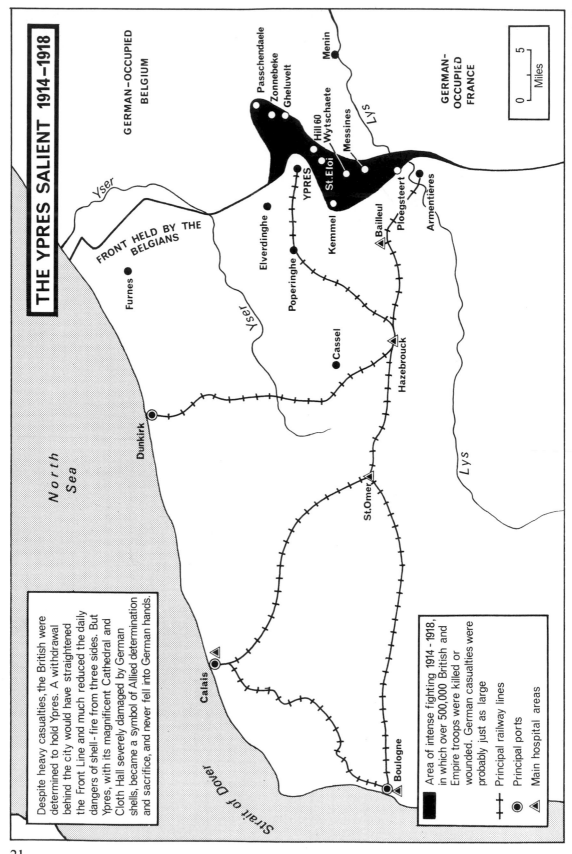

THE YPRES SALIENT 1914–1918

GERMAN-OCCUPIED BELGIUM

GERMAN-OCCUPIED FRANCE

North Sea

Strait of Dover

Yser

Yser

Lys

Lys

FRONT HELD BY THE BELGIANS

Menin

Passchendaele
Zonnebeke
Gheluvelt
Hill 60
Wytschaete
Messines
St. Eloi
YPRES
Kemmel
Bailleul
Ploegsteert
Armentières
Elverdinghe
Poperinghe
Furnes
Cassel
Hazebrouck
St. Omer
Dunkirk
Calais
Boulogne

0   5
Miles

Despite heavy casualties, the British were determined to hold Ypres. A withdrawal behind the city would have straightened the Front Line and much reduced the daily dangers of shell-fire from three sides. But Ypres, with its magnificent Cathedral and Cloth Hall severely damaged by German shells, became a symbol of Allied determination and sacrifice, and never fell into German hands.

Area of intense fighting 1914 - 1918, in which over 500,000 British and Empire troops were killed or wounded. German casualties were probably just as large

⊢ Principal railway lines
◉ Principal ports
▲ Main hospital areas

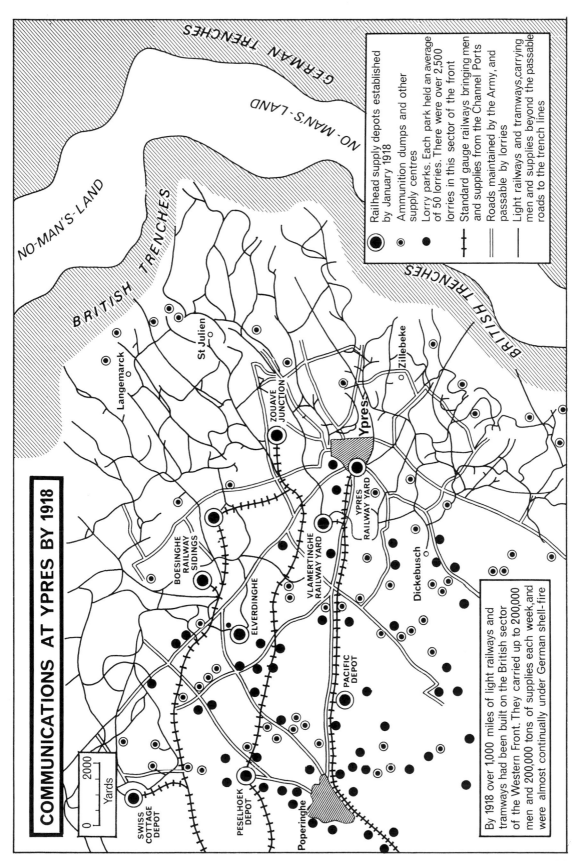

COMMUNICATIONS AT YPRES BY 1918

NO-MAN'S-LAND

GERMAN TRENCHES

NO-MAN'S-LAND

BRITISH TRENCHES

BRITISH TRENCHES

Langemarck

St Julien

Zillebeke

ZOUAVE JUNCTION

Ypres

YPRES RAILWAY YARD

BOESINGHE RAILWAY SIDINGS

ELVERDINGHE

VLAMERTINGHE RAILWAY YARD

Dickebusch

PACIFIC DEPOT

SWISS COTTAGE DEPOT

PESELHOEK DEPOT

Poperinghe

●	Railhead supply depots established by January 1918
⊙	Ammunition dumps and other supply centres
●	Lorry parks. Each park held an average of 50 lorries. There were over 2,500 lorries in this sector of the front
┼┼┼	Standard gauge railways bringing men and supplies from the Channel Ports
═	Roads maintained by the Army, and passable by lorries
—	Light railways and tramways, carrying men and supplies beyond the passable roads to the trench lines

Yards 0 — 2000

By 1918 over 1,000 miles of light railways and tramways had been built on the British sector of the Western Front. They carried up to 200,000 men and 200,000 tons of supplies each week, and were almost continually under German shell-fire

22

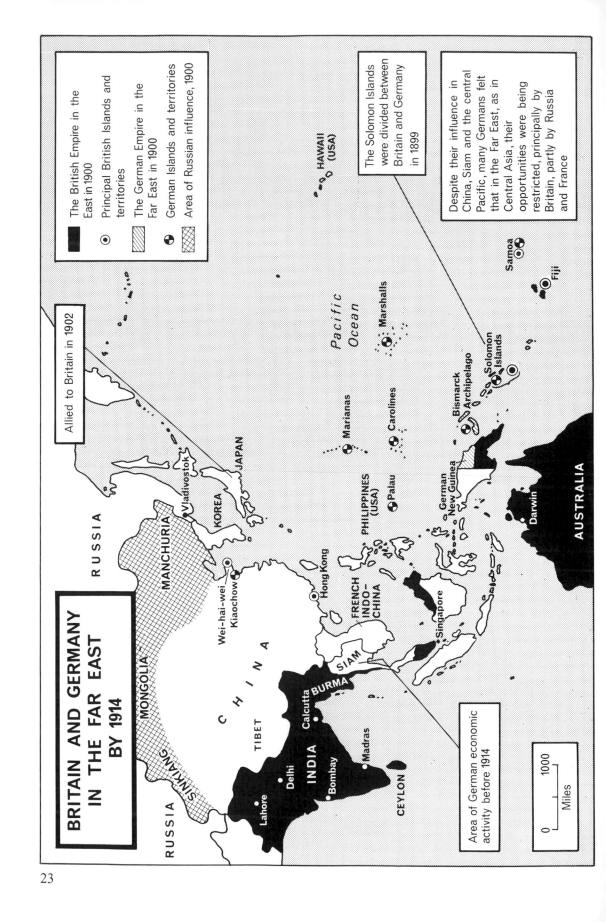

BRITAIN AND GERMANY IN THE FAR EAST BY 1914

Legend:

- The British Empire in the East in 1900
- Principal British Islands and territories
- The German Empire in the Far East in 1900
- German Islands and territories
- Area of Russian influence, 1900

The Solomon Islands were divided between Britain and Germany in 1899

Despite their influence in China, Siam and the central Pacific, many Germans felt that in the Far East, as in Central Asia, their opportunities were being restricted, principally by Britain, partly by Russia and France

Allied to Britain in 1902

Area of German economic activity before 1914

HAWAII (USA)

Samoa

Fiji

Pacific Ocean

Marshalls

Marianas

Carolines

Palau

Bismarck Archipelago

Solomon Islands

German New Guinea

Darwin

AUSTRALIA

PHILIPPINES (USA)

Singapore

RUSSIA

MONGOLIA

MANCHURIA

Vladivostok

KOREA

JAPAN

Wei-hai-wei

Kiaochow

Hong Kong

FRENCH INDO-CHINA

SIAM

BURMA

CHINA

TIBET

SINKIANG

RUSSIA

INDIA

Lahore

Delhi

Calcutta

Bombay

Madras

CEYLON

0   1000
Miles

23

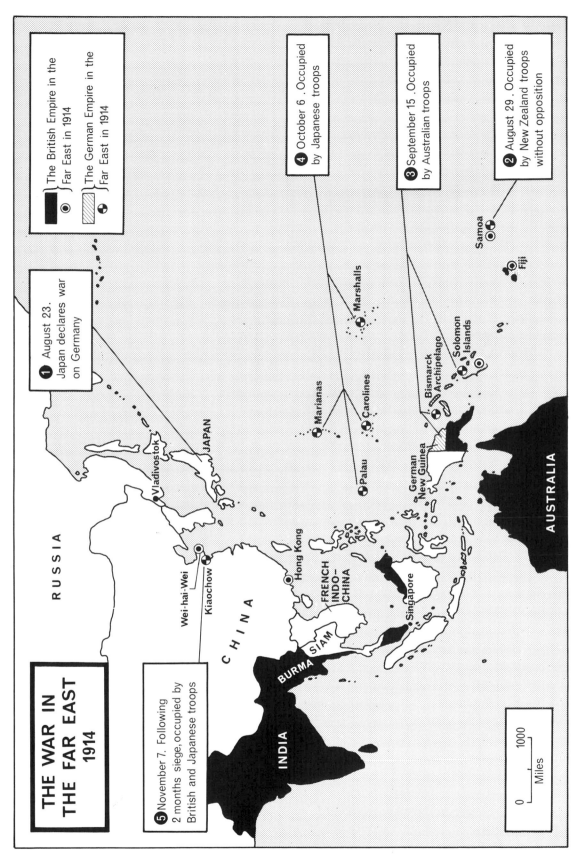

THE WAR IN
THE FAR EAST
1914

The British Empire in the Far East in 1914

The German Empire in the Far East in 1914

❶ August 23. Japan declares war on Germany

❷ August 29. Occupied by New Zealand troops without opposition

❸ September 15. Occupied by Australian troops

❹ October 6 . Occupied by Japanese troops

❺ November 7. Following 2 months siege, occupied by British and Japanese troops

RUSSIA

Vladivostok

JAPAN

Wei-hai-Wei

Kiaochow

CHINA

Hong Kong

FRENCH INDO-CHINA

BURMA

SIAM

INDIA

Singapore

Marianas

Palau

Carolines

Marshalls

German New Guinea

Bismarck Archipelago

Solomon Islands

Samoa

Fiji

AUSTRALIA

0   1000
Miles

24

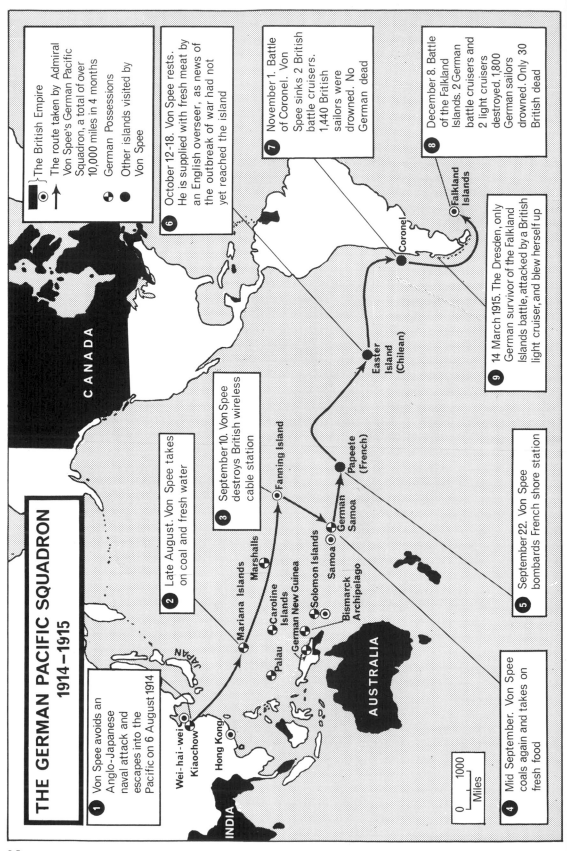

THE GERMAN PACIFIC SQUADRON 1914–1915

Legend:
- The British Empire
- The route taken by Admiral Von Spee's German Pacific Squadron, a total of over 10,000 miles in 4 months
- German Possessions
- Other islands visited by Von Spee

1 Von Spee avoids an Anglo-Japanese naval attack and escapes into the Pacific on 6 August 1914

2 Late August. Von Spee takes on coal and fresh water

3 September 10. Von Spee destroys British wireless cable station

4 Mid September. Von Spee coals again and takes on fresh food

5 September 22. Von Spee bombards French shore station

6 October 12-18. Von Spee rests. He is supplied with fresh meat by an English overseer, as news of the outbreak of war had not yet reached the island

7 November 1. Battle of Coronel. Von Spee sinks 2 British battle cruisers. 1,440 British sailors were drowned. No German dead

8 December 8. Battle of the Falkland Islands. 2 German battle cruisers and 2 light cruisers destroyed. 1,800 German sailors drowned. Only 30 British dead

9 14 March 1915. The Dresden, only German survivor of the Falkland Islands battle, attacked by a British light cruiser, and blew herself up

Map labels: CANADA, JAPAN, INDIA, AUSTRALIA, Wei-hai-wei, Kiaochow, Hong Kong, Palau, Mariana Islands, Caroline Islands, Marshalls, German New Guinea, Solomon Islands, Bismarck Archipelago, Samoa, German Samoa, Fanning Island, Papeete (French), Easter Island (Chilean), Coronel, Falkland Islands

0 1000 Miles

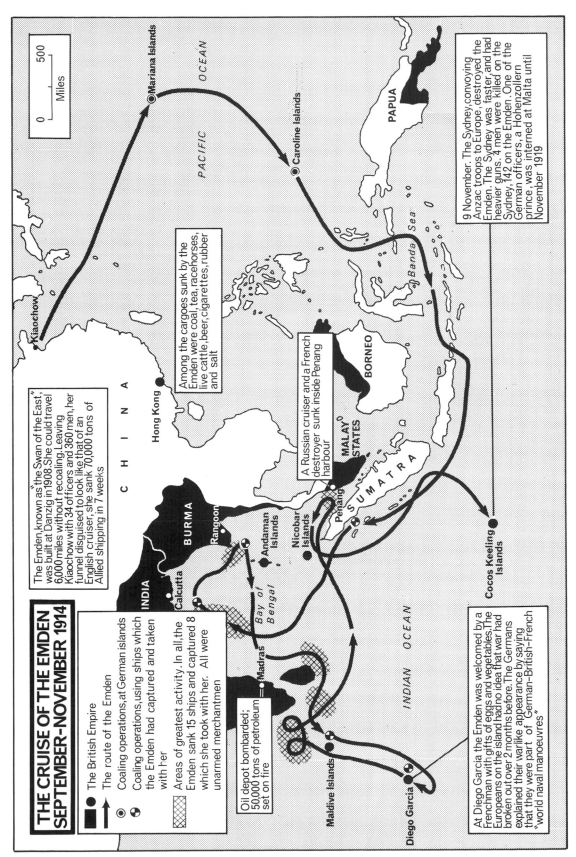

THE CRUISE OF THE EMDEN
SEPTEMBER–NOVEMBER 1914

● The British Empire

▲ The route of the Emden

◉ Coaling operations, at German islands

◑ Coaling operations, using ships which the Emden had captured and taken with her

▨ Areas of greatest activity. In all, the Emden sank 15 ships and captured 8 which she took with her. All were unarmed merchantmen

The Emden, known as the "Swan of the East," was built at Danzig in 1908. She could travel 6,000 miles without recoaling. Leaving Kiaochow with 34 officers and 360 men, her funnel disguised to look like that of an English cruiser, she sank 70,000 tons of Allied shipping in 7 weeks

Among the cargoes sunk by the Emden were coal, tea, racehorses, live cattle, beer, cigarettes, rubber and salt

A Russian cruiser and a French destroyer sunk inside Penang harbour

9 November. The Sydney, convoying Anzac troops to Europe, destroyed the Emden. The Sydney was faster, and had heavier guns. 4 men were killed on the Sydney, 142 on the Emden. One of the German officers, a Hohenzollern prince, was interned at Malta until November 1919

Oil depot bombarded; 50,000 tons of petroleum set on fire

At Diego Garcia the Emden was welcomed by a Frenchman with gifts of eggs and vegetables. The Europeans on the island had no idea that war had broken out over 2 months before. The Germans explained their warlike appearance by saying that they were part of "German–British–French world naval manoeuvres"

PACIFIC OCEAN

Mariana Islands

Caroline Islands

PAPUA

Banda Sea

BORNEO

Kiaochow

CHINA

Hong Kong

MALAY STATES

SUMATRA

Penang

Cocos Keeling Islands

BURMA

Rangoon

Andaman Islands

Nicobar Islands

INDIA

Calcutta

Bay of Bengal

Madras

INDIAN OCEAN

Maldive Islands

Diego Garcia

0 — 500 Miles

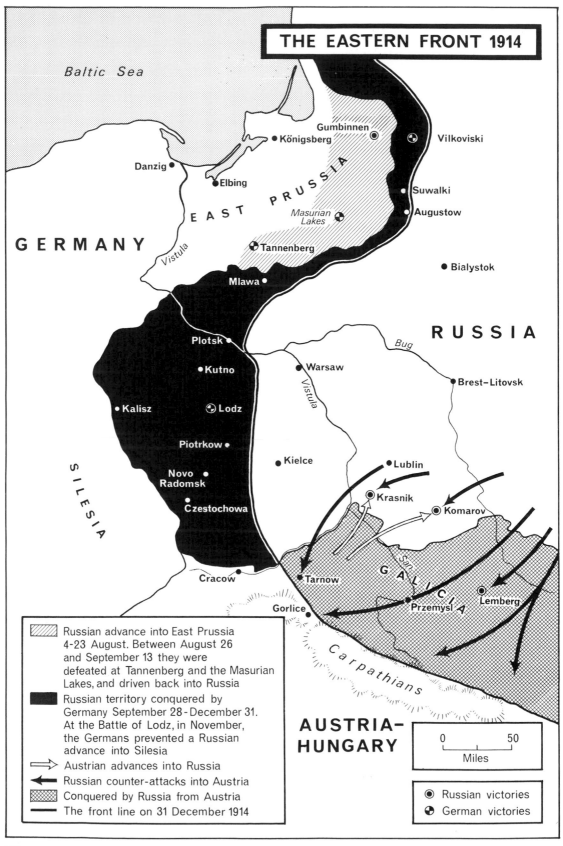

THE EASTERN FRONT 1914

Baltic Sea

GERMANY

EAST PRUSSIA

• Königsberg
Gumbinnen ⊙
⊛ Vilkoviski
Danzig •
• Elbing
Masurian Lakes ◓
Suwalki ○
Augustow ○
• Bialystok
• Tannenberg ◒
Vistula
Mlawa •

RUSSIA

Bug
Plotsk •
• Kutno
• Warsaw
Brest-Litovsk •
• Kalisz
◓ Lodz
Vistula
Piotrkow •
• Kielce
Novo Radomsk •
• Czestochowa
• Lublin
⊙ Krasnik
⊙ Komarov
S I L E S I A
Cracow •
• Tarnow
GALICIA
San
• Przemysl
◉ Lemberg
Gorlice •
Carpathians

AUSTRIA-HUNGARY

Russian advance into East Prussia 4-23 August. Between August 26 and September 13 they were defeated at Tannenberg and the Masurian Lakes, and driven back into Russia

Russian territory conquered by Germany September 28 - December 31. At the Battle of Lodz, in November, the Germans prevented a Russian advance into Silesia

⇨ Austrian advances into Russia

← Russian counter-attacks into Austria

Conquered by Russia from Austria

— The front line on 31 December 1914

0   50
Miles

⊙ Russian victories
◒ German victories

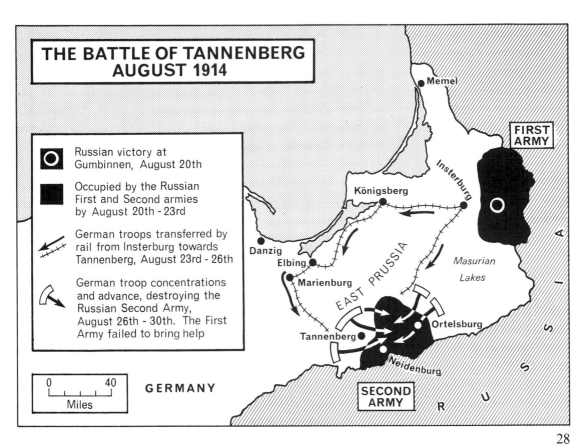

THE BATTLE OF TANNENBERG AUGUST 1914

Russian victory at Gumbinnen, August 20th

Occupied by the Russian First and Second armies by August 20th - 23rd

German troops transferred by rail from Insterburg towards Tannenberg, August 23rd - 26th

German troop concentrations and advance, destroying the Russian Second Army, August 26th - 30th. The First Army failed to bring help

0   40
Miles

GERMANY

FIRST ARMY

Memel

Königsberg

Insterburg

Danzig

Elbing

Marienburg

EAST PRUSSIA

Masurian Lakes

Tannenberg

Ortelsburg

Neidenburg

SECOND ARMY

R U S S I A

28

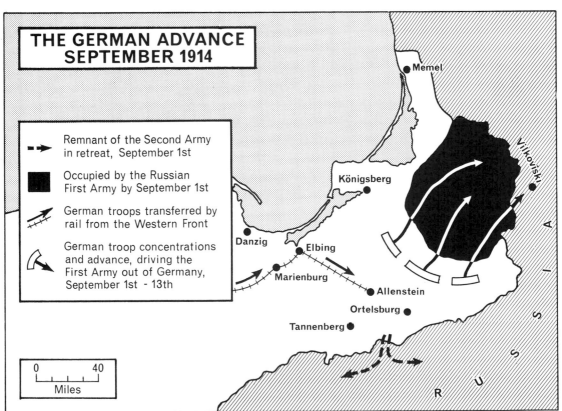

THE GERMAN ADVANCE SEPTEMBER 1914

Remnant of the Second Army in retreat, September 1st

Occupied by the Russian First Army by September 1st

German troops transferred by rail from the Western Front

German troop concentrations and advance, driving the First Army out of Germany, September 1st - 13th

0   40
Miles

Memel

Königsberg

Vilkoviski

Danzig

Elbing

Marienburg

Allenstein

Ortelsburg

Tannenberg

R U S S I A

29

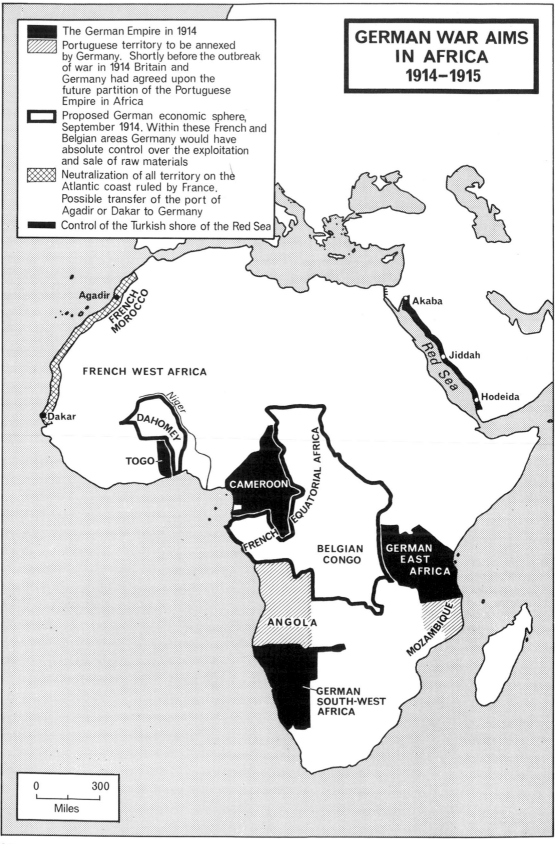

GERMAN WAR AIMS IN AFRICA 1914–1915

Legend:
- **The German Empire in 1914**
- Portuguese territory to be annexed by Germany. Shortly before the outbreak of war in 1914 Britain and Germany had agreed upon the future partition of the Portuguese Empire in Africa
- Proposed German economic sphere, September 1914. Within these French and Belgian areas Germany would have absolute control over the exploitation and sale of raw materials
- Neutralization of all territory on the Atlantic coast ruled by France. Possible transfer of the port of Agadir or Dakar to Germany
- Control of the Turkish shore of the Red Sea

Agadir
FRENCH MOROCCO
FRENCH WEST AFRICA
Niger
Dakar
DAHOMEY
TOGO
CAMEROON
FRENCH EQUATORIAL AFRICA
BELGIAN CONGO
ANGOLA
GERMAN EAST AFRICA
MOZAMBIQUE
GERMAN SOUTH-WEST AFRICA
Akaba
Red Sea
Jiddah
Hodeida

0   300
Miles

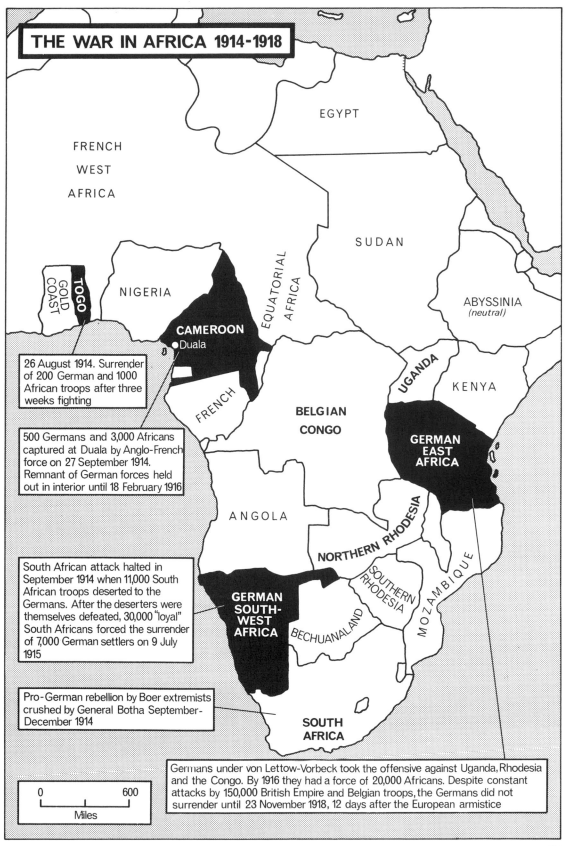

THE WAR IN AFRICA 1914-1918

EGYPT

FRENCH

WEST

AFRICA

SUDAN

GOLD COAST

TOGO

NIGERIA

EQUATORIAL AFRICA

ABYSSINIA
(neutral)

CAMEROON

●Duala

UGANDA

KENYA

FRENCH

26 August 1914. Surrender of 200 German and 1000 African troops after three weeks fighting

BELGIAN

CONGO

GERMAN EAST AFRICA

500 Germans and 3,000 Africans captured at Duala by Anglo-French force on 27 September 1914. Remnant of German forces held out in interior until 18 February 1916

ANGOLA

NORTHERN RHODESIA

SOUTHERN RHODESIA

MOZAMBIQUE

South African attack halted in September 1914 when 11,000 South African troops deserted to the Germans. After the deserters were themselves defeated, 30,000 "loyal" South Africans forced the surrender of 7,000 German settlers on 9 July 1915

GERMAN SOUTH-WEST AFRICA

BECHUANALAND

Pro-German rebellion by Boer extremists crushed by General Botha September-December 1914

SOUTH AFRICA

0   600

Miles

Germans under von Lettow-Vorbeck took the offensive against Uganda, Rhodesia and the Congo. By 1916 they had a force of 20,000 Africans. Despite constant attacks by 150,000 British Empire and Belgian troops, the Germans did not surrender until 23 November 1918, 12 days after the European armistice

Section Three

1915

A hundred thousand million mites we go
Wheeling and tacking o'er the eternal plain,
Some black with death—and some are white with woe.
Who sent us forth? Who takes us home again?

And there is sound of hymns of praise—to whom?
And curses—on whom curses?—snap the air.
And there is hope goes hand in hand with gloom,
And blood and indignation and despair. . . .

CHARLES SORLEY
"A HUNDRED THOUSAND MILLION MITES WE GO"

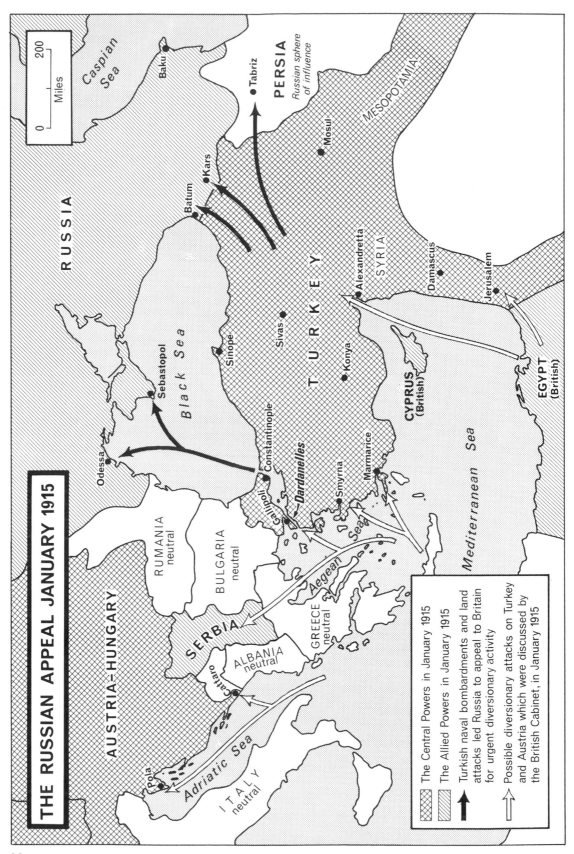

THE RUSSIAN APPEAL JANUARY 1915

200

Miles

0

*Caspian
Sea*

● Baku

● Tabriz

PERSIA

*Russian sphere
of influence*

MESOPOTAMIA

● Kars

Batum

RUSSIA

● Mosul

R **U** **S** **S** **I** **A**

Sebastopol ●

Black Sea

● Sinope

● Sivas

T U R K E Y

● Konya

● Alexandretta

SYRIA

● Damascus

● Jerusalem

**EGYPT
(British)**

Odessa ●

Constantinople ●

Dardanelles

Gallipoli

Smyrna ●

Marmarice ●

**CYPRUS
(British)**

*Mediterranean
Sea*

**RUMANIA
neutral**

**BULGARIA
neutral**

**GREECE
neutral**

*Aegean
Sea*

AUSTRIA-HUNGARY

SERBIA

**ALBANIA
neutral**

Cattaro ●

Adriatic Sea

Pola ●

**ITALY
neutral**

☐ The Central Powers in January 1915

☐ The Allied Powers in January 1915

➡ Turkish naval bombardments and land
attacks led Russia to appeal to Britain
for urgent diversionary activity

⇨ Possible diversionary attacks on Turkey
and Austria which were discussed by
the British Cabinet, in January 1915

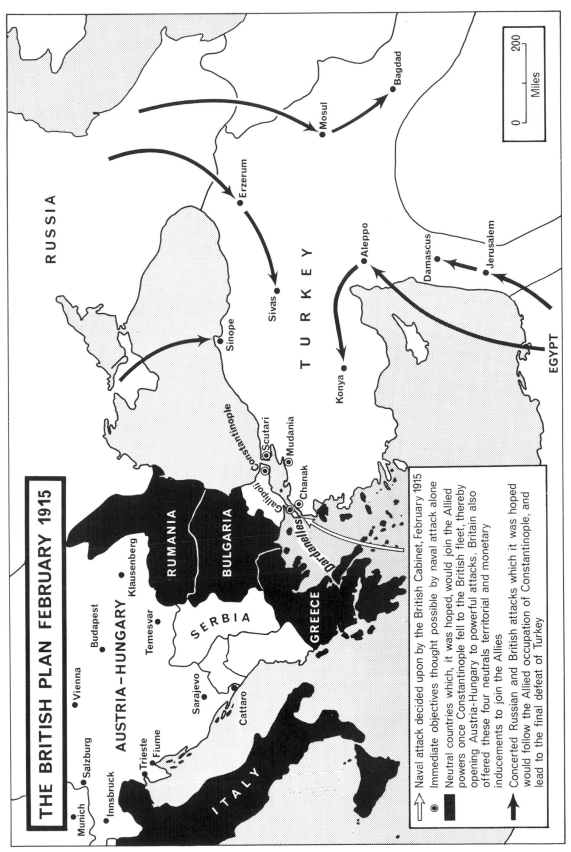

THE BRITISH PLAN FEBRUARY 1915

RUSSIA

TURKEY

AUSTRIA–HUNGARY

Munich
Innsbruck
Salzburg
Vienna
Budapest
Klausenberg
Temesvar
Trieste
Fiume
Sarajevo
Cattaro

ITALY

SERBIA

RUMANIA

BULGARIA

GREECE

Constantinople
Scutari
Mudania
Chanak
Gallipoli
Dardanelles

Sinope
Sivas
Konya
Erzerum
Mosul
Bagdad
Aleppo
Damascus
Jerusalem

EGYPT

0   200
Miles

Naval attack decided upon by the British Cabinet, February 1915

Immediate objectives thought possible by naval attack alone

Neutral countries which, it was hoped, would join the Allied powers once Constantinople fell to the British fleet, thereby opening Austria–Hungary to powerful attacks. Britain also offered these four neutrals territorial and monetary inducements to join the Allies

Concerted Russian and British attacks which it was hoped would follow the Allied occupation of Constantinople, and lead to the final defeat of Turkey

33

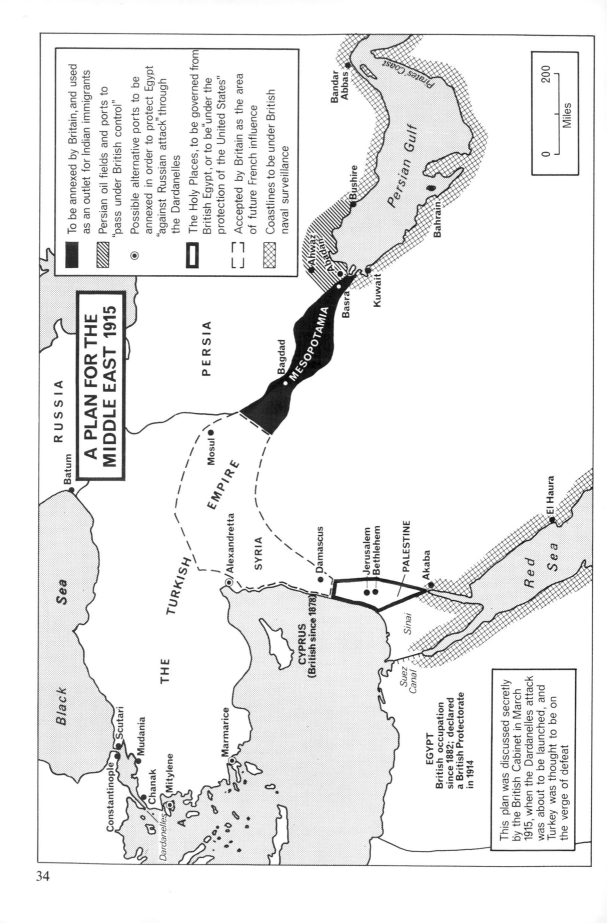

A PLAN FOR THE MIDDLE EAST 1915

Legend:

- ■ To be annexed by Britain, and used as an outlet for Indian immigrants
- ▨ Persian oil fields and ports to "pass under British control"
- ⊙ Possible alternative ports to be annexed in order to protect Egypt "against Russian attack" through the Dardanelles
- ▭ The Holy Places, to be governed from British Egypt, or to be "under the protection of the United States"
- ⊏⊐ Accepted by Britain as the area of future French influence
- ▦ Coastlines to be under British naval surveillance

RUSSIA

Batum

Black Sea

Constantinople
Scutari
Mudania
Chanak
Mitylene
Dardanelles
Marmarice

THE TURKISH EMPIRE

Mosul

PERSIA

Bagdad

MESOPOTAMIA

Ahwaz
Abadan
Basra
Kuwait

Bushire
Bahrain

Bandar Abbas

Persian Gulf

Pirates Coast

Alexandretta
SYRIA
Damascus
Jerusalem
Bethlehem
PALESTINE
Akaba
Sinai

CYPRUS
(British since 1878)

Suez Canal

EGYPT
British occupation since 1882; declared a British Protectorate in 1914

Red Sea

El Haura

Scale: 0 — 200 Miles

This plan was discussed secretly by the British Cabinet in March 1915, when the Dardanelles attack was about to be launched, and Turkey was thought to be on the verge of defeat

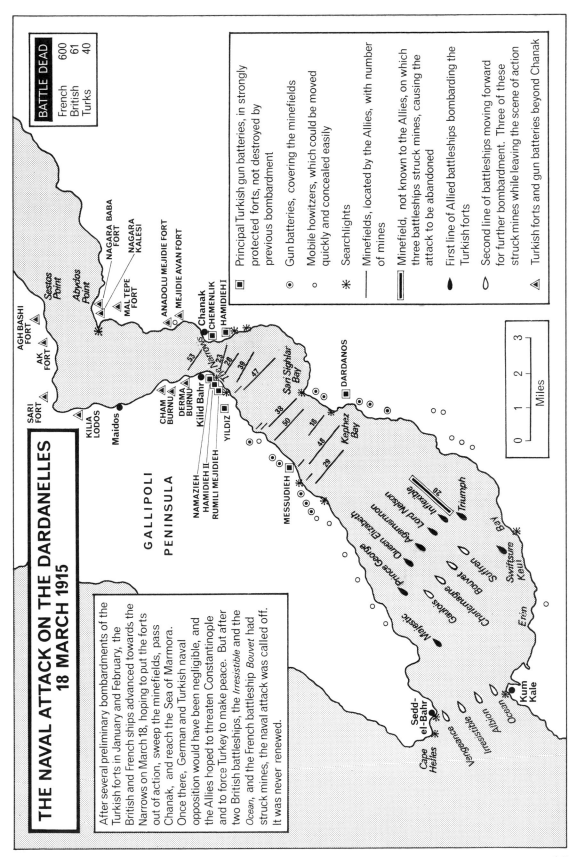

THE NAVAL ATTACK ON THE DARDANELLES 18 MARCH 1915

After several preliminary bombardments of the Turkish forts in January and February, the British and French ships advanced towards the Narrows on March 18, hoping to put the forts out of action, sweep the minefields, pass Chanak, and reach the Sea of Marmora. Once there, German and Turkish naval opposition would have been negligible, and the Allies hoped to threaten Constantinople and to force Turkey to make peace. But after two British battleships, the *Irresistible* and the *Ocean*, and the French battleship *Bouvet* had struck mines, the naval attack was called off. It was never renewed.

BATTLE DEAD	
French	600
British	61
Turks	40

■ Principal Turkish gun batteries, in strongly protected forts, not destroyed by previous bombardment

⊙ Gun batteries, covering the minefields

○ Mobile howitzers, which could be moved quickly and concealed easily

✻ Searchlights

— Minefields, located by the Allies, with number of mines

▭ Minefield, not known to the Allies, on which three battleships struck mines, causing the attack to be abandoned

● First line of Allied battleships bombarding the Turkish forts

◊ Second line of battleships moving forward for further bombardment. Three of these struck mines while leaving the scene of action

◁ Turkish forts and gun batteries beyond Chanak

GALLIPOLI PENINSULA

Miles
0 1 2 3

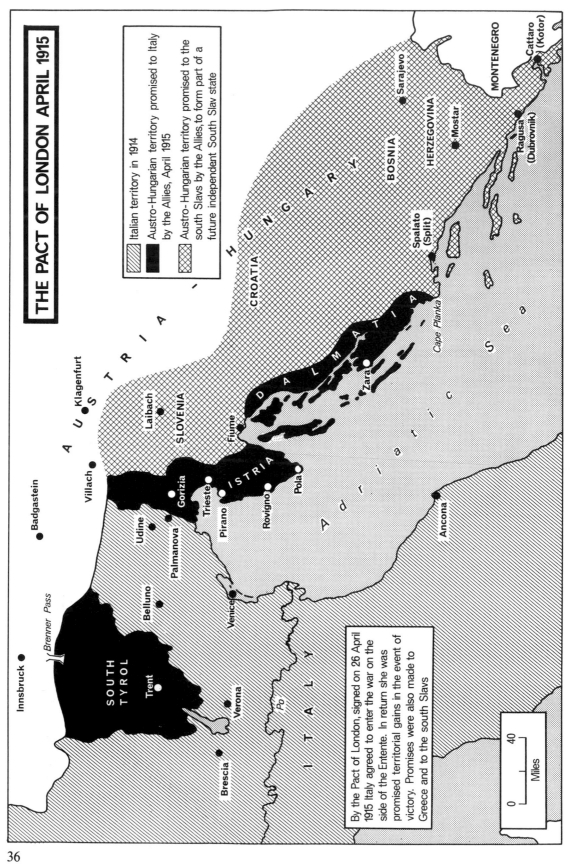

THE PACT OF LONDON APRIL 1915

Italian territory in 1914

Austro-Hungarian territory promised to Italy
by the Allies, April 1915

Austro-Hungarian territory promised to the
south Slavs by the Allies, to form part of a
future independent South Slav state

MONTENEGRO

Cattaro
(Kotor)

Sarajevo

BOSNIA

Mostar

HERZEGOVINA

Ragusa
(Dubrovnik)

Spalato
(Split)

A U S T R I A - H U N G A R Y

CROATIA

Cape Planka

Klagenfurt

Laibach

SLOVENIA

D A L M A T I A

Zara

A d r i a t i c   S e a

Villach

Fiume

ISTRIA

Gorizia

Trieste

Pirano

Rovigno

Pola

Badgastein

Udine

Palmanova

Ancona

Brenner Pass

Belluno

Venice

Po

Innsbruck

SOUTH
TYROL

Trent

Verona

I T A L Y

Brescia

By the Pact of London, signed on 26 April
1915 Italy agreed to enter the war on the
side of the Entente. In return she was
promised territorial gains in the event of
victory. Promises were also made to
Greece and to the south Slavs

0   40

Miles

36

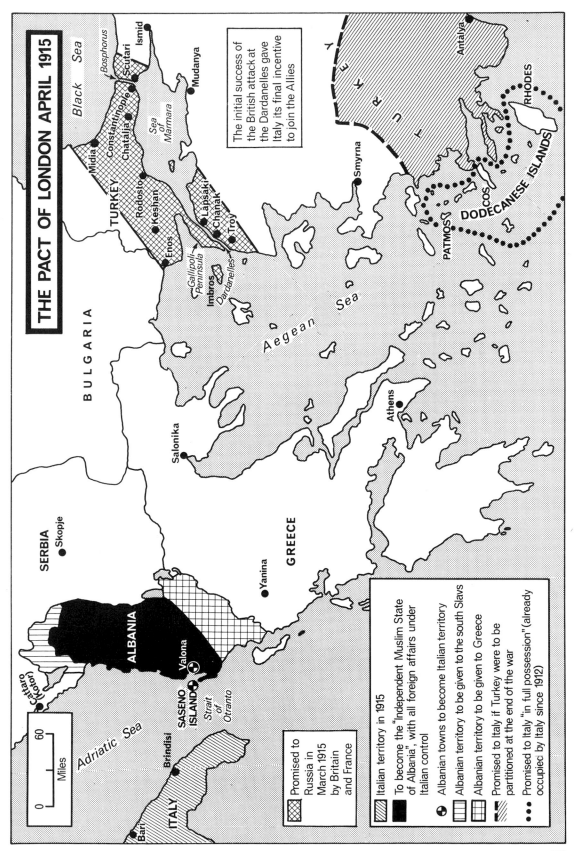

THE PACT OF LONDON APRIL 1915

Black Sea

Bosphorus

Ismid

Scutari

Mudanya

The initial success of the British attack at the Dardanelles gave Italy its final incentive to join the Allies

TURKEY

Midia

Constantinople

Chatalja

Sea of Marmara

Rodosto

Keshan

Lapsaki

Chanak

Troy

Enos

Smyrna

Gallipoli Peninsula

Imbros

Dardanelles

Antalya

RHODES

COS

DODECANESE ISLANDS

PATMOS

Aegean Sea

BULGARIA

Salonika

Athens

SERBIA

Skopje

GREECE

Yanina

Cattaro (Kotor)

ALBANIA

Valona

SASENO ISLAND

Strait of Otranto

Brindisi

Bari

ITALY

Adriatic Sea

60

Miles

0

Promised to Russia in March 1915 by Britain and France

Italian territory in 1915

To become the "Independent Muslim State of Albania", with all foreign affairs under Italian control

Albanian towns to become Italian territory

Albanian territory to be given to the south Slavs

Albanian territory to be given to Greece

Promised to Italy if Turkey were to be partitioned at the end of the war

Promised to Italy "in full possession" (already occupied by Italy since 1912)

37

THE MILITARY LANDINGS ON THE GALLIPOLI PENINSULA APRIL AND AUGUST 1915

After the failure of the naval attack of 18 March 1915, Allied troops landed on 25 April, hoping to capture the high ground of Achi Baba and Sari Bair, and to reach the shore of the Narrows. But a tenacious Turkish defence kept them pinned down to their tiny beachheads. A second landing on 6 August likewise failed to reach the Narrows. After more than eight months of heroism, frustration, muddle, incompetence, disease and death, the Allied armies withdrew in January 1916 and the enterprise was abandoned. The Turkish successes both in April and August owed much to the military genius of Mustafa Kemal, later, as Atatürk, President of Turkey

The two areas on the Gallipoli Peninsula held by Allied troops were known as 'Helles' (after the Cape) and 'Anzac' (after the colloquial Australian name for the Australian and New Zealand Army Corps, or Anzacs, who took a leading part in the northern landings

Map labels

Kiretch Tepe
Tekke Tepe
Suvla Point
Anafarta Sagir
Suvla Bay
Salt Lake (dry in summer)
Biyuk Anafarta
Nibrunesi Point
Lala Baba
Hill 60
Sari Bair Ridge
Chunuk Bair 850ft
Koja Chemen Tepe 971ft
Ocean Beach
Ari Burnu
Anzac Cove
Hell Spit
Brighton Beach
Gaba Tepe
Boghali
Mal Tepe 534ft
Maidos
Kilid Bahr Plateau
Kilid Bahr
Chanak
The Narrows
Achi Baba 709ft
Krithia
Gully Ravine
Kereves Dere
Tekke Burnu
Sedd-el-Bahr
Morto Bay
Cape Helles

ESTIMATED BATTLE DEAD

Turkish	100,000
Allied	46,000

Legend

- ● Landing beaches at 'Helles' on April 25
- ◉ Landing beaches at 'Anzac' on April 25
- ꙍꙍꙍ Objectives for April 25, not reached in 8 months of fighting
- ⊠ Ground held at 'Helles' from May 1915 until the evacuation in January 1916
- ▨ Ground held at 'Anzac' from May 1915 until August 1915
- △ Landing beaches at Suvla on August 6
- ▥ Ground held until evacuated in December
- ▧ Ground gained at 'Anzac' and 'Suvla' in August 1915 and held until the evacuation in January 1916
- ▲▲▲ Furthest advance in August, held only for a few hours, when the Turks counter-attacked successfully and drove the Allied troops off the crest of Chunuk Bair

0   1   2
Miles

ALLIED TRENCHES ON GALLIPOLI
THE 'HELLES' FRONT IN JULY 1915

Aegean Sea

Fusilier Bluff

Ghurka Mule Track

Western Birdcage

Forward Inch

Gully Ravine

Eastern Birdcage

Holborn Circus

Eastern Mule Trench

Lancashire St.

Chelmsford St.

Rue de Paris

Worcester Barricade

Leith Walk

Munster Terr.

No 1 Australian Line

Oldham Rd.

Ardwick Gn.

Princes St

Clapham Junction

No 2 Australian Line

Wigan Road

Hope St.

The Vineyard

KRITHIA VILLAGE

Sauchiehall Street

Oxford Street

Plymouth Ave

Main Street

Nelson Ave.

Piccadilly Circus

Central St.

Leicester Square

Park Lane

Hyde Park Corner

Regent St

Avenue de Paris

Esplanade

Avenue de Constantinople

The Haricot

N

Boyau Central

Withered Tree

0   500
Yards

- - - Turkish Front Line
⊓⊔⊓⊔ } Allied trenches
⊙   Dressing stations and first aid post

Dardanelles

39

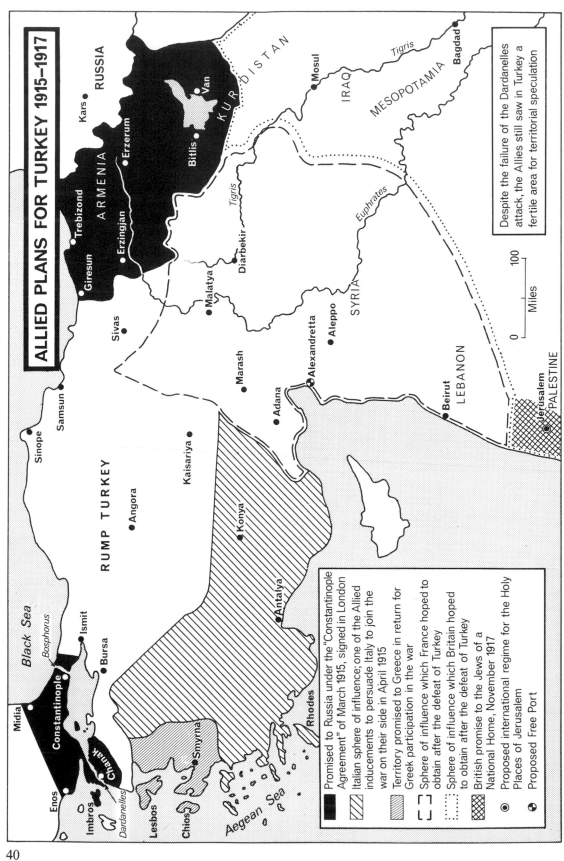

ALLIED PLANS FOR TURKEY 1915–1917

Despite the failure of the Dardanelles attack, the Allies still saw in Turkey a fertile area for territorial speculation

RUSSIA

Kars

Mosul

IRAQ

MESOPOTAMIA

Bagdad

Tigris

KURDISTAN

Van

Bitlis

Erzerum

ARMENIA

Erzingjan

Tigris

Diarbekir

Euphrates

SYRIA

Trebizond

Giresun

Malatya

Aleppo

Marash

Adana

Alexandretta

Beirut

LEBANON

Sivas

Jerusalem

PALESTINE

0   100
Miles

Samsun

Sinope

Kaisariya

RUMP TURKEY

Angora

Konya

Antalya

Ismit

Bursa

Black Sea

Bosphorus

Constantinople

Chanak

Dardanelles

Midia

Enos

Imbros

Lesbos

Chios

Smyrna

Rhodes

Aegean Sea

Promised to Russia under the "Constantinople Agreement" of March 1915, signed in London

Italian sphere of influence; one of the Allied inducements to persuade Italy to join the war on their side in April 1915

Territory promised to Greece in return for Greek participation in the war

Sphere of influence which France hoped to obtain after the defeat of Turkey

Sphere of influence which Britain hoped to obtain after the defeat of Turkey

British promise to the Jews of a National Home, November 1917

Proposed international regime for the Holy Places of Jerusalem

Proposed Free Port

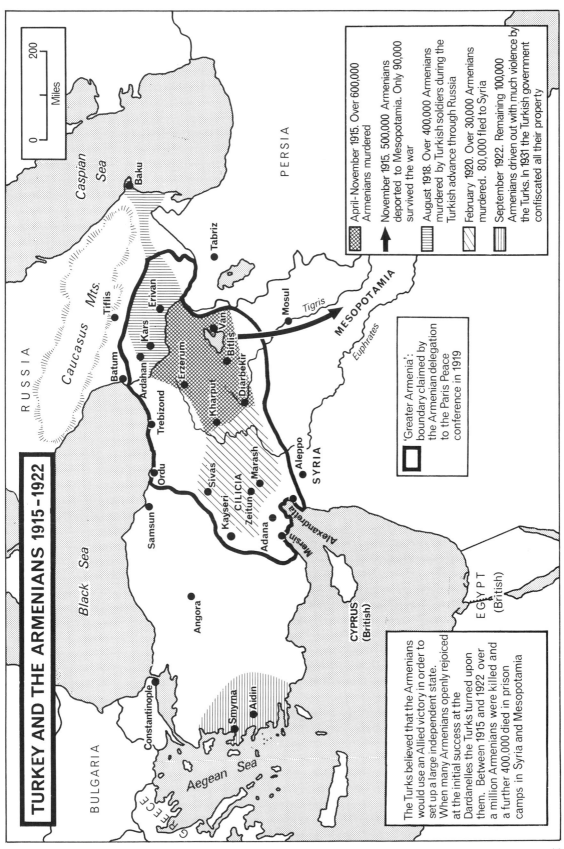

TURKEY AND THE ARMENIANS 1915-1922

April-November 1915. Over 600,000 Armenians murdered

November 1915. 500,000 Armenians deported to Mesopotamia. Only 90,000 survived the war

August 1918. Over 400,000 Armenians murdered by Turkish soldiers during the Turkish advance through Russia

February 1920. Over 30,000 Armenians murdered. 80,000 fled to Syria

September 1922. Remaining 100,000 Armenians driven out with much violence by the Turks. In 1931 the Turkish government confiscated all their property

'Greater Armenia': boundary claimed by the Armenian delegation to the Paris Peace conference in 1919

The Turks believed that the Armenians would use an Allied victory in order to set up a large independent state. When many Armenians openly rejoiced at the initial success at the Dardanelles the Turks turned upon them. Between 1915 and 1922 over a million Armenians were killed and a further 400,000 died in prison camps in Syria and Mesopotamia

RUSSIA

PERSIA

BULGARIA

GREECE

EGYPT (British)

CYPRUS (British)

SYRIA

MESOPOTAMIA

Caspian Sea

Black Sea

Aegean Sea

Caucasus Mts.

Tigris

Euphrates

Baku
Tabriz
Mosul
Tiflis
Erivan
Van
Kars
Bitlis
Erzerum
Diarbekir
Ardahan
Batum
Kharput
Trebizond
Ordu
Sivas
Marash
Aleppo
Samsun
Kayseri
Zeitun
CILICIA
Adana
Mersin
Alexandretta
Angora
Constantinople
Smyrna
Aidin

Miles
0   200

41

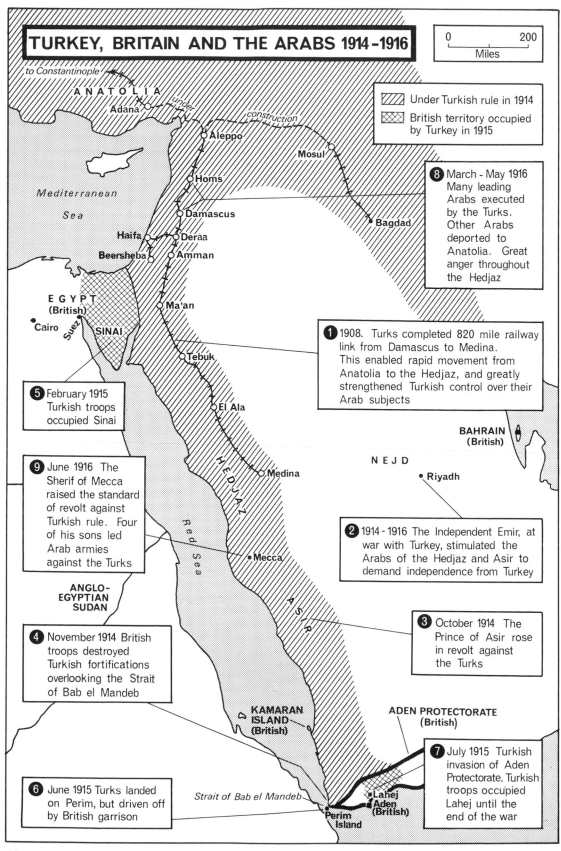

TURKEY, BRITAIN AND THE ARABS 1914-1916

0   200

Miles

to Constantinople

A N A T O L I A

Adana

under

construction

Aleppo

Mosul

Homs

Mediterranean

Sea

Damascus

Haifa

Deraa

Bagdad

Beersheba

Amman

E G Y P T
(British)

Ma'an

Cairo

Suez

SINAI

Tebuk

El Ala

H E D J A Z

Medina

Red Sea

A S I R

Riyadh

N E J D

ANGLO-
EGYPTIAN
SUDAN

Mecca

Perim
Island

Strait of Bab el Mandeb

KAMARAN
ISLAND
(British)

ADEN PROTECTORATE
(British)

Lahej

Aden
(British)

BAHRAIN
(British)

☐ Under Turkish rule in 1914

☒ British territory occupied by Turkey in 1915

❽ March - May 1916 Many leading Arabs executed by the Turks. Other Arabs deported to Anatolia. Great anger throughout the Hedjaz

❶ 1908. Turks completed 820 mile railway link from Damascus to Medina. This enabled rapid movement from Anatolia to the Hedjaz, and greatly strengthened Turkish control over their Arab subjects

❺ February 1915 Turkish troops occupied Sinai

❾ June 1916 The Sherif of Mecca raised the standard of revolt against Turkish rule. Four of his sons led Arab armies against the Turks

❷ 1914 - 1916 The Independent Emir, at war with Turkey, stimulated the Arabs of the Hedjaz and Asir to demand independence from Turkey

❸ October 1914 The Prince of Asir rose in revolt against the Turks

❹ November 1914 British troops destroyed Turkish fortifications overlooking the Strait of Bab el Mandeb

❼ July 1915 Turkish invasion of Aden Protectorate. Turkish troops occupied Lahej until the end of the war

❻ June 1915 Turks landed on Perim, but driven off by British garrison

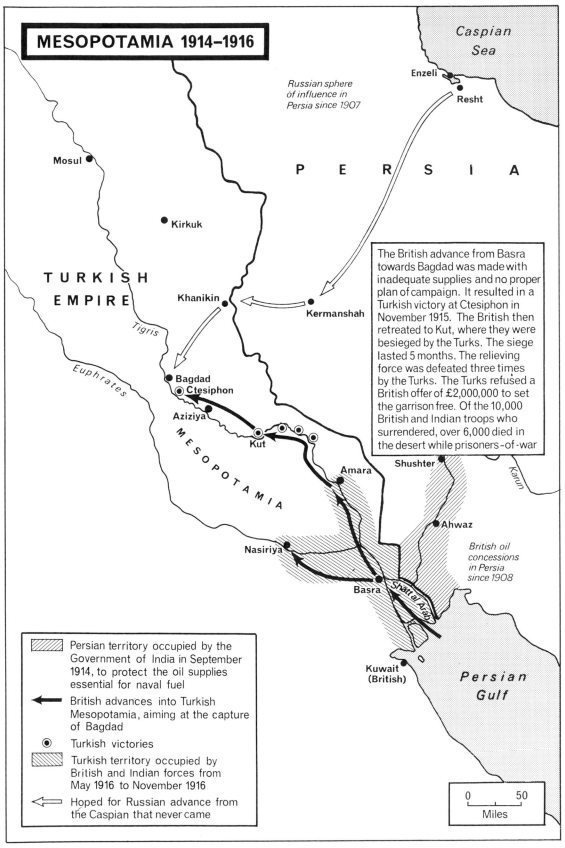

MESOPOTAMIA 1914–1916

Caspian Sea

Enzeli
Resht

Russian sphere of influence in Persia since 1907

P E R S I A

Mosul

Kirkuk

T U R K I S H

E M P I R E

Khanikin

Kermanshah

Tigris

Euphrates

Bagdad
Ctesiphon

Aziziya

M E S O P O T A M I A

Kut

Amara

Shushter

Karun

Ahwaz

Nasiriya

British oil concessions in Persia since 1908

Basra

Shatt al Arab

The British advance from Basra towards Bagdad was made with inadequate supplies and no proper plan of campaign. It resulted in a Turkish victory at Ctesiphon in November 1915. The British then retreated to Kut, where they were besieged by the Turks. The siege lasted 5 months. The relieving force was defeated three times by the Turks. The Turks refused a British offer of £2,000,000 to set the garrison free. Of the 10,000 British and Indian troops who surrendered, over 6,000 died in the desert while prisoners-of-war

Kuwait
(British)

Persian Gulf

▨ Persian territory occupied by the Government of India in September 1914, to protect the oil supplies essential for naval fuel

◀ British advances into Turkish Mesopotamia, aiming at the capture of Bagdad

◉ Turkish victories

▨ Turkish territory occupied by British and Indian forces from May 1916 to November 1916

⇐ Hoped for Russian advance from the Caspian that never came

0   50
Miles

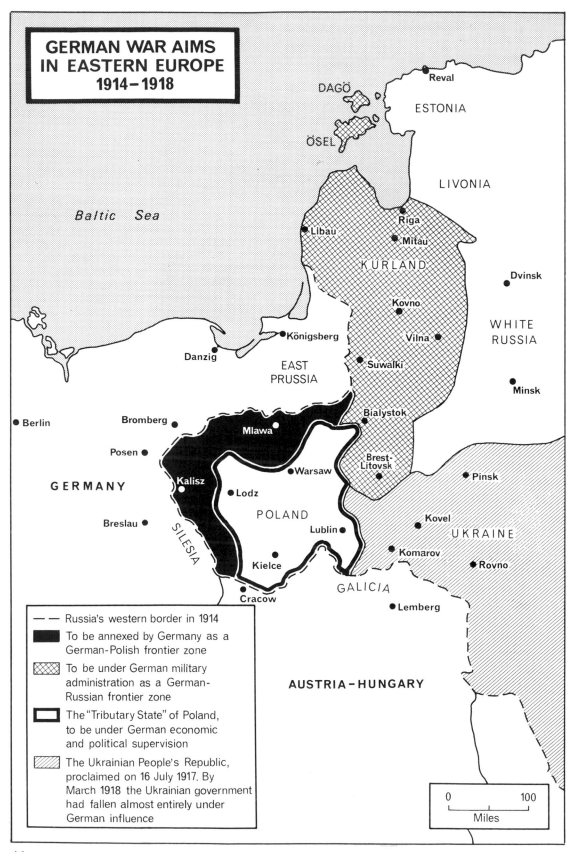

GERMAN WAR AIMS IN EASTERN EUROPE 1914–1918

DAGÖ

Reval

ESTONIA

ÖSEL

LIVONIA

Baltic Sea

Riga

Libau

Mitau

Dvinsk

KURLAND

Kovno

WHITE RUSSIA

Königsberg

Vilna

Danzig

EAST PRUSSIA

Suwalki

Minsk

Berlin

Bromberg

Bialystok

Mlawa

Posen

Brest-Litovsk

Pinsk

Warsaw

GERMANY

Kalisz

Lodz

Breslau

POLAND

Kovel

SILESIA

Lublin

UKRAINE

Kielce

Komarov

Rovno

GALICIA

Cracow

Lemberg

AUSTRIA – HUNGARY

— — Russia's western border in 1914

To be annexed by Germany as a German-Polish frontier zone

To be under German military administration as a German-Russian frontier zone

The "Tributary State" of Poland, to be under German economic and political supervision

The Ukrainian People's Republic, proclaimed on 16 July 1917. By March 1918 the Ukrainian government had fallen almost entirely under German influence

0   100

Miles

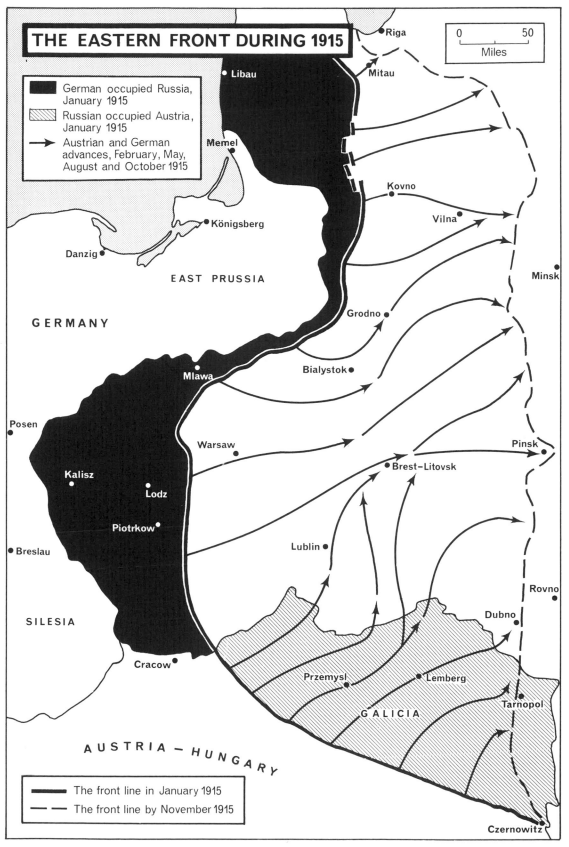

THE EASTERN FRONT DURING 1915

0   50
Miles

- ■ German occupied Russia, January 1915
- ▨ Russian occupied Austria, January 1915
- → Austrian and German advances, February, May, August and October 1915

Riga

Libau

Mitau

Memel

Kovno

Königsberg

Vilna

Danzig

Minsk

EAST PRUSSIA

GERMANY

Grodno

Mlawa

Bialystok

Posen

Warsaw

Pinsk

Kalisz

Brest–Litovsk

Lodz

Piotrkow

Breslau

Lublin

Rovno

SILESIA

Dubno

Cracow

Przemysl

Lemberg

Tarnopol

GALICIA

AUSTRIA – HUNGARY

Czernowitz

— The front line in January 1915

--- The front line by November 1915

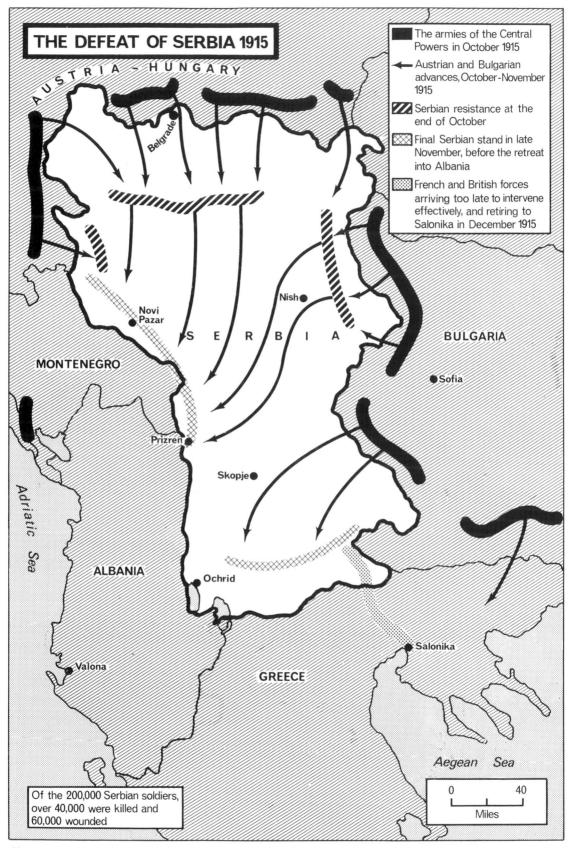

THE DEFEAT OF SERBIA 1915

AUSTRIA - HUNGARY

Belgrade

■ The armies of the Central Powers in October 1915

← Austrian and Bulgarian advances, October-November 1915

▨ Serbian resistance at the end of October

▧ Final Serbian stand in late November, before the retreat into Albania

▨ French and British forces arriving too late to intervene effectively, and retiring to Salonika in December 1915

MONTENEGRO

Novi Pazar

S E R B I A

Nish

BULGARIA

Sofia

Prizren

Skopje

Adriatic Sea

ALBANIA

Ochrid

Valona

GREECE

Salonika

Aegean Sea

Of the 200,000 Serbian soldiers, over 40,000 were killed and 60,000 wounded

0   40
Miles

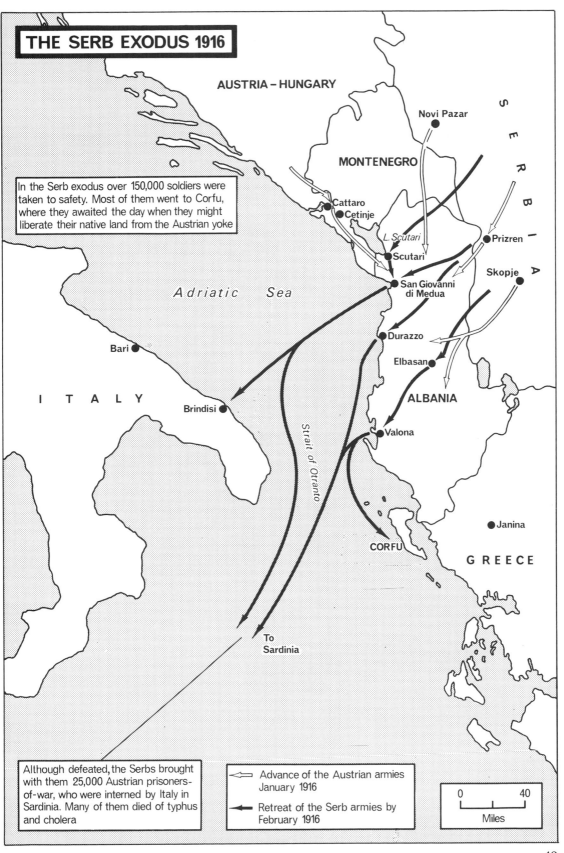

THE SERB EXODUS 1916

AUSTRIA – HUNGARY

MONTENEGRO

Novi Pazar

S
E
R
B
I
A

Cattaro
Cetinje

In the Serb exodus over 150,000 soldiers were taken to safety. Most of them went to Corfu, where they awaited the day when they might liberate their native land from the Austrian yoke

L. Scutari

Scutari

Prizren

Skopje

A d r i a t i c   S e a

San Giovanni di Medua

Bari

Durazzo

Elbasan

I T A L Y

Brindisi

ALBANIA

Strait of Otranto

Valona

Janina

CORFU

G R E E C E

To Sardinia

Although defeated, the Serbs brought with them 25,000 Austrian prisoners-of-war, who were interned by Italy in Sardinia. Many of them died of typhus and cholera

⇐ Advance of the Austrian armies January 1916

◄ Retreat of the Serb armies by February 1916

0   40

Miles

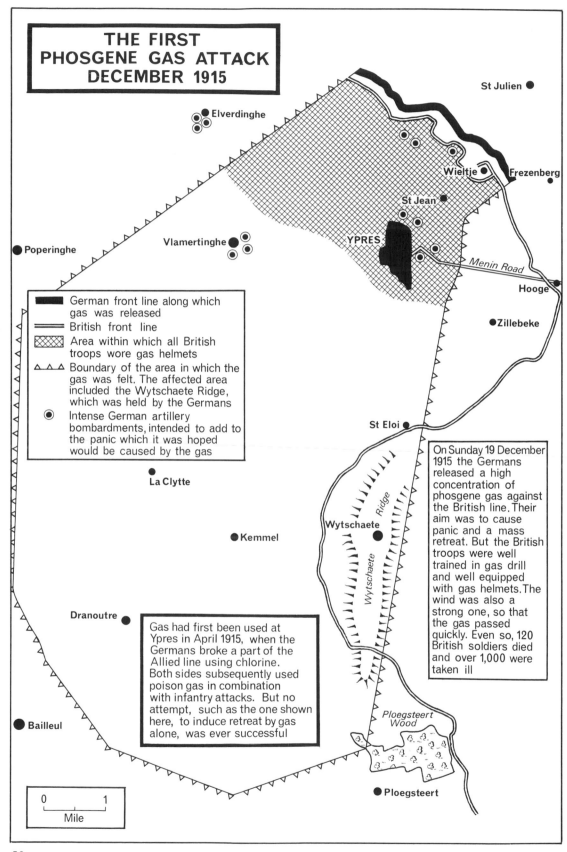

THE FIRST PHOSGENE GAS ATTACK DECEMBER 1915

St Julien

Elverdinghe

Wieltje   Frezenberg

St Jean

YPRES

Menin Road

Poperinghe

Vlamertinghe

Hooge

Zillebeke

German front line along which gas was released

British front line

Area within which all British troops wore gas helmets

Boundary of the area in which the gas was felt. The affected area included the Wytschaete Ridge, which was held by the Germans

Intense German artillery bombardments, intended to add to the panic which it was hoped would be caused by the gas

St Eloi

La Clytte

On Sunday 19 December 1915 the Germans released a high concentration of phosgene gas against the British line. Their aim was to cause panic and a mass retreat. But the British troops were well trained in gas drill and well equipped with gas helmets. The wind was also a strong one, so that the gas passed quickly. Even so, 120 British soldiers died and over 1,000 were taken ill

Kemmel

Wytschaete

Wytschaete Ridge

Dranoutre

Gas had first been used at Ypres in April 1915, when the Germans broke a part of the Allied line using chlorine. Both sides subsequently used poison gas in combination with infantry attacks. But no attempt, such as the one shown here, to induce retreat by gas alone, was ever successful

Ploegsteert Wood

Bailleul

0   1
Mile

Ploegsteert

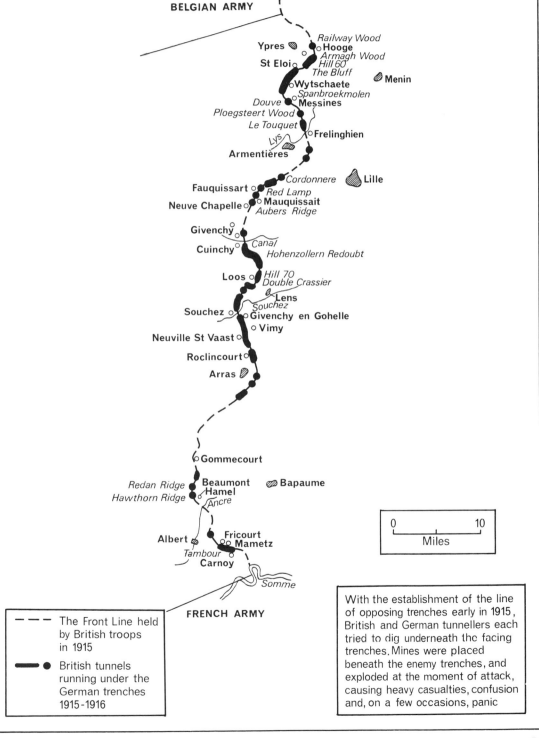

THE TUNNELLERS OF THE WESTERN FRONT
1915–1916

BELGIAN ARMY

Railway Wood
Ypres
Hooge
Armagh Wood
St Eloi
Hill 60
The Bluff
Menin
Wytschaete
Spanbroekmolen
Douve
Messines
Ploegsteert Wood
Le Touquet
Frelinghien
Lys
Armentières

Cordonnere
Lille
Fauquissart
Red Lamp
Neuve Chapelle
Mauquissait
Aubers Ridge

Givenchy
Canal
Cuinchy
Hohenzollern Redoubt

Loos
Hill 70
Double Crassier
Lens
Souchez
Souchez
Givenchy en Gohelle
Vimy
Neuville St Vaast
Roclincourt
Arras

Gommecourt

Redan Ridge
Beaumont
Bapaume
Hamel
Hawthorn Ridge
Ancre

Albert
Fricourt
Mametz
Tambour
Carnoy
Somme

FRENCH ARMY

	Scale
0	10
	Miles

- - - The Front Line held by British troops in 1915

●━━● British tunnels running under the German trenches 1915-1916

With the establishment of the line of opposing trenches early in 1915, British and German tunnellers each tried to dig underneath the facing trenches. Mines were placed beneath the enemy trenches, and exploded at the moment of attack, causing heavy casualties, confusion and, on a few occasions, panic

Section Four

1916

... Lines of grey, muttering faces, masked with fear,
They leave their trenches, going over the top,
While time ticks blank and busy on their wrists,
And hope, with furtive eyes and grappling fists,
Flounders in mud. O Jesus, make it stop!

— SIEGFRIED SASSOON
"ATTACK"

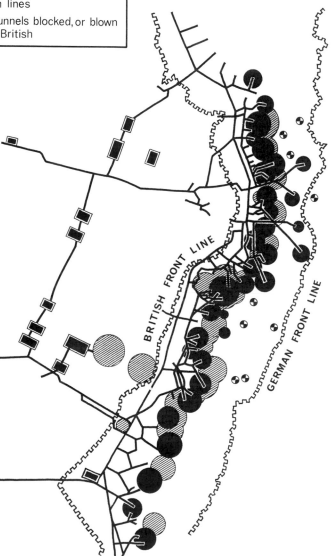

UNDERGROUND ACTIVITY ON THE WESTERN FRONT 1916

Legend:
- ᴖᴖᴖ The British and German front lines
- ▬ British dugouts, underground stores and explosive supplies
- — British tunnels below ground
- ● Craters blown by the British in no-man's-land
- ◉ Craters blown by the Germans in no-man's-land, and behind the British lines
- ◕ German tunnels blocked, or blown in, by the British

BRITISH FRONT LINE

GERMAN FRONT LINE

Once the opposing armies had established their trench fortifications, sappers and miners began digging under no-man's-land, and even behind enemy lines. At regular intervals explosive charges were set off, destroying enemy forward positions and trench fortifications. The subsequent craters themselves became military objectives. Within a year there were over 60 craters blown in the mile long section of no-man's-land in the sector of the trenches shown here

0   200
Feet

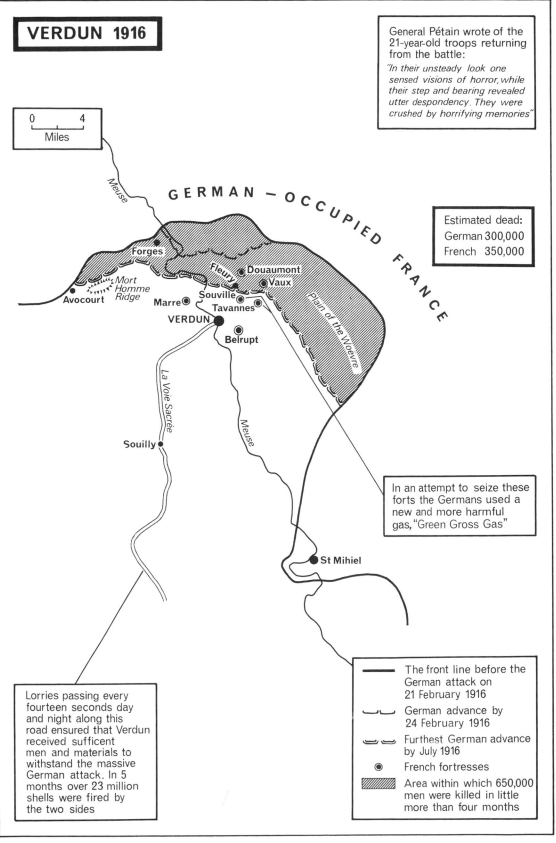

VERDUN 1916

General Pétain wrote of the 21-year-old troops returning from the battle:

"In their unsteady look one sensed visions of horror, while their step and bearing revealed utter despondency. They were crushed by horrifying memories"

0   4
Miles

Meuse

GERMAN — OCCUPIED FRANCE

Forges

Mort Homme Ridge

Avocourt

Fleury

Douaumont

Vaux

Souville

Marre

Tavannes

VERDUN

Belrupt

Plain of the Woevre

La Voie Sacrée

Meuse

Souilly

St Mihiel

Estimated dead:
German 300,000
French   350,000

In an attempt to seize these forts the Germans used a new and more harmful gas, "Green Gross Gas"

Lorries passing every fourteen seconds day and night along this road ensured that Verdun received sufficent men and materials to withstand the massive German attack. In 5 months over 23 million shells were fired by the two sides

—————— The front line before the German attack on 21 February 1916

German advance by 24 February 1916

Furthest German advance by July 1916

◉   French fortresses

▨   Area within which 650,000 men were killed in little more than four months

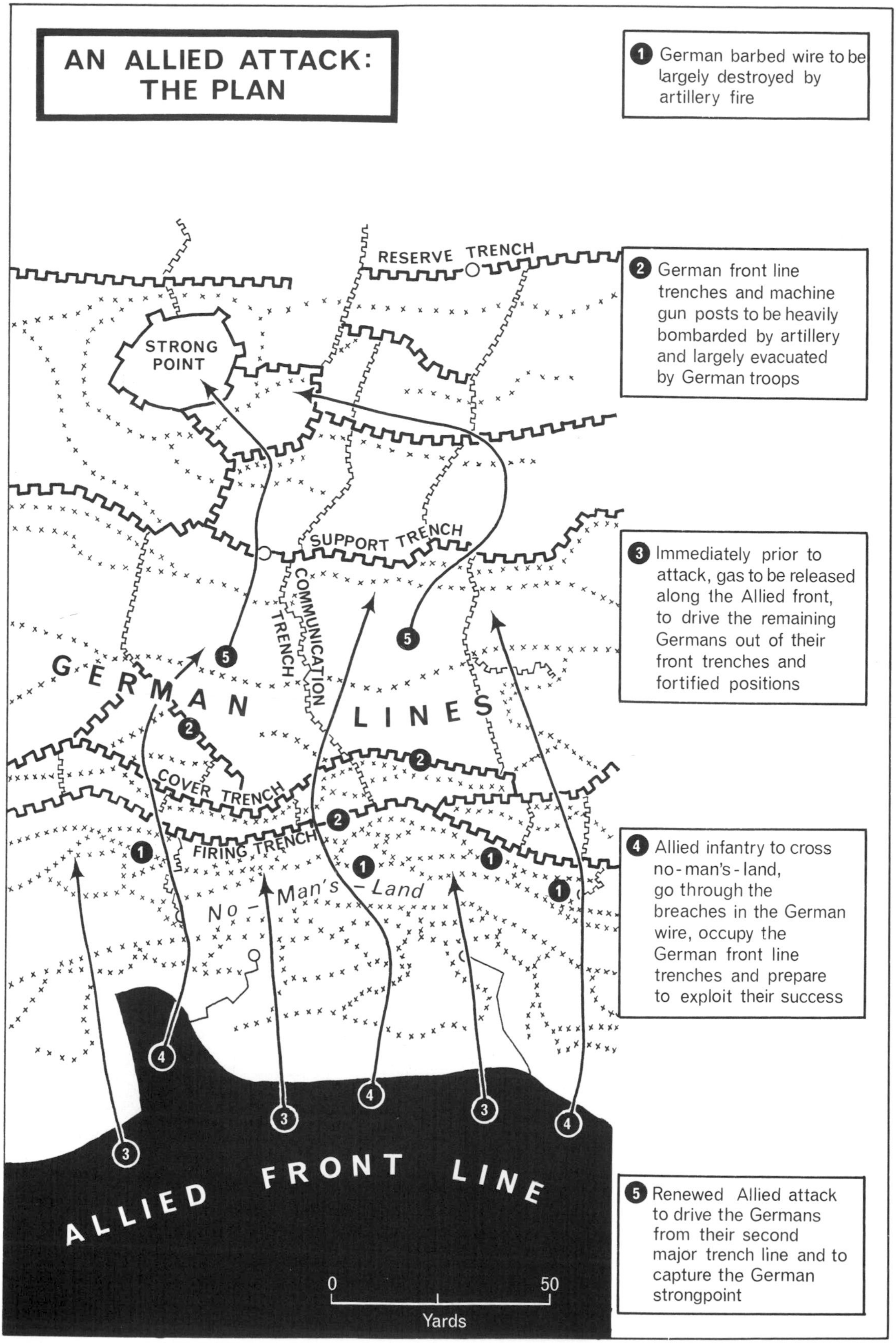

AN ALLIED ATTACK: THE PLAN

1 German barbed wire to be largely destroyed by artillery fire

2 German front line trenches and machine gun posts to be heavily bombarded by artillery and largely evacuated by German troops

3 Immediately prior to attack, gas to be released along the Allied front, to drive the remaining Germans out of their front trenches and fortified positions

4 Allied infantry to cross no-man's-land, go through the breaches in the German wire, occupy the German front line trenches and prepare to exploit their success

5 Renewed Allied attack to drive the Germans from their second major trench line and to capture the German strongpoint

RESERVE TRENCH

STRONG POINT

SUPPORT TRENCH

COMMUNICATION TRENCH

G E R M A N   L I N E S

COVER TRENCH

FIRING TRENCH

No - Man's - Land

ALLIED FRONT LINE

0   50

Yards

1 Insufficiently accurate or heavy artillery barrage fails to make any significant breaks in the German barbed wire

2 German concrete dugouts and well-constructed trenches not destroyed by Allied artillery, but remain occupied by German troops

3 Change of wind blows the gas back towards the Allied front line

4 The Allied troops are partly caught by their own gas, which has blown back, or has lingered in no-man's-land. Other men are trapped by the unbroken barbed wire and are then machine-gunned from German strongpoints which survived Allied artillery fire

5 A few Allied troops enter the first German trenches, but after gallant individual efforts are captured or killed. No troops reach the second German line. The Germans send up re-inforcements who rapidly repair what damage has been done. The Allied artillery, having exhausted its meagre supplies of shells, is unable to renew its heavy bombardment

RESERVE TRENCH

STRONG POINT

SUPPORT TRENCH

GERMAN LINES

COMMUNICATION TRENCH

COVER TRENCH

FIRING TRENCH

No - Man's - Land

ALLIED FRONT LINE

0   50
Yards

THE SOMME 1916

Legend:
- Allied front line on 1 July 1916
- German front line on 1 July
- German front line by the end of July
- German front line on 1 September
- German front line on 1 October
- German front line on 20 November

Scale: 0 — 2 Miles

Gommecourt
Hébuterne
Bapaume
Miraumont
Beaumont Hamel
Warlencourt
Le Sars
le Transloy
Thiepval
Courcelette
Gueudecourt
Martinpuich
High wood
Delville wood
Sailly
Pozières
Longueval
Morval
Ovillers
Ginchy
Contalmaison
Mametz wood
Guillemont
Combles
Montauban
Trones wood
Albert
Fricourt
Mametz
Maurepas
Bouchavesnes
Maricourt
Somme
Somme
Péronne
BRITISH FRONT LINE
FRENCH FRONT LINE
Dompierre
Barleux
Estrées

On the first day of the battle, July 1, German machine guns, often hidden in armoured emplacements, prevented any British gains. 20,000 British troops were killed on that day: amounting to 60% of all the officers and 40% of all the men engaged. The battle continued fiercely for five months, and included the first use of tanks, by the British, in September

The British had 460, the French 850 heavy guns to maintain a continuous artillery barrage. In the preliminary bombardment alone, 1,700,000 shells were fired. By September, stocks of artillery shell were seriously low. Even on the first day, poor quality shells resulted in a general failure to destroy German dug-outs

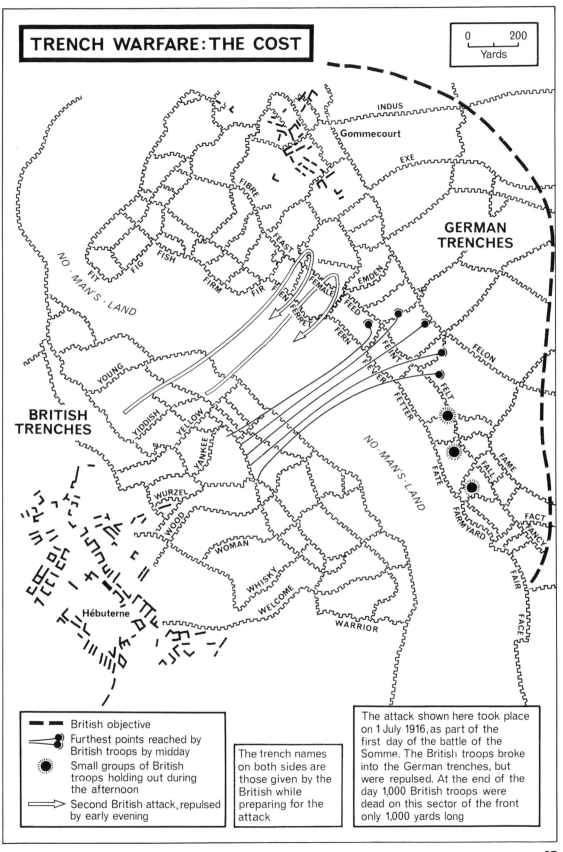

TRENCH WARFARE: THE COST

0   200
Yards

INDUS

Gommecourt

EXE

FIBRE

GERMAN
TRENCHES

NO-MAN'S-LAND

FIT
FIG   FISH   FEAST
            FIRM   FIR FIEN FEMALE   EMDEN
                         FFERRET FEED
                                  FERN   FEINT   FELON
BRITISH
TRENCHES   FEVER   FELT
                                          FETTER
                   YOUNG
                                                      FAME
            YIDDISH   NO-MAN'S-LAND   FALL
                   YELLOW   FATE
                YANKEE   FARMYARD   FACT
                                                                FANCY
            WURZEL
            WOOD
                   WOMAN   FAIR

                         WHISKY
                   WELCOME   FACE
Hébuterne
                         WARRIOR

British objective

Furthest points reached by
British troops by midday

Small groups of British
troops holding out during
the afternoon

Second British attack, repulsed
by early evening

The trench names
on both sides are
those given by the
British while
preparing for the
attack

The attack shown here took place
on 1 July 1916, as part of the
first day of the battle of the
Somme. The British troops broke
into the German trenches, but
were repulsed. At the end of the
day 1,000 British troops were
dead on this sector of the front
only 1,000 yards long

57

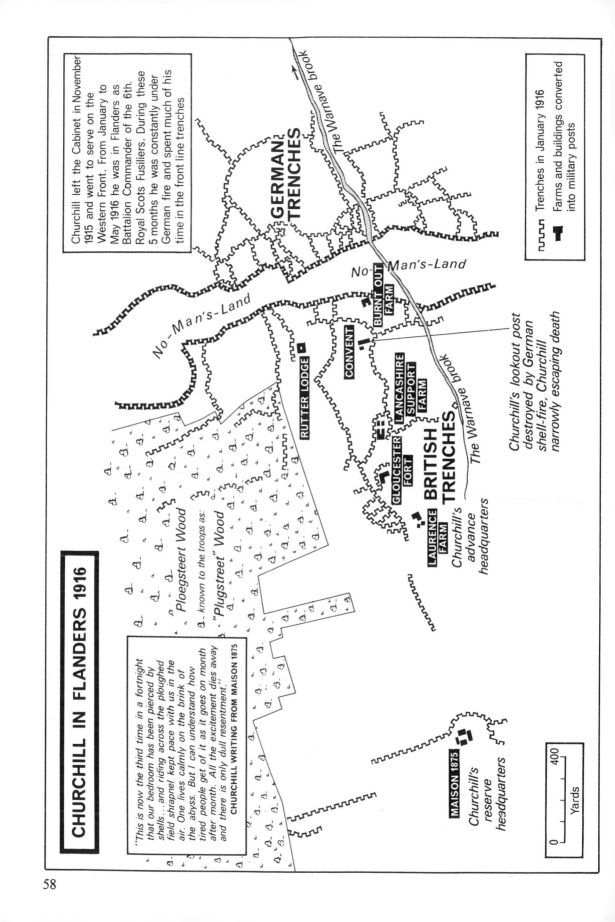

CHURCHILL IN FLANDERS 1916

Churchill left the Cabinet in November 1915 and went to serve on the Western Front. From January to May 1916 he was in Flanders as Battalion Commander of the 6th. Royal Scots Fusiliers. During these 5 months he was constantly under German fire and spent much of his time in the front line trenches

Trenches in January 1916

Farms and buildings converted into military posts

The Warnave brook

GERMAN TRENCHES

No-Man's-Land

No-Man's-Land

BURNT OUT FARM

CONVENT

RUTTER LODGE

LANCASHIRE SUPPORT FARM

GLOUCESTER FORT

BRITISH TRENCHES

The Warnave brook

LAURENCE FARM
Churchill's advance headquarters

Churchill's lookout post destroyed by German shell-fire, Churchill narrowly escaping death

Ploegsteert Wood

— known to the troops as:
"Plugstreet" Wood

MAISON 1875
Churchill's reserve headquarters

"This is now the third time in a fortnight that our bedroom has been pierced by shells...and riding across the ploughed field shrapnel kept pace with us in the air. One lives calmly on the brink of the abyss. But I can understand how tired people get of it as it goes on month after month. All the excitement dies away and there is only dull resentment."
CHURCHILL WRITING FROM MAISON 1875

0   400
Yards

58

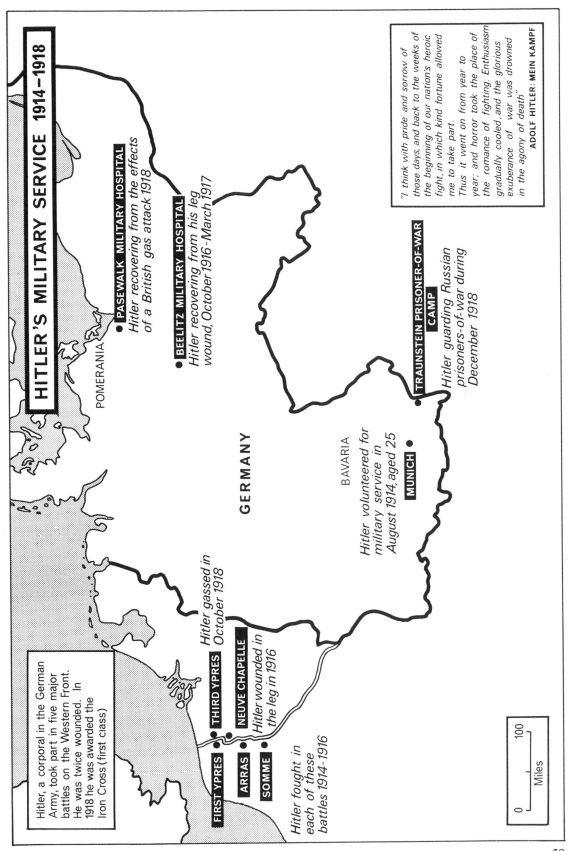

HITLER'S MILITARY SERVICE 1914–1918

"I think with pride and sorrow of those days, and back to the weeks of the beginning of our nation's heroic fight, in which kind fortune allowed me to take part.
Thus it went on from year to year; and horror took the place of the romance of fighting. Enthusiasm gradually cooled, and the glorious exuberance of war was drowned in the agony of death"
ADOLF HITLER: MEIN KAMPF

PASEWALK MILITARY HOSPITAL
Hitler recovering from the effects of a British gas attack 1918

BEELITZ MILITARY HOSPITAL
Hitler recovering from his leg wound, October 1916 - March 1917

POMERANIA

TRAUNSTEIN PRISONER-OF-WAR CAMP
Hitler guarding Russian prisoners-of-war during December 1918

GERMANY

BAVARIA

Hitler volunteered for military service in August 1914, aged 25

MUNICH

Hitler gassed in October 1918

THIRD YPRES

NEUVE CHAPELLE
Hitler wounded in the leg in 1916

FIRST YPRES

ARRAS

SOMME

Hitler fought in each of these battles 1914-1916

Hitler, a corporal in the German Army, took part in five major battles on the Western Front. He was twice wounded. In 1918 he was awarded the Iron Cross (first class)

0   100
Miles

59

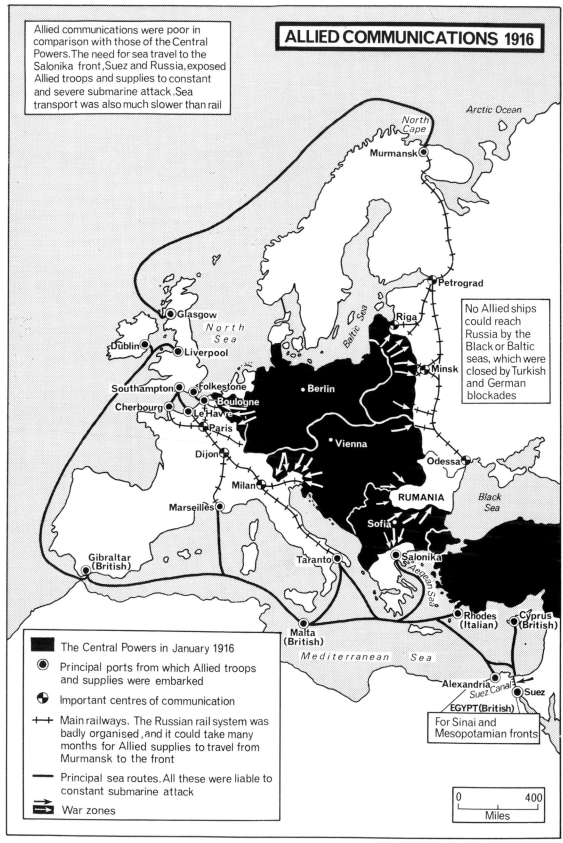

Allied communications were poor in comparison with those of the Central Powers. The need for sea travel to the Salonika front, Suez and Russia, exposed Allied troops and supplies to constant and severe submarine attack. Sea transport was also much slower than rail

ALLIED COMMUNICATIONS 1916

Arctic Ocean

North Cape

Murmansk

Petrograd

Riga

Baltic Sea

No Allied ships could reach Russia by the Black or Baltic seas, which were closed by Turkish and German blockades

Glasgow

North Sea

Dublin

Liverpool

Minsk

Southampton

Folkestone

Boulogne

Berlin

Cherbourg

Le Havre

Paris

Vienna

Dijon

Odessa

Milan

Black Sea

RUMANIA

Marseilles

Sofia

Gibraltar (British)

Taranto

Salonika

Aegean Sea

Malta (British)

Rhodes (Italian)

Cyprus (British)

Mediterranean Sea

Alexandria

Suez Canal

Suez

EGYPT (British)

For Sinai and Mesopotamian fronts

▮ The Central Powers in January 1916

◉ Principal ports from which Allied troops and supplies were embarked

◕ Important centres of communication

+++ Main railways. The Russian rail system was badly organised, and it could take many months for Allied supplies to travel from Murmansk to the front

— Principal sea routes. All these were liable to constant submarine attack

⇒ War zones

0   400
Miles

RAIL COMMUNICATIONS OF THE CENTRAL POWERS 1916

0   200

Miles

North Sea

Baltic Sea

Libau

Memel

Vilna

Kiel

Danzig

Königsberg

Hamburg

Stettin

Zeebrugge

Berlin

Warsaw

GERMANY

Brussels

Frankfurt

Metz

AUSTRIA – HUNGARY

Vienna

Budapest

Trieste

Fiume

Adriatic Sea

RUMANIA

Nish

Varna

Sofia

BULGARIA

Black Sea

Constantinople

Aegean Sea

TURKEY

—— The Central Powers in December 1915

⊙ Principal ports

◓ Important railway centres

→ War zones

▨ Serbia, whose conquest in 1915 made it possible to link Turkey and Bulgaria with Austria and Germany

▧ Rumania, whose conquest in 1916 was made easier by being accessible at four different points by rail

+++ Principal railways

The Central Powers were able to make use of a pre-war railway network which was ideal for the rapid movement of troops and supplies, both from the centre to the war zones, and from zone to zone. The system was immune from Allied attack

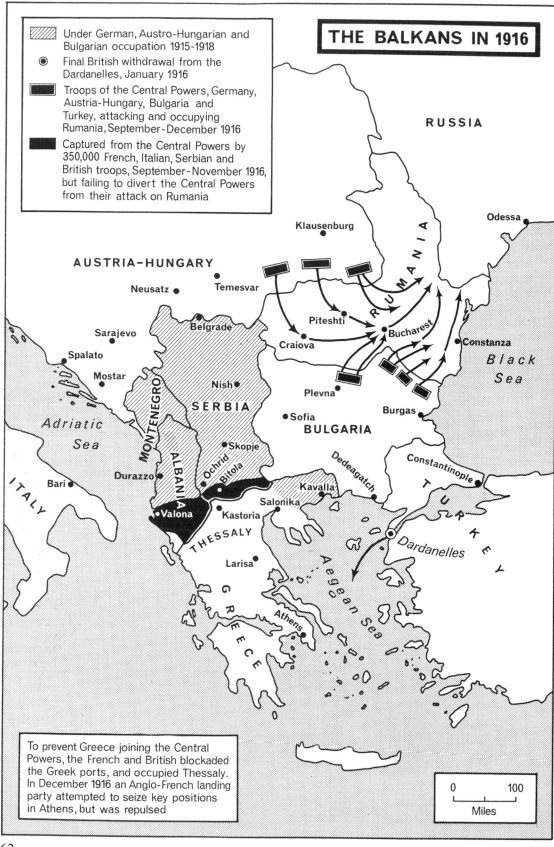

THE BALKANS IN 1916

Legend:

- Under German, Austro-Hungarian and Bulgarian occupation 1915-1918
- Final British withdrawal from the Dardanelles, January 1916
- Troops of the Central Powers, Germany, Austria-Hungary, Bulgaria and Turkey, attacking and occupying Rumania, September-December 1916
- Captured from the Central Powers by 350,000 French, Italian, Serbian and British troops, September-November 1916, but failing to divert the Central Powers from their attack on Rumania

RUSSIA

Odessa

Klausenburg

AUSTRIA-HUNGARY

Neusatz
Temesvar

R U M A N I A

Piteshti
Craiova
Bucharest
Constanza

Black Sea

Sarajevo
Belgrade

Spalato
Mostar

M O N T E N E G R O

Nish
S E R B I A

Plevna
Burgas

Sofia
BULGARIA

Adriatic Sea

Skopje

A L B A N I A

Ochrid
Bitola

Dedeagatch
Constantinople

T U R K E Y

Bari
Durazzo

Kavalla
Salonika

Valona
Kastoria

T H E S S A L Y

Dardanelles

G R E E C E

Larisa

Aegean Sea

Athens

To prevent Greece joining the Central Powers, the French and British blockaded the Greek ports, and occupied Thessaly. In December 1916 an Anglo-French landing party attempted to seize key positions in Athens, but was repulsed

```
0        100
|_____|
   Miles
```

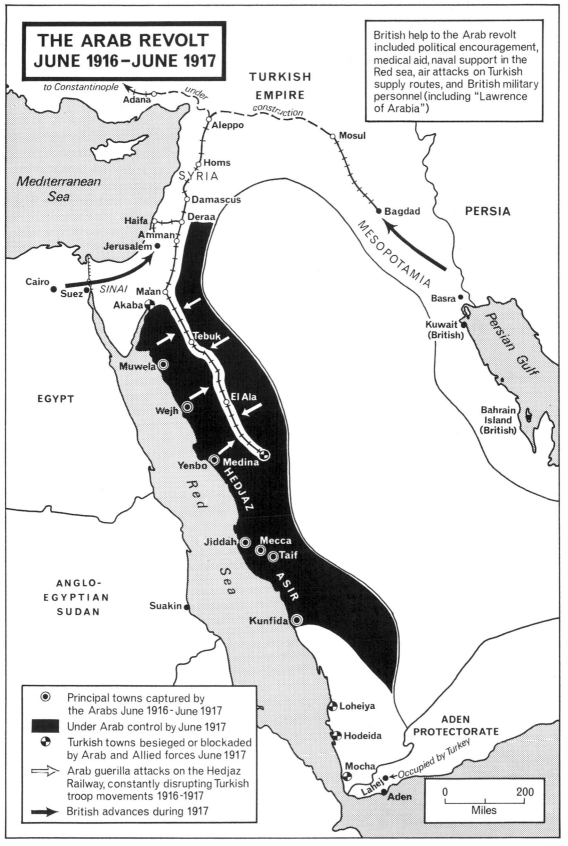

THE ARAB REVOLT
JUNE 1916 – JUNE 1917

British help to the Arab revolt included political encouragement, medical aid, naval support in the Red sea, air attacks on Turkish supply routes, and British military personnel (including "Lawrence of Arabia")

to Constantinople

Adana

under construction

TURKISH EMPIRE

Aleppo

Mosul

Homs

SYRIA

Mediterranean Sea

Damascus

Deraa

Haifa

Amman

Jerusalem

Bagdad

PERSIA

MESOPOTAMIA

Cairo

Suez

SINAI

Ma'an

Akaba

Basra

Kuwait (British)

Tebuk

Muwela

Persian Gulf

EGYPT

El Ala

Wejh

Bahrain Island (British)

Yenbo

Medina

HEDJAZ

Red Sea

Jiddah

Mecca

Taif

ANGLO-
EGYPTIAN
SUDAN

ASIR

Suakin

Kunfida

Loheiya

ADEN
PROTECTORATE

Hodeida

Mocha

Occupied by Turkey

Lahej

Aden

	Principal towns captured by the Arabs June 1916 – June 1917
	Under Arab control by June 1917
	Turkish towns besieged or blockaded by Arab and Allied forces June 1917
⇨	Arab guerilla attacks on the Hedjaz Railway, constantly disrupting Turkish troop movements 1916–1917
➡	British advances during 1917

0   200
Miles

Section Five

THE WAR IN THE AIR

Night shatters in mid-heaven—the bark of guns,
The roar of planes, the crash of bombs, and all
The unshackled skyey pandemonium stuns
The senses to indifference, when a fall
Of masonry nearby startles awake,
Tingling, wide-eyed, prick-eared, with bristling hair,
Each sense within the body, crouched aware
Like some sore-hunted creature in the brake. . . .

WILFRED GIBSON
"AIR-RAID"

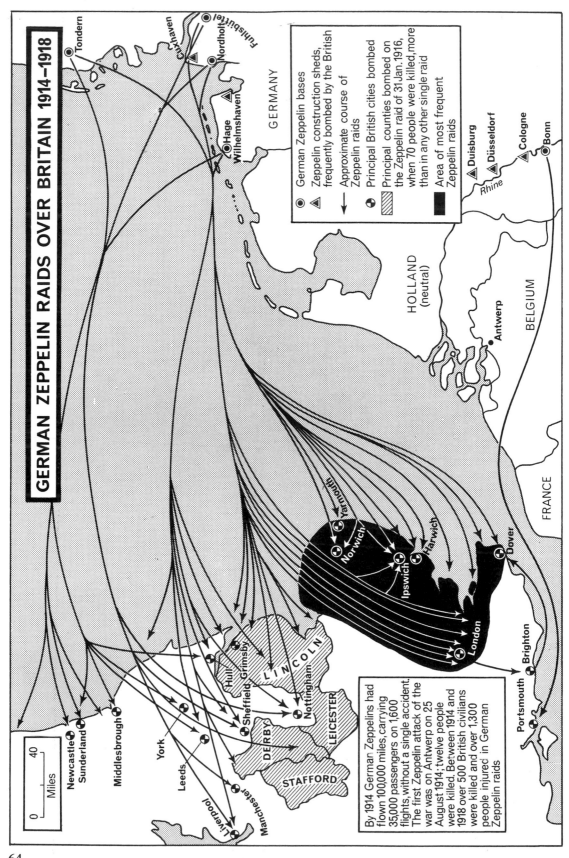

GERMAN ZEPPELIN RAIDS OVER BRITAIN 1914–1918

GERMANY

Tondern

Cuxhaven
Nordholt
Fuhlsbüttel

Hage
Wilhelmshaven

Rhine
Duisburg
Düsseldorf
Cologne
Bonn

HOLLAND
(neutral)

Antwerp

BELGIUM

FRANCE

⊙ German Zeppelin bases

◁ Zeppelin construction sheds, frequently bombed by the British

↓ Approximate course of Zeppelin raids

⊕ Principal British cities bombed

◕ Principal counties bombed on the Zeppelin raid of 31 Jan.1916, when 70 people were killed, more than in any other single raid

▨ Area of most frequent Zeppelin raids

Newcastle
Sunderland

Middlesbrough

York

Leeds

Liverpool

Manchester

Sheffield
Hull
Grimsby

LINCOLN

Nottingham

DERBY

LEICESTER

STAFFORD

Yarmouth
Norwich
Ipswich
Harwich

London

Dover

Portsmouth
Brighton

0   40
Miles

By 1914 German Zeppelins had flown 100,000 miles, carrying 35,000 passengers on 1,600 flights, without a single accident. The first Zeppelin attack of the war was on Antwerp on 25 August 1914; twelve people were killed. Between 1914 and 1918 over 500 British civilians were killed and over 1,300 people injured in German Zeppelin raids.

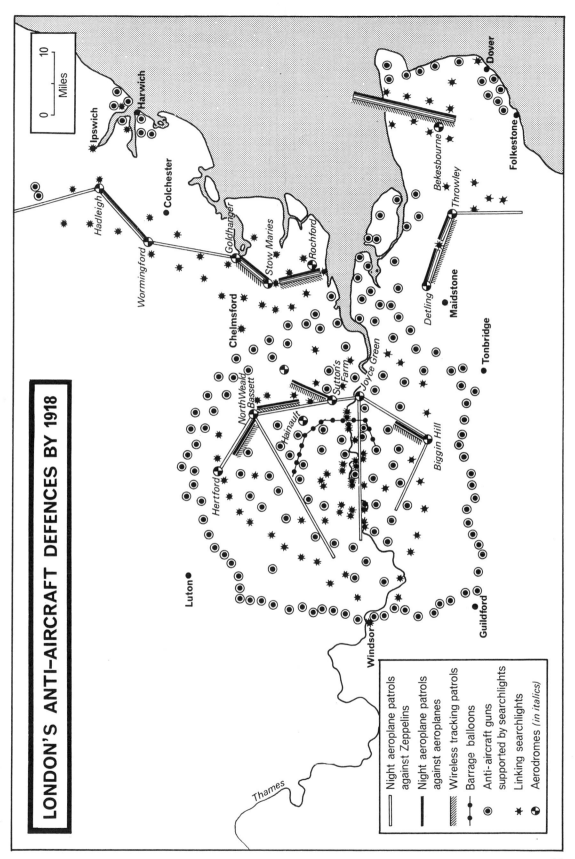

LONDON'S ANTI-AIRCRAFT DEFENCES BY 1918

0 | 10
Miles

Dover
Folkestone
Bekesbourne
Throwley
Harwich
Ipswich
Detling
Maidstone
Colchester
Tonbridge
Hadleigh
Wormingford
Goldhanger
Stow Maries
Rochford
Chelmsford
Sutton's Farm
Joyce Green
North Weald Bassett
Hainault
Biggin Hill
Hertford
Luton
Windsor
Guildford
Thames

Night aeroplane patrols against Zeppelins
Night aeroplane patrols against aeroplanes
Wireless tracking patrols
Barrage balloons
Anti-aircraft guns supported by searchlights
Linking searchlights
Aerodromes (in italics)

65

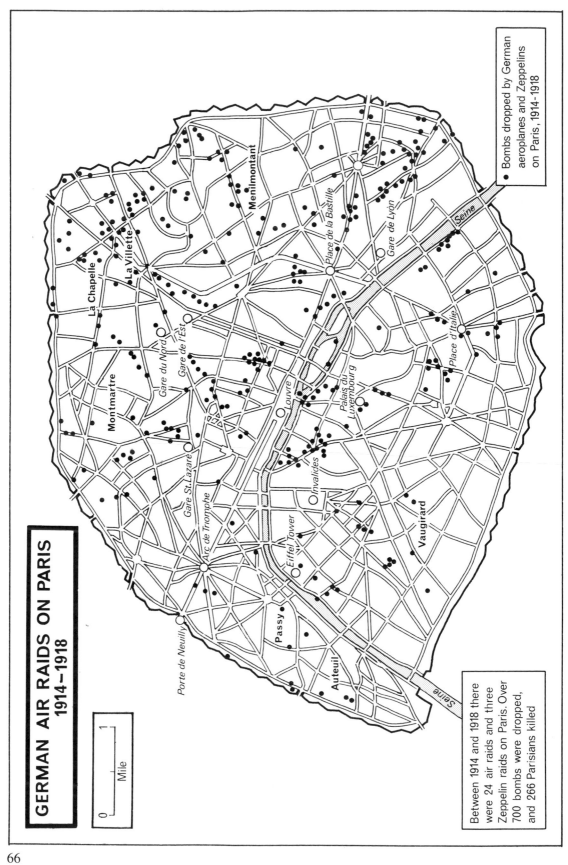

GERMAN AIR RAIDS ON PARIS
1914–1918

Bombs dropped by German aeroplanes and Zeppelins on Paris, 1914–1918

Between 1914 and 1918 there were 24 air raids and three Zeppelin raids on Paris. Over 700 bombs were dropped, and 266 Parisians killed

0 ___ 1
Mile

Menilmontant

Place de la Bastille

Gare de Lyon

Seine

La Chapelle

La Villette

Gare du Nord

Gare de l'Est

Montmartre

Place d'Italie

Gare St. Lazare

Louvre

Palais du Luxembourg

Arc de Triomphe

Invalides

Eiffel Tower

Vaugirard

Porte de Neuilly

Passy

Auteuil

Seine

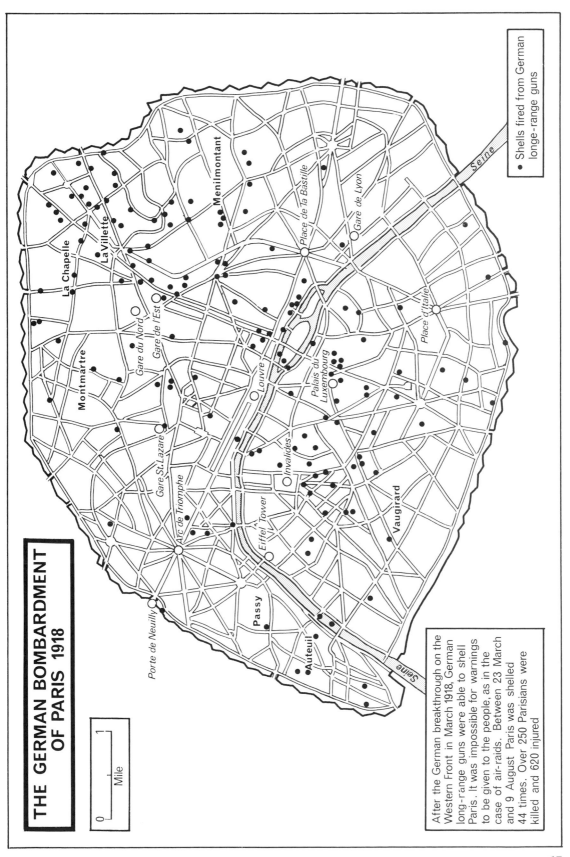

THE GERMAN BOMBARDMENT OF PARIS 1918

0 — 1
Mile

- Shells fired from German longe-range guns

Porte de Neuilly

Montmartre

La Chapelle

La Villette

Menilmontant

Gare du Nord

Gare de l'Est

Place de la Bastille

Gare de Lyon

Seine

Gare St.Lazare

Arc de Triomphe

Louvre

Palais du Luxembourg

Place d'Italie

Invalides

Eiffel Tower

Passy

Vaugirard

Auteuil

Seine

After the German breakthrough on the Western Front in March 1918, German long-range guns were able to shell Paris. It was impossible for warnings to be given to the people, as in the case of air-raids. Between 23 March and 9 August Paris was shelled 44 times. Over 250 Parisians were killed and 620 injured

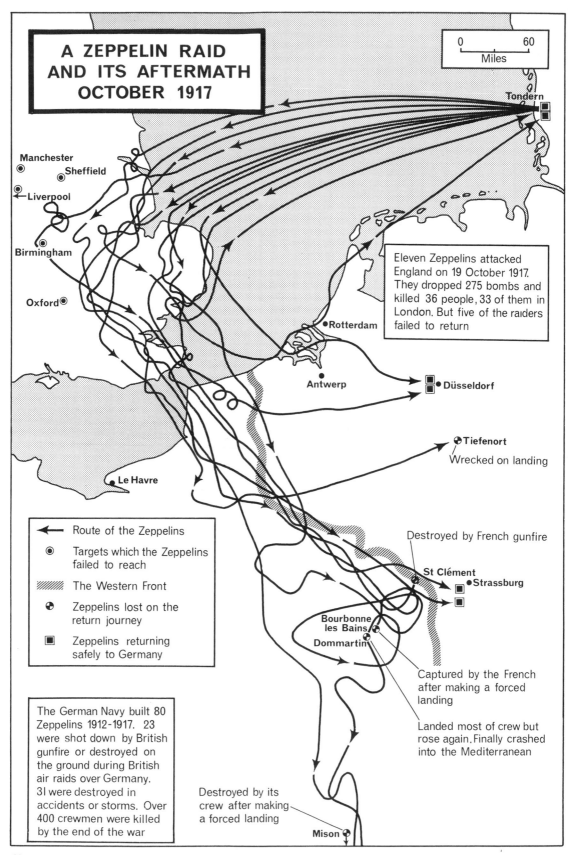

A ZEPPELIN RAID AND ITS AFTERMATH OCTOBER 1917

0   60
Miles

Tondern

Manchester
Sheffield
Liverpool
Birmingham
Oxford

Eleven Zeppelins attacked
England on 19 October 1917.
They dropped 275 bombs and
killed 36 people, 33 of them in
London. But five of the raiders
failed to return

● Rotterdam

Antwerp

■● Düsseldorf

⊕ Tiefenort
Wrecked on landing

Le Havre

← Route of the Zeppelins

◉ Targets which the Zeppelins failed to reach

▨ The Western Front

⊕ Zeppelins lost on the return journey

■ Zeppelins returning safely to Germany

Destroyed by French gunfire

St Clément
■ ●Strassburg
■

Bourbonne
les Bains
Dommartin

Captured by the French
after making a forced
landing

Landed most of crew but
rose again. Finally crashed
into the Mediterranean

The German Navy built 80
Zeppelins 1912-1917. 23
were shot down by British
gunfire or destroyed on
the ground during British
air raids over Germany.
31 were destroyed in
accidents or storms. Over
400 crewmen were killed
by the end of the war

Destroyed by its
crew after making
a forced landing

Mison ⊕

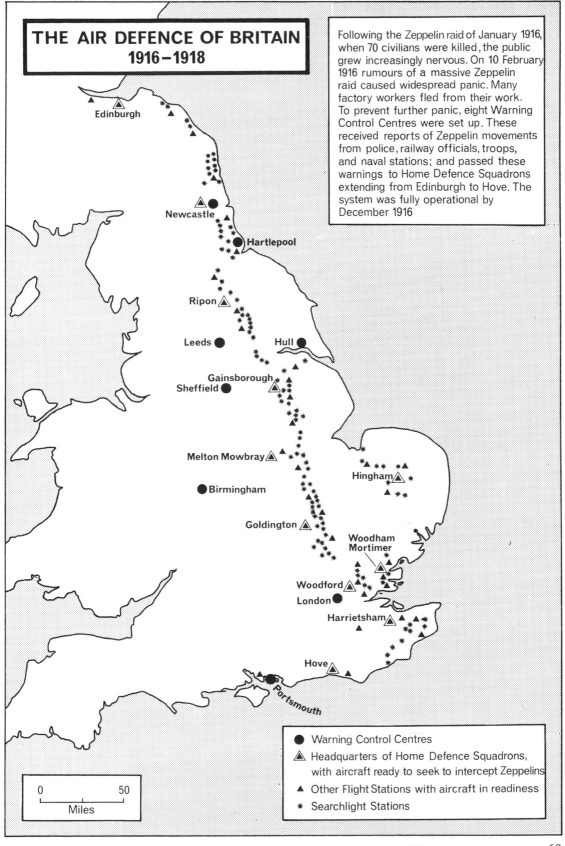

THE AIR DEFENCE OF BRITAIN
1916–1918

Following the Zeppelin raid of January 1916, when 70 civilians were killed, the public grew increasingly nervous. On 10 February 1916 rumours of a massive Zeppelin raid caused widespread panic. Many factory workers fled from their work. To prevent further panic, eight Warning Control Centres were set up. These received reports of Zeppelin movements from police, railway officials, troops, and naval stations; and passed these warnings to Home Defence Squadrons extending from Edinburgh to Hove. The system was fully operational by December 1916

Edinburgh

Newcastle

Hartlepool

Ripon

Leeds   Hull

Gainsborough
Sheffield

Melton Mowbray

Hingham

Birmingham

Goldington

Woodham
Mortimer

Woodford

London

Harrietsham

Hove

Portsmouth

0   50
Miles

● Warning Control Centres
△ Headquarters of Home Defence Squadrons, with aircraft ready to seek to intercept Zeppelins
▲ Other Flight Stations with aircraft in readiness
✳ Searchlight Stations

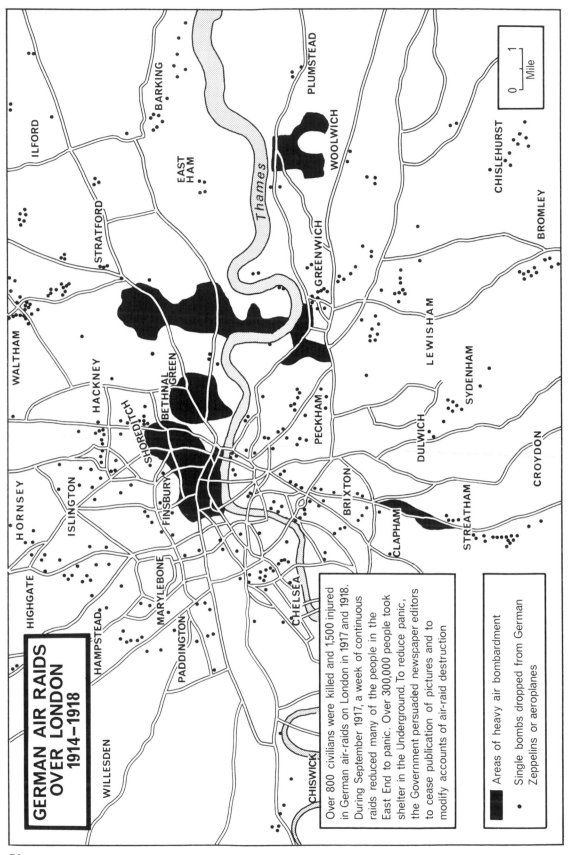

GERMAN AIR RAIDS OVER LONDON 1914–1918

Over 800 civilians were killed and 1,500 injured in German air-raids on London in 1917 and 1918. During September 1917, a week of continuous raids reduced many of the people in the East End to panic. Over 300,000 people took shelter in the Underground. To reduce panic, the Government persuaded newspaper editors to cease publication of pictures and to modify accounts of air-raid destruction

■ Areas of heavy air bombardment

• Single bombs dropped from German Zeppelins or aeroplanes

ILFORD

BARKING

PLUMSTEAD

WOOLWICH

EAST HAM

Thames

CHISLEHURST

STRATFORD

GREENWICH

BROMLEY

WALTHAM

LEWISHAM

HACKNEY

BETHNAL GREEN

SYDENHAM

SHOREDITCH

PECKHAM

HORNSEY

ISLINGTON

FINSBURY

DULWICH

CROYDON

BRIXTON

STREATHAM

HIGHGATE

CLAPHAM

MARYLEBONE

HAMPSTEAD

PADDINGTON

CHELSEA

WILLESDEN

CHISWICK

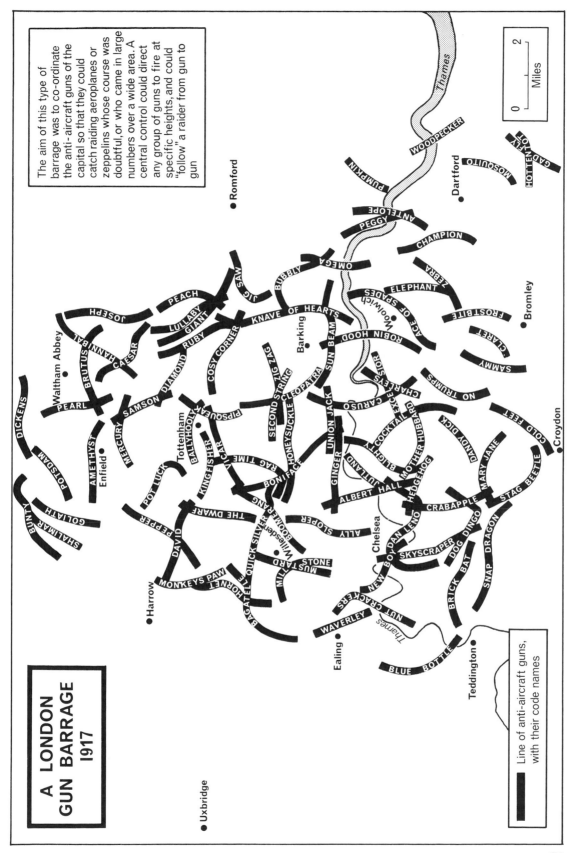

A LONDON GUN BARRAGE 1917

The aim of this type of barrage was to co-ordinate the anti-aircraft guns of the capital so that they could catch raiding aeroplanes or zeppelins whose course was doubtful, or who came in large numbers over a wide area. A central control could direct any group of guns to fire at specific heights, and could "follow" a raider from gun to gun

Line of anti-aircraft guns, with their code names

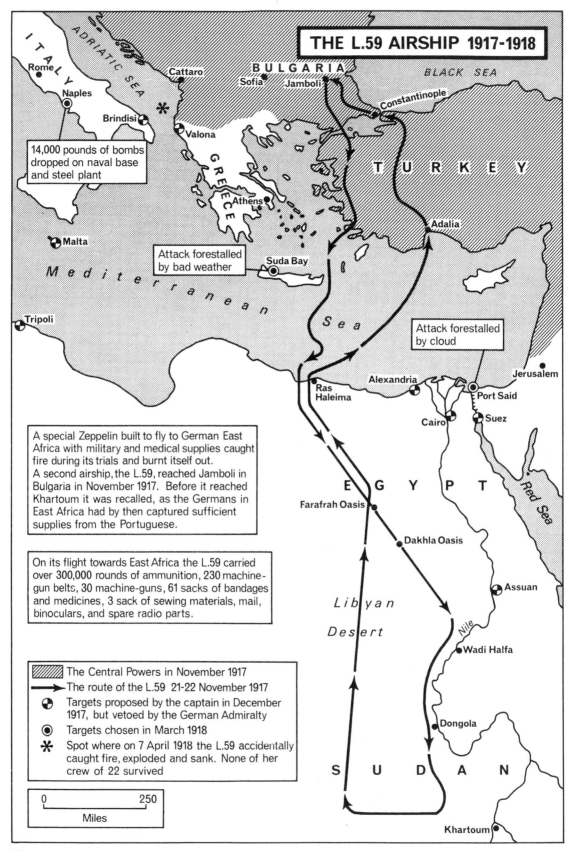

THE L.59 AIRSHIP 1917-1918

14,000 pounds of bombs dropped on naval base and steel plant

Attack forestalled by bad weather

Attack forestalled by cloud

A special Zeppelin built to fly to German East Africa with military and medical supplies caught fire during its trials and burnt itself out.
A second airship, the L.59, reached Jamboli in Bulgaria in November 1917. Before it reached Khartoum it was recalled, as the Germans in East Africa had by then captured sufficient supplies from the Portuguese.

On its flight towards East Africa the L.59 carried over 300,000 rounds of ammunition, 230 machine-gun belts, 30 machine-guns, 61 sacks of bandages and medicines, 3 sack of sewing materials, mail, binoculars, and spare radio parts.

⬛⬛⬛ The Central Powers in November 1917

➤ The route of the L.59 21-22 November 1917

◉ Targets proposed by the captain in December 1917, but vetoed by the German Admiralty

◉ Targets chosen in March 1918

✳ Spot where on 7 April 1918 the L.59 accidentally caught fire, exploded and sank. None of her crew of 22 survived

0 — 250
Miles

Labels on map: ITALY, ADRIATIC SEA, Rome, Naples, Brindisi, Cattaro, Valona, BULGARIA, Sofia, Jamboli, BLACK SEA, Constantinople, TURKEY, GREECE, Athens, Adalia, Malta, Mediterranean Sea, Suda Bay, Tripoli, Ras Haleima, Alexandria, Jerusalem, Port Said, Cairo, Suez, EGYPT, Farafrah Oasis, Dakhla Oasis, Red Sea, Assuan, Libyan Desert, Nile, Wadi Halfa, Dongola, SUDAN, Khartoum

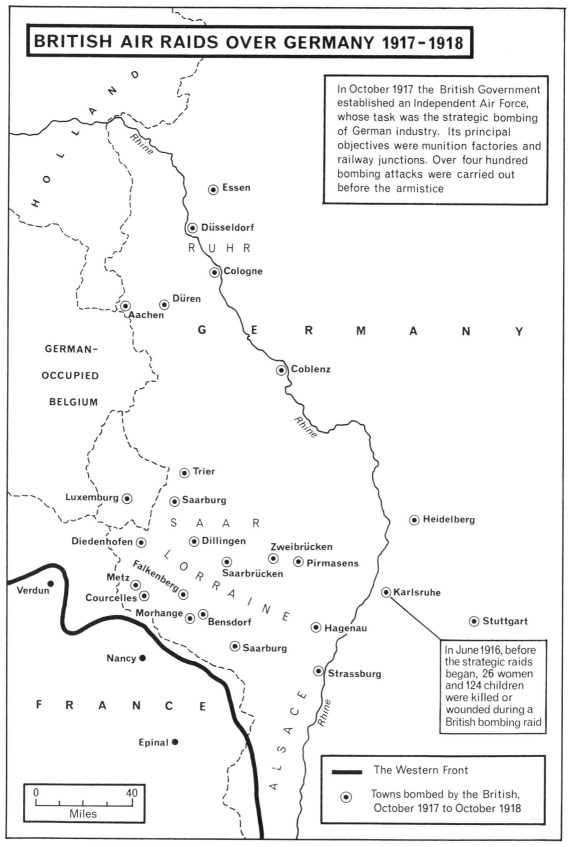

BRITISH AIR RAIDS OVER GERMANY 1917-1918

In October 1917 the British Government established an Independent Air Force, whose task was the strategic bombing of German industry. Its principal objectives were munition factories and railway junctions. Over four hundred bombing attacks were carried out before the armistice

HOLLAND

Rhine

⊙ Essen

⊙ Düsseldorf

R U H R

⊙ Cologne

⊙ Düren

⊙ Aachen

G E R M A N Y

GERMAN-

OCCUPIED

BELGIUM

⊙ Coblenz

Rhine

⊙ Trier

Luxemburg ⊙

⊙ Saarburg

S A A R

⊙ Heidelberg

Diedenhofen ⊙

⊙ Dillingen

Zweibrücken

⊙

⊙ Pirmasens

L O R R A I N E

Falkenberg

⊙ Saarbrücken

Metz

⊙

Verdun ●

Courcelles ⊙

⊙ Karlsruhe

Morhange ⊙ ⊙

⊙ Bensdorf

⊙ Stuttgart

⊙ Saarburg

⊙ Hagenau

Nancy ●

⊙ Strassburg

F R A N C E

In June 1916, before the strategic raids began, 26 women and 124 children were killed or wounded during a British bombing raid

A L S A C E

Rhine

Epinal ●

—— The Western Front

⊙ Towns bombed by the British, October 1917 to October 1918

0   40

Miles

Section Six

THE WAR AT SEA

We sift the drifting sea,
   and blindly grope beneath;
obscure and toilsome we,
   he fishermen of death.

E. HILTON-YOUNG
'MINE-SWEEPING TRAWLERS''

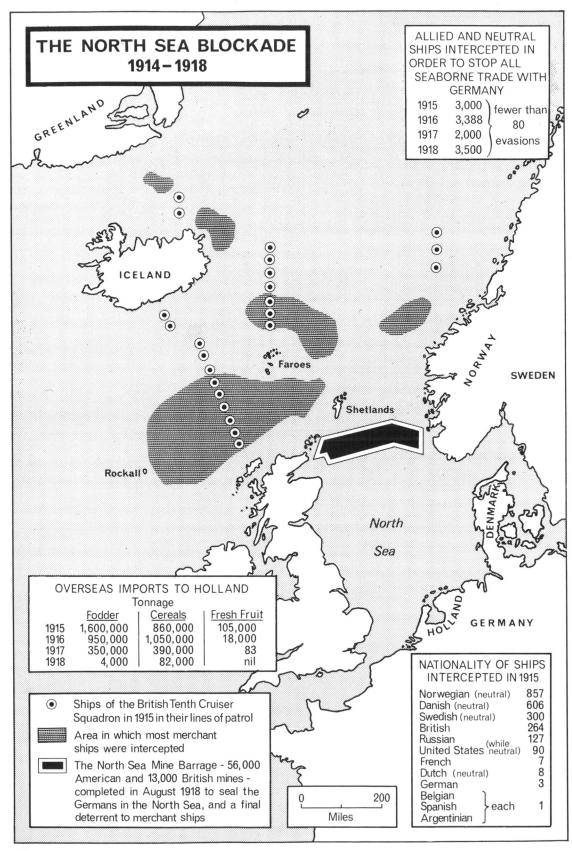

THE NORTH SEA BLOCKADE
1914–1918

ALLIED AND NEUTRAL
SHIPS INTERCEPTED IN
ORDER TO STOP ALL
SEABORNE TRADE WITH
GERMANY

1915	3,000	fewer than
1916	3,388	80
1917	2,000	evasions
1918	3,500	

GREENLAND

ICELAND

Faroes

Shetlands

Rockall °

NORWAY

SWEDEN

DENMARK

North

Sea

HOLLAND

GERMANY

OVERSEAS IMPORTS TO HOLLAND
Tonnage

	Fodder	Cereals	Fresh Fruit
1915	1,600,000	860,000	105,000
1916	950,000	1,050,000	18,000
1917	350,000	390,000	83
1918	4,000	82,000	nil

NATIONALITY OF SHIPS
INTERCEPTED IN 1915

Norwegian (neutral)	857
Danish (neutral)	606
Swedish (neutral)	300
British	264
Russian (while	127
United States neutral)	90
French	7
Dutch (neutral)	8
German	3
Belgian	
Spanish } each	1
Argentinian	

⊙ Ships of the British Tenth Cruiser
Squadron in 1915 in their lines of patrol

▦ Area in which most merchant
ships were intercepted

■ The North Sea Mine Barrage - 56,000
American and 13,000 British mines -
completed in August 1918 to seal the
Germans in the North Sea, and a final
deterrent to merchant ships

0   200
Miles

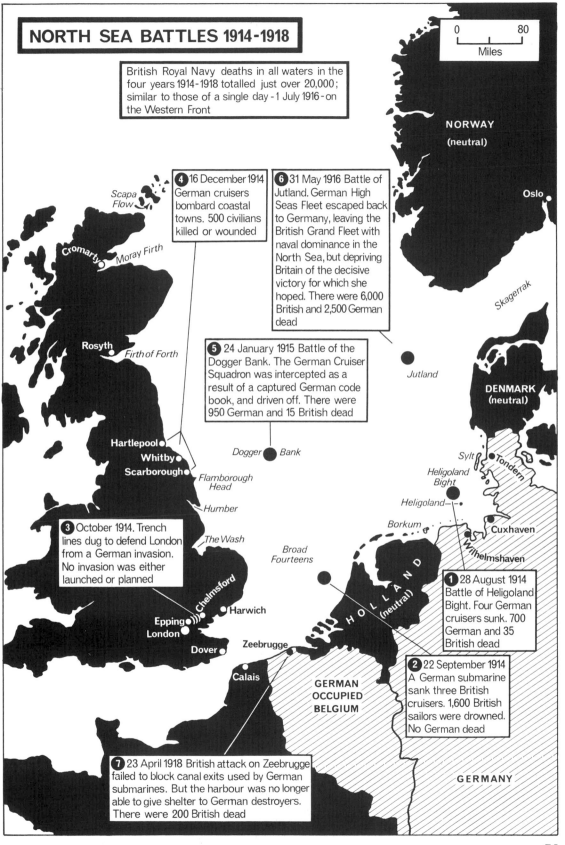

NORTH SEA BATTLES 1914-1918

British Royal Navy deaths in all waters in the four years 1914-1918 totalled just over 20,000; similar to those of a single day - 1 July 1916 - on the Western Front

0 ———— 80
Miles

NORWAY
(neutral)

Oslo

Scapa Flow

(4) 16 December 1914 German cruisers bombard coastal towns. 500 civilians killed or wounded

(6) 31 May 1916 Battle of Jutland. German High Seas Fleet escaped back to Germany, leaving the British Grand Fleet with naval dominance in the North Sea, but depriving Britain of the decisive victory for which she hoped. There were 6,000 British and 2,500 German dead

Cromarty
Moray Firth

Skagerrak

(5) 24 January 1915 Battle of the Dogger Bank. The German Cruiser Squadron was intercepted as a result of a captured German code book, and driven off. There were 950 German and 15 British dead

Jutland

DENMARK
(neutral)

Rosyth
Firth of Forth

Hartlepool•
Whitby•
Scarborough•
Flamborough Head

Dogger • Bank

Sylt •Tondern

Heligoland Bight

Heligoland — •-•
Borkum

Cuxhaven

Humber

(3) October 1914. Trench lines dug to defend London from a German invasion. No invasion was either launched or planned

The Wash

Broad Fourteens

Wilhelmshaven

(1) 28 August 1914 Battle of Heligoland Bight. Four German cruisers sunk. 700 German and 35 British dead

H O L L A N D (neutral)

Chelmsford
Epping•)))•
London•
Harwich

Dover•
Zeebrugge
Calais

(2) 22 September 1914 A German submarine sank three British cruisers. 1,600 British sailors were drowned. No German dead

GERMAN OCCUPIED BELGIUM

(7) 23 April 1918 British attack on Zeebrugge failed to block canal exits used by German submarines. But the harbour was no longer able to give shelter to German destroyers. There were 200 British dead

GERMANY

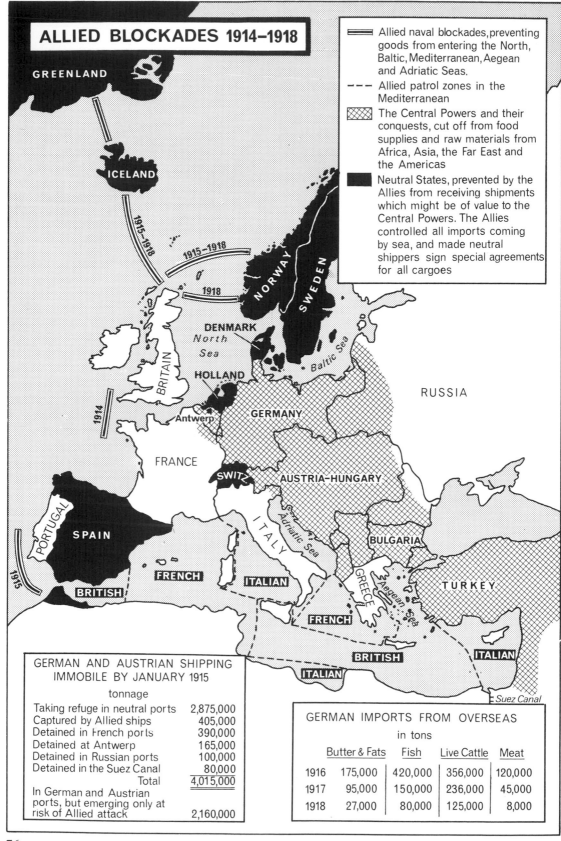

ALLIED BLOCKADES 1914–1918

GREENLAND

ICELAND

1915–1918

1915–1918

1918

NORWAY

SWEDEN

DENMARK

North Sea

Baltic Sea

HOLLAND

Antwerp

BRITAIN

GERMANY

RUSSIA

1914

FRANCE

SWITZ

AUSTRIA–HUNGARY

PORTUGAL

SPAIN

ITALY

Adriatic Sea

BULGARIA

1915

GREECE

Aegean Sea

TURKEY

FRENCH

ITALIAN

FRENCH

BRITISH

BRITISH

ITALIAN

ITALIAN

Suez Canal

Allied naval blockades, preventing goods from entering the North, Baltic, Mediterranean, Aegean and Adriatic Seas.

--- Allied patrol zones in the Mediterranean

The Central Powers and their conquests, cut off from food supplies and raw materials from Africa, Asia, the Far East and the Americas

Neutral States, prevented by the Allies from receiving shipments which might be of value to the Central Powers. The Allies controlled all imports coming by sea, and made neutral shippers sign special agreements for all cargoes

GERMAN AND AUSTRIAN SHIPPING IMMOBILE BY JANUARY 1915

tonnage

Taking refuge in neutral ports	2,875,000
Captured by Allied ships	405,000
Detained in French ports	390,000
Detained at Antwerp	165,000
Detained in Russian ports	100,000
Detained in the Suez Canal	80,000
Total	4,015,000
In German and Austrian ports, but emerging only at risk of Allied attack	2,160,000

GERMAN IMPORTS FROM OVERSEAS

in tons

	Butter & Fats	Fish	Live Cattle	Meat
1916	175,000	420,000	356,000	120,000
1917	95,000	150,000	236,000	45,000
1918	27,000	80,000	125,000	8,000

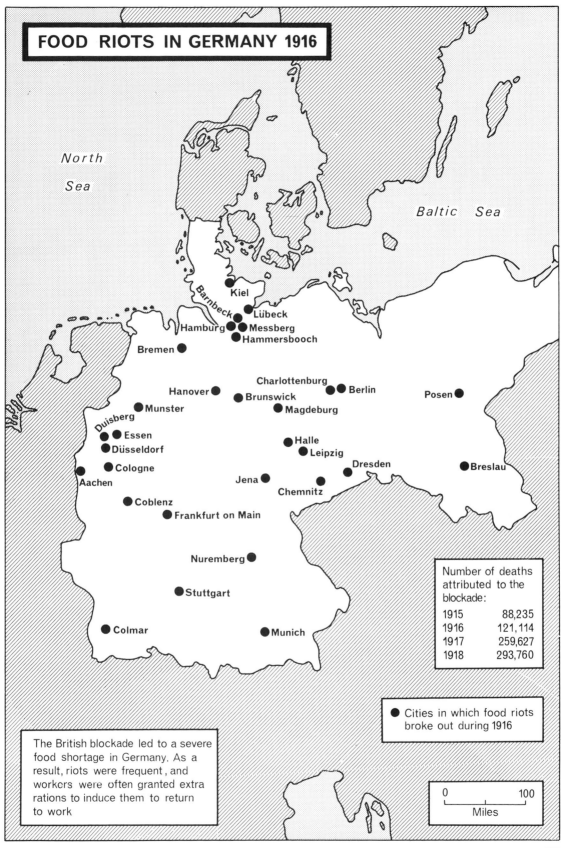

FOOD RIOTS IN GERMANY 1916

North
Sea

Baltic Sea

Barnbeck

● Kiel

● Lübeck

Hamburg ● ● Messberg
● Hammersbooch

Bremen ●

Charlottenburg
Hanover ● ● ● Berlin
● Brunswick Posen ●
Munster ● ● Magdeburg

Duisberg
● Essen ● Halle
● Düsseldorf ● Leipzig

● Cologne Dresden ●
Aachen ● ● Breslau
Jena ● ●
● Coblenz Chemnitz
● Frankfurt on Main

Nuremberg ●

● Stuttgart

● Colmar ● Munich

Number of deaths
attributed to the
blockade:
1915   88,235
1916   121,114
1917   259,627
1918   293,760

● Cities in which food riots
broke out during 1916

The British blockade led to a severe
food shortage in Germany. As a
result, riots were frequent, and
workers were often granted extra
rations to induce them to return
to work

0   100
Miles

THE WESTERN APPROACHES 1914-1918

⊕ German submarines sunk by Britain 1914-1918: total 48

▲ Convoy collection points, with the number of convoys leaving every 16 days. Following the introduction of convoys in June 1917, submarine sinkings of merchant shipping fell sharply

With the introduction of the convoy system in June 1917, German submarines attacking merchant ships were liable to be set upon by Allied escort vessels and even attacked from the air

SCOTLAND

△2 Lamlash

ATLANTIC

OCEAN

IRELAND

Irish Sea

△7 Liverpool

W A L E S

ENGLAND

△4 Milford

△2 Falmouth △4 Devonport

English

Channel

FRANCE

Between 1914 and 1918 German submarines sank over 11 million tons of Allied shipping, of which nearly 8 million tons were British. Over 2,000 British naval and merchant ships and 578 fishing boats were torpedoed, killing 12,723 sailors, 908 civilians and 63 fishermen. The British sank 178 U-boats, killing 515 officers and 4,849 men

0   100
Miles

BRITISH MERCHANT SHIPS SUNK MAY–DECEMBER 1917

⊙ British merchant ships sunk by German submarines. Each symbol represents a single British ship

SCOTLAND

IRELAND

WALES

ENGLAND

FRANCE

In the eight months May–December 1917, German submarines sank five hundred British merchant ships. These sinkings gravely jeopardized Britain's ability to continue the war, which was only ensured by the introduction of the convoy system in June 1917. But it was not until the end of the year that it had become fully effective, by which time over 2,400,000 tons of shipping had been sunk

0   100
Miles

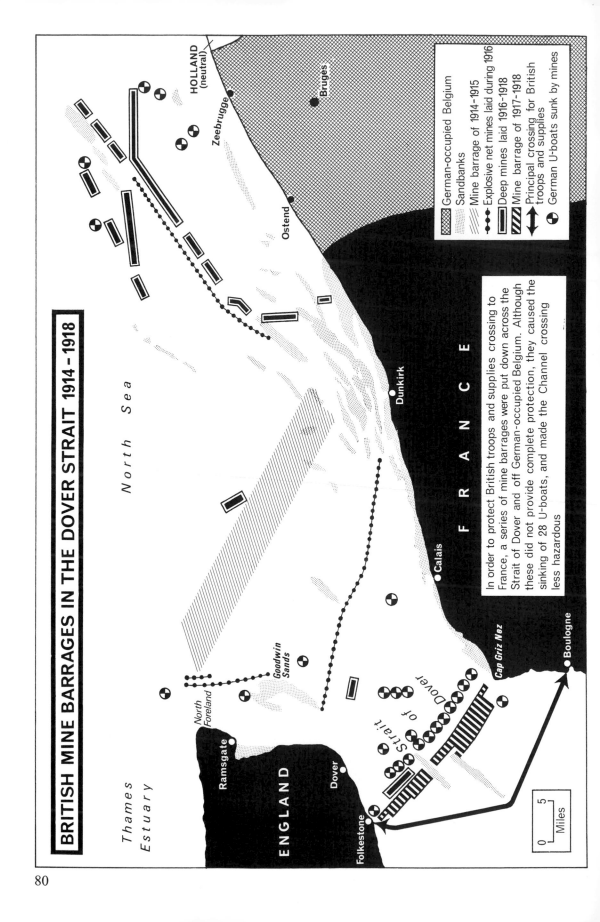

BRITISH MINE BARRAGES IN THE DOVER STRAIT 1914–1918

Legend:
- German-occupied Belgium
- Sandbanks
- Mine barrage of 1914–1915
- Explosive net mines laid during 1916
- Deep mines laid 1916–1918
- Mine barrage of 1917–1918
- Principal crossing for British troops and supplies
- German U-boats sunk by mines

In order to protect British troops and supplies crossing to France, a series of mine barrages were put down across the Strait of Dover and off German-occupied Belgium. Although these did not provide complete protection, they caused the sinking of 28 U-boats, and made the Channel crossing less hazardous

North Sea

Thames Estuary

HOLLAND (neutral)

Bruges

Zeebrugge

Ostend

Dunkirk

Calais

Cap Griz Nez

Boulogne

Goodwin Sands

North Foreland

Ramsgate

Dover

Folkestone

ENGLAND

FRANCE

Strait of Dover

0   5
Miles

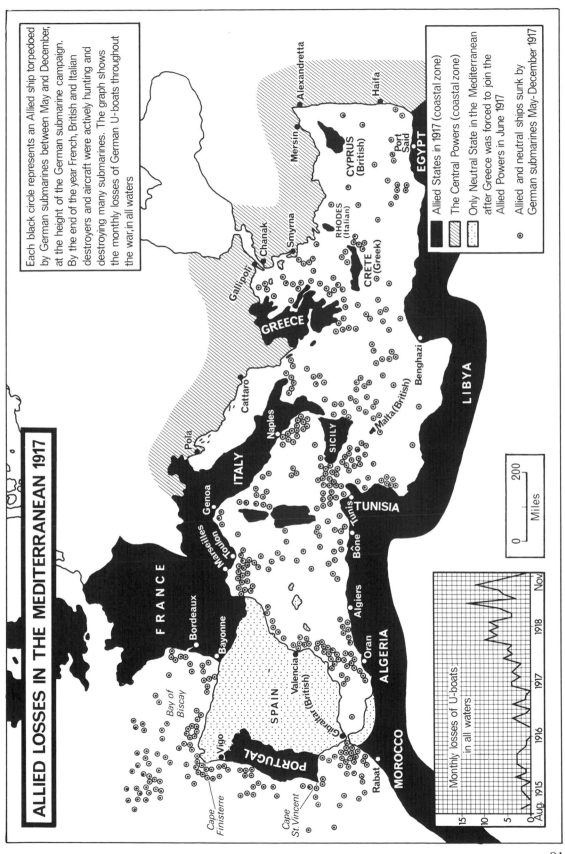

ALLIED LOSSES IN THE MEDITERRANEAN 1917

Each black circle represents an Allied ship torpedoed by German submarines between May and December, at the height of the German submarine campaign. By the end of the year French, British and Italian destroyers and aircraft were actively hunting and destroying many submarines. The graph shows the monthly losses of German U-boats throughout the war, in all waters

Allied States in 1917 (coastal zone)

The Central Powers (coastal zone)

Only Neutral State in the Mediterranean after Greece was forced to join the Allied Powers in June 1917

Allied and neutral ships sunk by German submarines May-December 1917

Bay of Biscay

Cape Finisterre

Cape St. Vincent

FRANCE

Bordeaux

Bayonne

PORTUGAL

SPAIN

Vigo

Valencia

Rabat

MOROCCO

Gibraltar (British)

Oran

Algiers

ALGERIA

Marseilles

Toulon

Genoa

ITALY

Naples

Pola

Cattaro

Bône

Tunis

TUNISIA

SICILY

Malta (British)

GREECE

Gallipoli

Chanak

Smyrna

Benghazi

LIBYA

CRETE (Greek)

RHODES (Italian)

CYPRUS (British)

Mersin

Alexandretta

Haifa

Port Said

EGYPT

Monthly losses of U-boats in all waters

0   5   10   15

Aug. 1915   1916   1917   1918   Nov

0   200   Miles

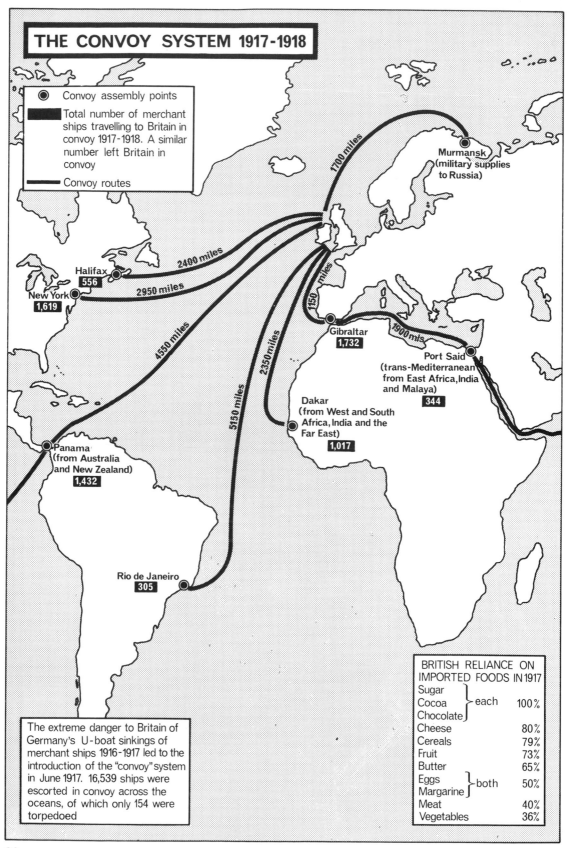

THE CONVOY SYSTEM 1917-1918

⊙ Convoy assembly points

▬ Total number of merchant ships travelling to Britain in convoy 1917-1918. A similar number left Britain in convoy

▬ Convoy routes

Murmansk
(military supplies to Russia)

1700 miles

Halifax
556

2400 miles

New York
1,619

2950 miles

1150 miles

Gibraltar
1,732

1900 mls

Port Said
(trans-Mediterranean from East Africa, India and Malaya)
344

4550 miles

2350 miles

5150 miles

Dakar
(from West and South Africa, India and the Far East)
1,017

Panama
(from Australia and New Zealand)
1,432

Rio de Janeiro
305

BRITISH RELIANCE ON IMPORTED FOODS IN 1917

Sugar	} each	100%
Cocoa		
Chocolate		
Cheese		80%
Cereals		79%
Fruit		73%
Butter		65%
Eggs	} both	50%
Margarine		
Meat		40%
Vegetables		36%

The extreme danger to Britain of Germany's U-boat sinkings of merchant ships 1916-1917 led to the introduction of the "convoy" system in June 1917. 16,539 ships were escorted in convoy across the oceans, of which only 154 were torpedoed

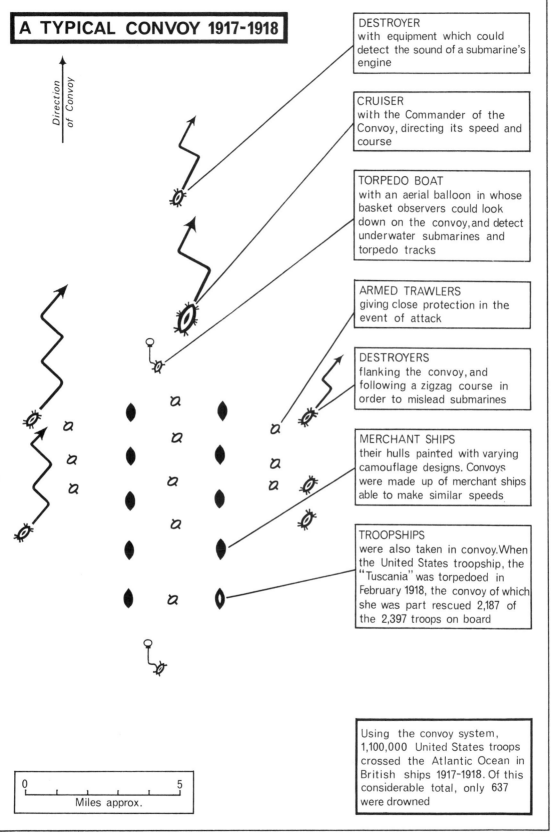

A TYPICAL CONVOY 1917-1918

Direction of Convoy

DESTROYER
with equipment which could detect the sound of a submarine's engine

CRUISER
with the Commander of the Convoy, directing its speed and course

TORPEDO BOAT
with an aerial balloon in whose basket observers could look down on the convoy, and detect underwater submarines and torpedo tracks

ARMED TRAWLERS
giving close protection in the event of attack

DESTROYERS
flanking the convoy, and following a zigzag course in order to mislead submarines

MERCHANT SHIPS
their hulls painted with varying camouflage designs. Convoys were made up of merchant ships able to make similar speeds.

TROOPSHIPS
were also taken in convoy. When the United States troopship, the "Tuscania" was torpedoed in February 1918, the convoy of which she was part rescued 2,187 of the 2,397 troops on board

Using the convoy system, 1,100,000 United States troops crossed the Atlantic Ocean in British ships 1917-1918. Of this considerable total, only 637 were drowned

0   5
Miles approx.

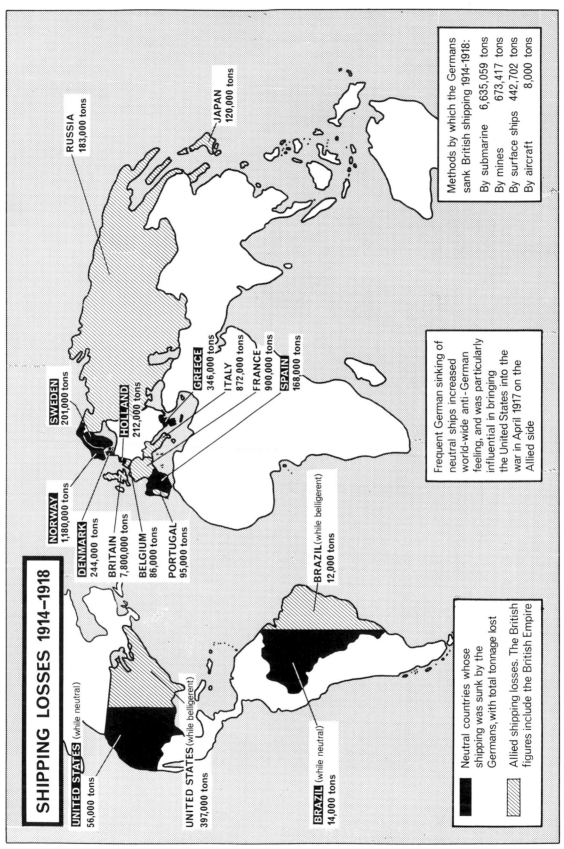

SHIPPING LOSSES 1914–1918

RUSSIA 183,000 tons

JAPAN 120,000 tons

SWEDEN 201,000 tons

HOLLAND 212,000 tons

GREECE 346,000 tons

ITALY 872,000 tons

FRANCE 900,000 tons

SPAIN 168,000 tons

NORWAY 1,180,000 tons

DENMARK 244,000 tons

BRITAIN 7,800,000 tons

BELGIUM 86,000 tons

PORTUGAL 95,000 tons

BRAZIL (while belligerent) 12,000 tons

BRAZIL (while neutral) 14,000 tons

UNITED STATES (while neutral) 56,000 tons

UNITED STATES (while belligerent) 397,000 tons

Methods by which the Germans sank British shipping 1914–1918:

By submarine   6,635,059 tons
By mines   673,417 tons
By surface ships 442,702 tons
By aircraft   8,000 tons

Frequent German sinking of neutral ships increased world-wide anti-German feeling, and was particularly influential in bringing the United States into the war in April 1917 on the Allied side

Neutral countries whose shipping was sunk by the Germans, with total tonnage lost

Allied shipping losses. The British figures include the British Empire

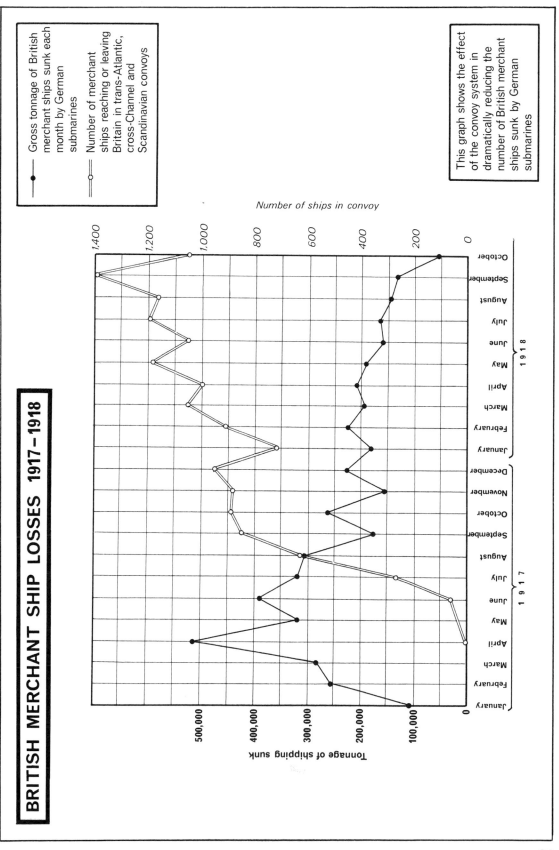

BRITISH MERCHANT SHIP LOSSES 1917–1918

- Gross tonnage of British merchant ships sunk each month by German submarines
- Number of merchant ships reaching or leaving Britain in trans-Atlantic, cross-Channel and Scandinavian convoys

This graph shows the effect of the convoy system in dramatically reducing the number of British merchant ships sunk by German submarines

Number of ships in convoy

1,400
1,200
1,000
800
600
400
200
0

Tonnage of shipping sunk

500,000
400,000
300,000
200,000
100,000
0

January February March April May June July August September October November December January February March April May June July August September October

1 9 1 7

1 9 1 8

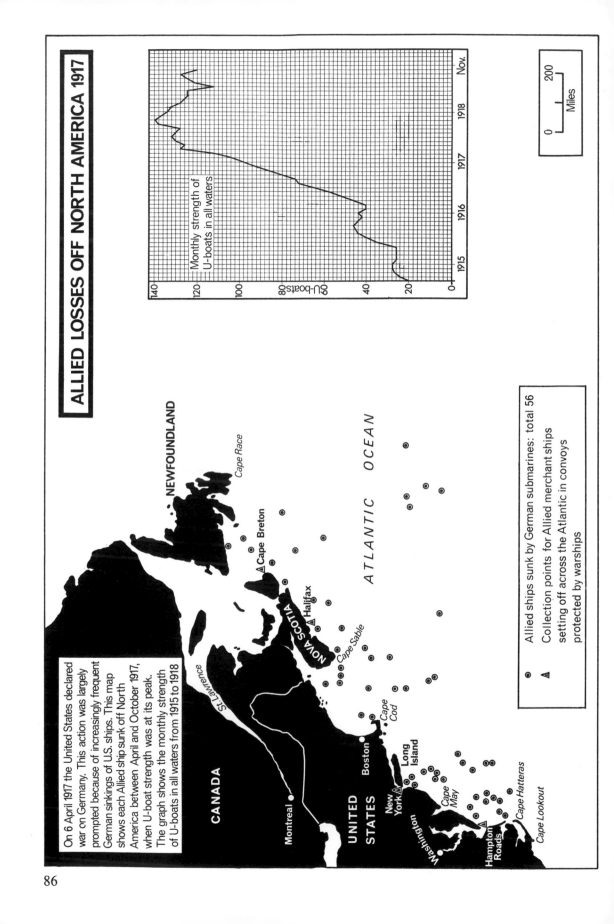

ALLIED LOSSES OFF NORTH AMERICA 1917

On 6 April 1917 the United States declared war on Germany. This action was largely prompted because of increasingly frequent German sinkings of U.S. ships. This map shows each Allied ship sunk off North America between April and October 1917, when U-boat strength was at its peak. The graph shows the monthly strength of U-boats in all waters from 1915 to 1918.

Monthly strength of U-boats in all waters

U-boats

140
120
100
80
60
40
20
0

1915   1916   1917   1918   Nov.

NEWFOUNDLAND

Cape Race

Cape Breton

NOVA SCOTIA

Halifax

Cape Sable

ATLANTIC OCEAN

CANADA

St. Lawrence

Montreal

UNITED STATES

Boston

Cape Cod

Long Island

New York

Cape May

Washington

Hampton Roads

Cape Hatteras

Cape Lookout

⊚   Allied ships sunk by German submarines: total 56

▲   Collection points for Allied merchant ships setting off across the Atlantic in convoys protected by warships

0   200
Miles

86

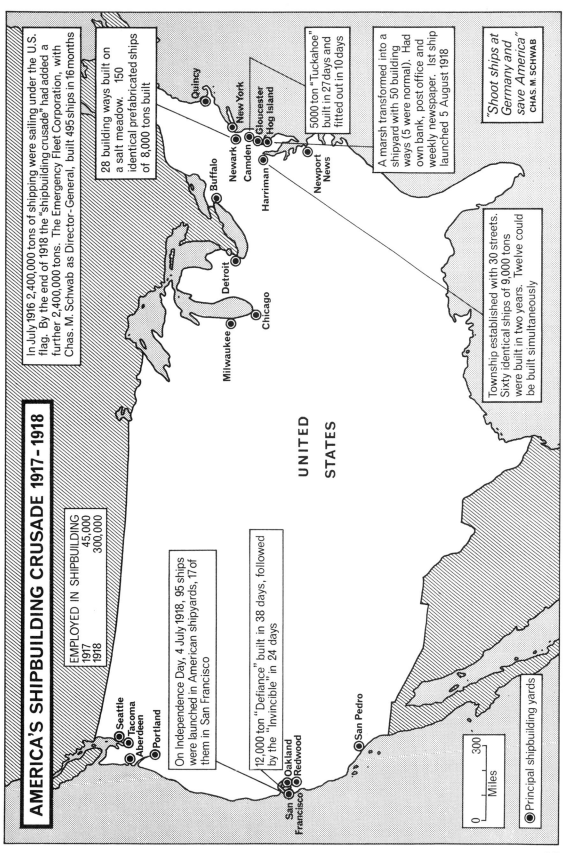

AMERICA'S SHIPBUILDING CRUSADE 1917-1918

In July 1916 2,400,000 tons of shipping were sailing under the U.S. flag. By the end of 1918 the "shipbuilding crusade" had added a further 2,400,000 tons. The Emergency Fleet Corporation, with Chas. M. Schwab as Director-General, built 495 ships in 16 months

28 building ways built on a salt meadow. 150 identical prefabricated ships of 8,000 tons built

5000 ton "Tuckahoe" built in 27 days and fitted out in 10 days

A marsh transformed into a shipyard with 50 building ways (5 were normal). Had own bank, post office and weekly newspaper. 1st ship launched 5 August 1918

"Shoot ships at Germany and save America"
CHAS. M. SCHWAB

Quincy
New York
Newark
Camden Gloucester
Hog Island
Buffalo
Harriman
Newport News
Detroit
Milwaukee
Chicago

UNITED STATES

Township established with 30 streets. Sixty identical ships of 9,000 tons were built in two years. Twelve could be built simultaneously

EMPLOYED IN SHIPBUILDING
1917   45,000
1918   300,000

On Independence Day, 4 July 1918, 95 ships were launched in American shipyards, 17 of them in San Francisco

12,000 ton "Defiance" built in 38 days, followed by the "Invincible" in 24 days

Seattle
Tacoma
Aberdeen
Portland

San Francisco
Oakland
Redwood

San Pedro

300
Miles
0

● Principal shipbuilding yards

87

Section Seven

1917

. . . Light many lamps and gather round his bed
Lend him your eyes, warm blood, and will to live
Speak to him; rouse him; you may save him yet.
He's young; he hated War; how should he die
When cruel old campaigners win safe through?

But death replied: "I choose him." So he went.
And there was silence in the summer night;
Silence and safety; and the veils of sleep.
Then, far away, the thudding of the guns.

SIEGFRIED SASSOON
"THE DEATH-BED"

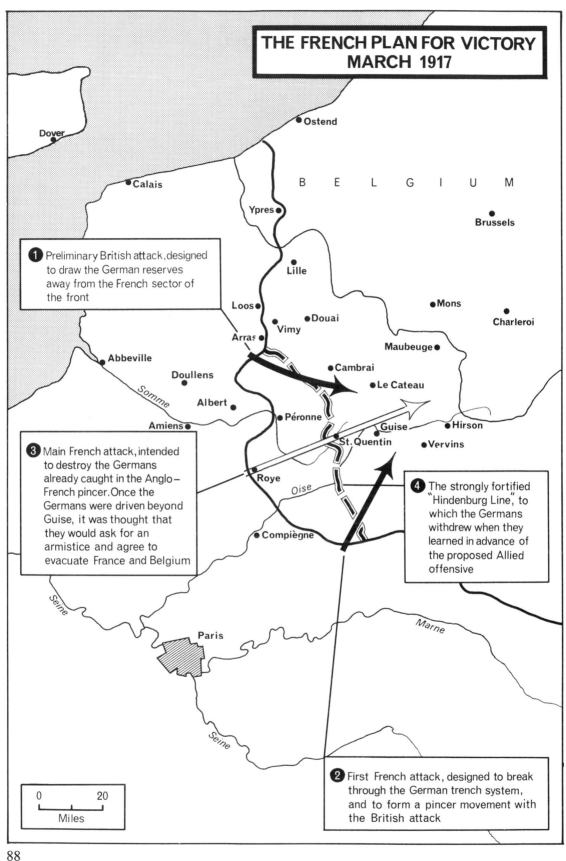

THE FRENCH PLAN FOR VICTORY MARCH 1917

Dover

Ostend

Calais

B E L G I U M

Ypres

Brussels

1 Preliminary British attack, designed to draw the German reserves away from the French sector of the front

Lille

Loos

Mons

Charleroi

Douai

Vimy

Arras

Maubeuge

Cambrai

Abbeville

Le Cateau

Doullens

Somme

Albert

Péronne

Amiens

Guise

Hirson

St. Quentin

Vervins

3 Main French attack, intended to destroy the Germans already caught in the Anglo–French pincer. Once the Germans were driven beyond Guise, it was thought that they would ask for an armistice and agree to evacuate France and Belgium

Roye

Oise

4 The strongly fortified "Hindenburg Line", to which the Germans withdrew when they learned in advance of the proposed Allied offensive

Compiègne

Seine

Marne

Paris

Seine

0   20

Miles

2 First French attack, designed to break through the German trench system, and to form a pincer movement with the British attack

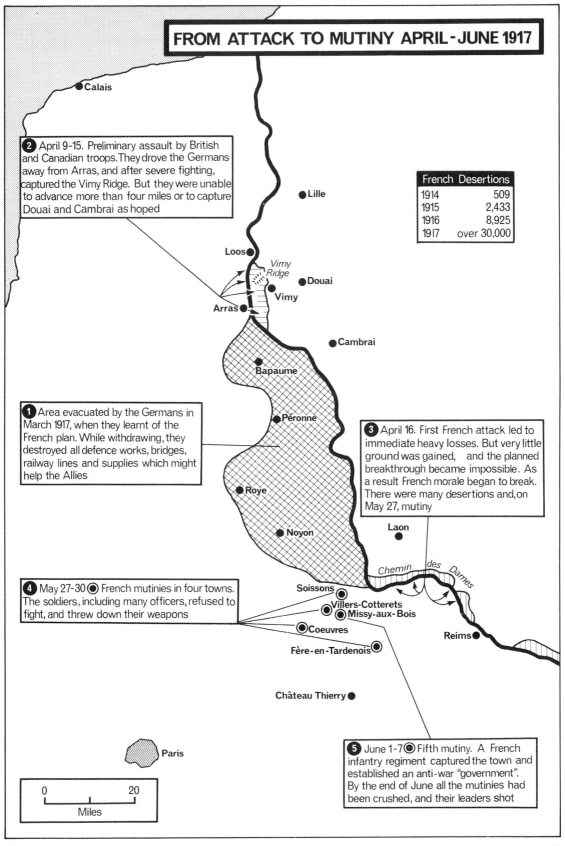

FROM ATTACK TO MUTINY APRIL - JUNE 1917

● Calais

2 April 9-15. Preliminary assault by British and Canadian troops. They drove the Germans away from Arras, and after severe fighting, captured the Vimy Ridge. But they were unable to advance more than four miles or to capture Douai and Cambrai as hoped

● Lille

French Desertions	
1914	509
1915	2,433
1916	8,925
1917	over 30,000

Loos ●

Vimy Ridge

● Douai

● Vimy

Arras ●

● Cambrai

● Bapaume

1 Area evacuated by the Germans in March 1917, when they learnt of the French plan. While withdrawing, they destroyed all defence works, bridges, railway lines and supplies which might help the Allies

● Péronne

3 April 16. First French attack led to immediate heavy losses. But very little ground was gained, and the planned breakthrough became impossible. As a result French morale began to break. There were many desertions and, on May 27, mutiny

● Roye

● Noyon

● Laon

Chemin des Dames

4 May 27-30 ◉ French mutinies in four towns. The soldiers, including many officers, refused to fight, and threw down their weapons

Soissons ◉

◉ Villers-Cotterets
◉ Missy-aux-Bois

◉ Coeuvres

Reims ●

Fère-en-Tardenois ◉

Château Thierry ●

Paris

5 June 1-7 ◉ Fifth mutiny. A French infantry regiment captured the town and established an anti-war "government". By the end of June all the mutinies had been crushed, and their leaders shot

0   20
Miles

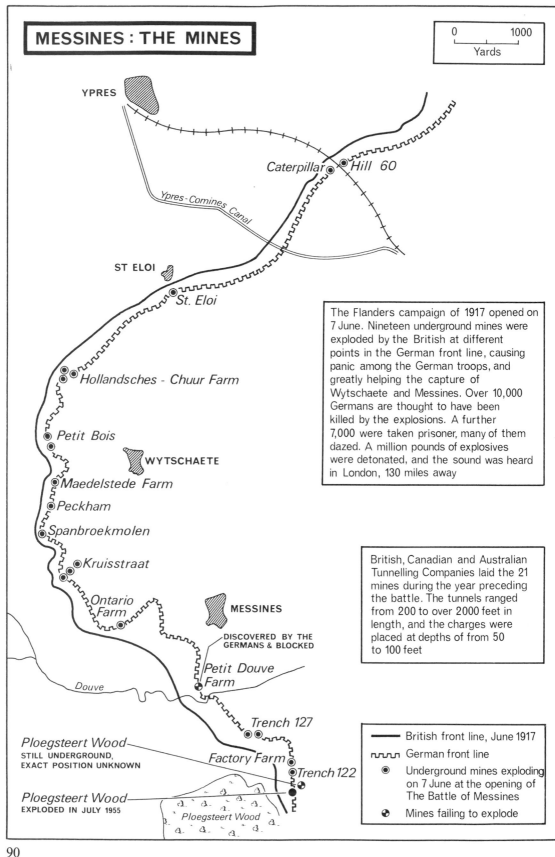

MESSINES : THE MINES

0   1000
Yards

YPRES

Caterpillar ◎ Hill 60

Ypres-Comines Canal

ST ELOI

◉ *St. Eloi*

◉◉ *Hollandsches - Chuur Farm*

◉ *Petit Bois*

WYTSCHAETE

◉ *Maedelstede Farm*

◉ *Peckham*

◉ *Spanbroekmolen*

◉ *Kruisstraat*

Ontario Farm

MESSINES

DISCOVERED BY THE
GERMANS & BLOCKED

Petit Douve Farm ⊕

Douve

Trench 127

Ploegsteert Wood
STILL UNDERGROUND,
EXACT POSITION UNKNOWN

Factory Farm

◉ *Trench 122*

Ploegsteert Wood
EXPLODED IN JULY 1955

Ploegsteert Wood

The Flanders campaign of 1917 opened on 7 June. Nineteen underground mines were exploded by the British at different points in the German front line, causing panic among the German troops, and greatly helping the capture of Wytschaete and Messines. Over 10,000 Germans are thought to have been killed by the explosions. A further 7,000 were taken prisoner, many of them dazed. A million pounds of explosives were detonated, and the sound was heard in London, 130 miles away

British, Canadian and Australian Tunnelling Companies laid the 21 mines during the year preceding the battle. The tunnels ranged from 200 to over 2000 feet in length, and the charges were placed at depths of from 50 to 100 feet

———— British front line, June 1917
ᴧᴧᴧᴧ German front line
◎ Underground mines exploding on 7 June at the opening of The Battle of Messines
◑ Mines failing to explode

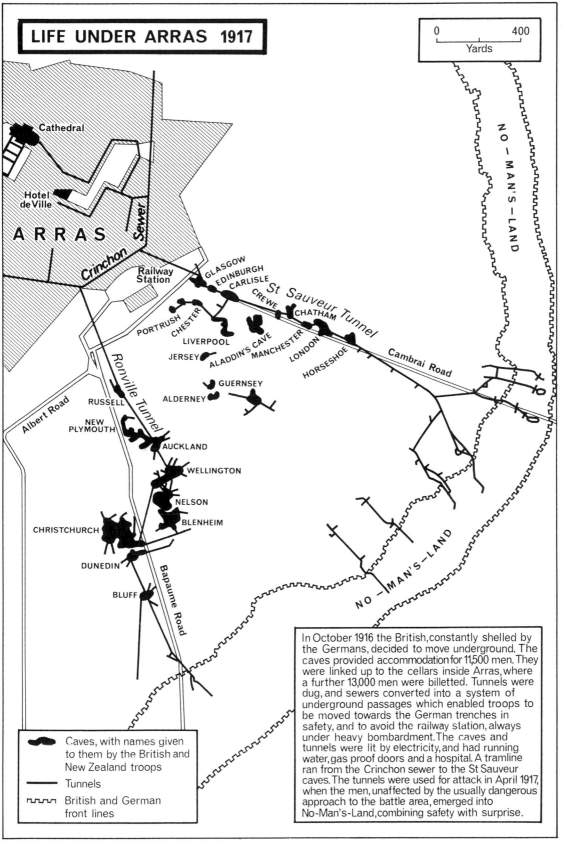

LIFE UNDER ARRAS 1917

0   400
Yards

Cathedral

Hotel de Ville

A R R A S

Crinchon Sewer

Railway Station

GLASGOW
EDINBURGH
CARLISLE
St Sauveur Tunnel
CREWE
CHATHAM
PORTRUSH
CHESTER
LIVERPOOL
ALADDIN'S CAVE
MANCHESTER
LONDON
JERSEY
HORSESHOE
Cambrai Road

GUERNSEY
ALDERNEY

Albert Road
RUSSELL
Ronville Tunnel
NEW PLYMOUTH
AUCKLAND
WELLINGTON
NELSON
BLENHEIM
CHRISTCHURCH
DUNEDIN
Bapaume Road
BLUFF

NO – MAN'S – LAND

NO – MAN'S – LAND

Caves, with names given to them by the British and New Zealand troops

Tunnels

British and German front lines

In October 1916 the British, constantly shelled by the Germans, decided to move underground. The caves provided accommodation for 11,500 men. They were linked up to the cellars inside Arras, where a further 13,000 men were billetted. Tunnels were dug, and sewers converted into a system of underground passages which enabled troops to be moved towards the German trenches in safety, and to avoid the railway station, always under heavy bombardment. The caves and tunnels were lit by electricity, and had running water, gas proof doors and a hospital. A tramline ran from the Crinchon sewer to the St Sauveur caves. The tunnels were used for attack in April 1917, when the men, unaffected by the usually dangerous approach to the battle area, emerged into No-Man's-Land, combining safety with surprise.

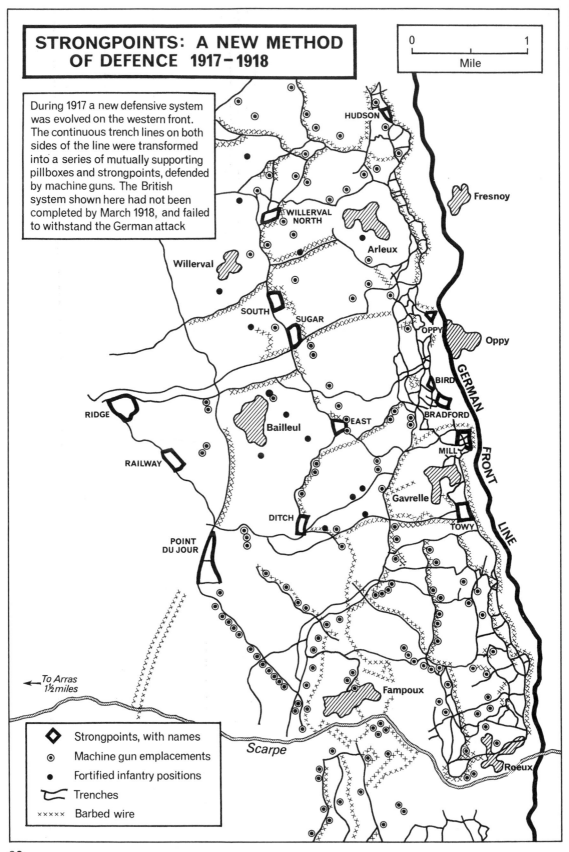

STRONGPOINTS: A NEW METHOD OF DEFENCE 1917–1918

0   1
Mile

During 1917 a new defensive system was evolved on the western front. The continuous trench lines on both sides of the line were transformed into a series of mutually supporting pillboxes and strongpoints, defended by machine guns. The British system shown here had not been completed by March 1918, and failed to withstand the German attack

HUDSON

Fresnoy

WILLERVAL NORTH

Arleux

Willerval

SOUTH

SUGAR

OPPY

Oppy

BIRD

RIDGE

BRADFORD

Bailleul

EAST

MILL

RAILWAY

Gavrelle

DITCH

TOWY

POINT DU JOUR

← To Arras
1½ miles

Fampoux

Scarpe

Roeux

◇   Strongpoints, with names

◉   Machine gun emplacements

●   Fortified infantry positions

⊐   Trenches

××××   Barbed wire

GERMAN FRONT LINE

TANKS: A NEW METHOD OF ATTACK 1917–1918

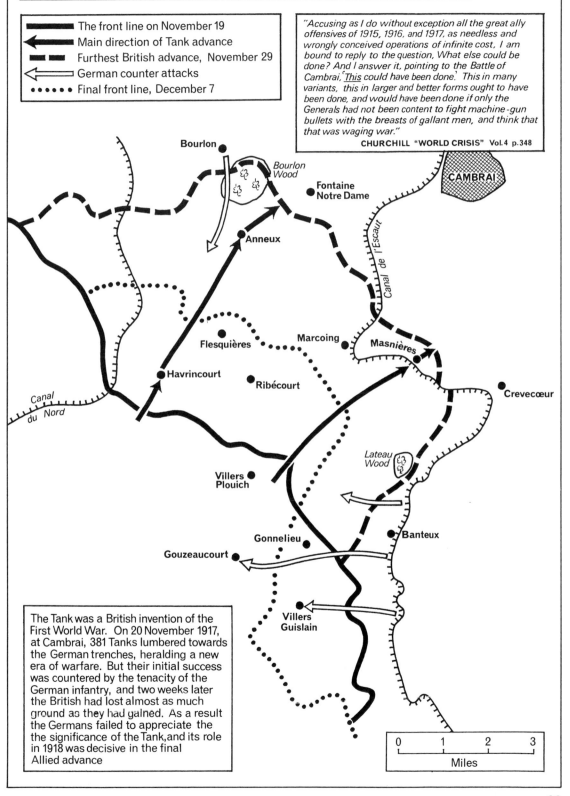

Legend:
- The front line on November 19
- Main direction of Tank advance
- Furthest British advance, November 29
- German counter attacks
- Final front line, December 7

"Accusing as I do without exception all the great ally offensives of 1915, 1916, and 1917, as needless and wrongly conceived operations of infinite cost, I am bound to reply to the question, What else could be done? And I answer it, pointing to the Battle of Cambrai, 'This could have been done.' This in many variants, this in larger and better forms ought to have been done, and would have been done if only the Generals had not been content to fight machine-gun bullets with the breasts of gallant men, and think that that was waging war."
CHURCHILL "WORLD CRISIS" Vol. 4 p.348

Bourlon
Bourlon Wood
CAMBRAI
Fontaine Notre Dame
Anneux
Canal de l'Escaut
Flesquières
Marcoing
Masnières
Havrincourt
Ribécourt
Crevecœur
Canal du Nord
Villers Plouich
Lateau Wood
Gonnelieu
Banteux
Gouzeaucourt
Villers Guislain

The Tank was a British invention of the First World War. On 20 November 1917, at Cambrai, 381 Tanks lumbered towards the German trenches, heralding a new era of warfare. But their initial success was countered by the tenacity of the German infantry, and two weeks later the British had lost almost as much ground as they had gained. As a result the Germans failed to appreciate the the significance of the Tank, and its role in 1918 was decisive in the final Allied advance

0   1   2   3
Miles

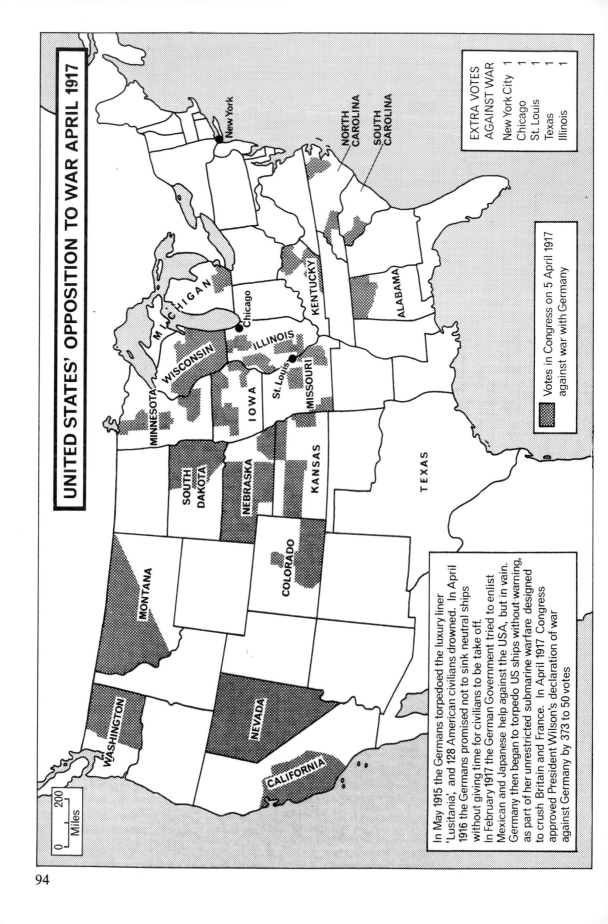

UNITED STATES' OPPOSITION TO WAR APRIL 1917

New York

NORTH CAROLINA

SOUTH CAROLINA

M I C H I G A N

Chicago

ILLINOIS

WISCONSIN

ALABAMA

KENTUCKY

MINNESOTA

IOWA

St. Louis

MISSOURI

MONTANA

SOUTH DAKOTA

NEBRASKA

KANSAS

COLORADO

TEXAS

WASHINGTON

NEVADA

CALIFORNIA

0 200
Miles

Votes in Congress on 5 April 1917
against war with Germany

In May 1915 the Germans torpedoed the luxury liner 'Lusitania', and 128 American civilians drowned. In April 1916 the Germans promised not to sink neutral ships without giving time for civilians to be take off.
In February 1917 the German Government tried to enlist Mexican and Japanese help against the USA, but in vain. Germany then began to torpedo US ships without warning, as part of her unrestricted submarine warfare designed to crush Britain and France. In April 1917 Congress approved President Wilson's declaration of war against Germany by 373 to 50 votes

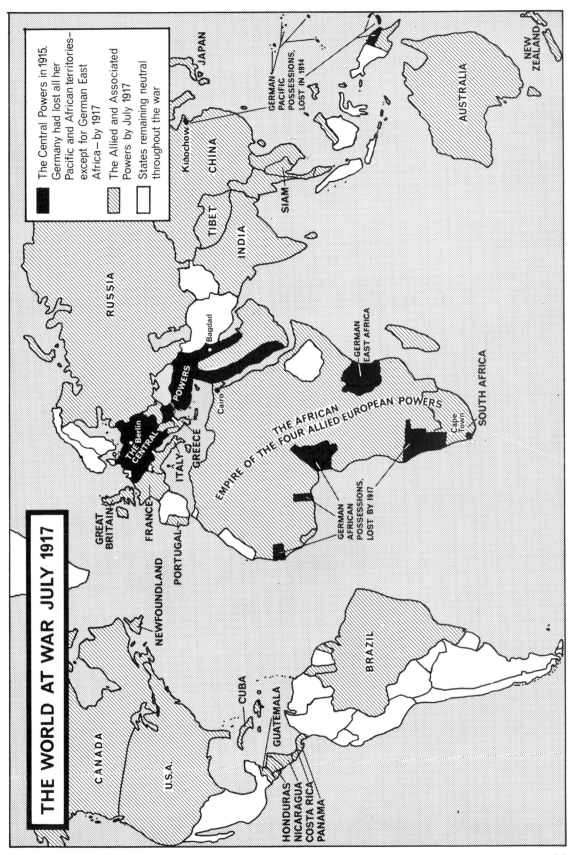

THE WORLD AT WAR JULY 1917

The Central Powers in 1915.
Germany had lost all her
Pacific and African territories–
except for German East
Africa– by 1917

The Allied and Associated
Powers by July 1917

States remaining neutral
throughout the war

CANADA

NEWFOUNDLAND

U.S.A.

CUBA

GUATEMALA

HONDURAS
NICARAGUA
COSTA RICA
PANAMA

BRAZIL

GREAT
BRITAIN

FRANCE

PORTUGAL

THE Berlin
CENTRAL

POWERS

ITALY
GREECE

Cairo

Bagdad

RUSSIA

TIBET

INDIA

CHINA

Kiaochow

SIAM

JAPAN

GERMAN
PACIFIC
POSSESSIONS,
LOST IN 1914

AUSTRALIA

NEW
ZEALAND

THE AFRICAN
EMPIRE OF THE FOUR ALLIED EUROPEAN POWERS

GERMAN
EAST
AFRICA

GERMAN AFRICAN
POSSESSIONS,
LOST BY 1917

Cape
Town

SOUTH AFRICA

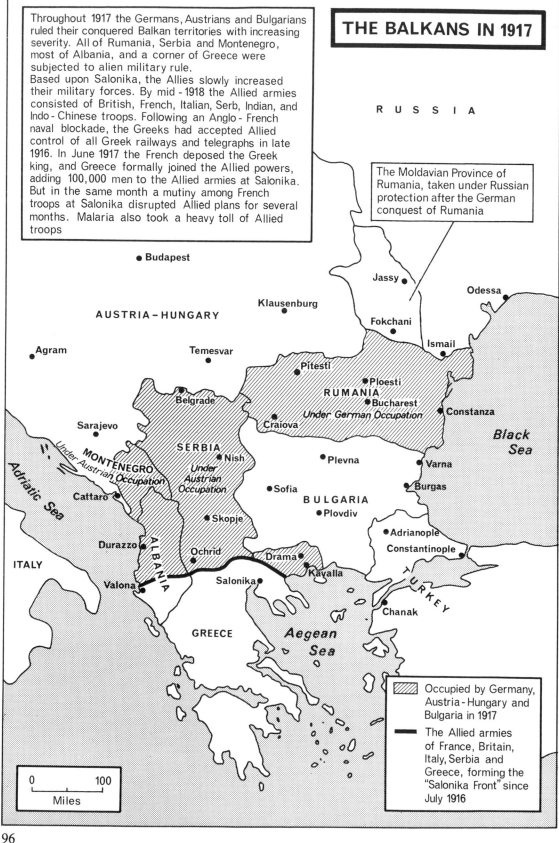

THE BALKANS IN 1917

Throughout 1917 the Germans, Austrians and Bulgarians ruled their conquered Balkan territories with increasing severity. All of Rumania, Serbia and Montenegro, most of Albania, and a corner of Greece were subjected to alien military rule.

Based upon Salonika, the Allies slowly increased their military forces. By mid-1918 the Allied armies consisted of British, French, Italian, Serb, Indian, and Indo-Chinese troops. Following an Anglo-French naval blockade, the Greeks had accepted Allied control of all Greek railways and telegraphs in late 1916. In June 1917 the French deposed the Greek king, and Greece formally joined the Allied powers, adding 100,000 men to the Allied armies at Salonika. But in the same month a mutiny among French troops at Salonika disrupted Allied plans for several months. Malaria also took a heavy toll of Allied troops

The Moldavian Province of Rumania, taken under Russian protection after the German conquest of Rumania

RUSSIA

● Budapest

AUSTRIA – HUNGARY

● Klausenburg

● Jassy

● Odessa

● Fokchani

● Agram

● Temesvar

● Pitesti

● Ismail

● Ploesti

RUMANIA

● Belgrade

● Bucharest

Under German Occupation

● Constanza

● Sarajevo

● Craiova

Black Sea

MONTENEGRO
Under Austrian Occupation

SERBIA

● Nish

Under Austrian Occupation

● Plevna

● Varna

● Cattaro

● Sofia

BULGARIA

● Burgas

Adriatic Sea

● Skopje

● Plovdiv

● Adrianople

● Durazzo

ALBANIA

● Ochrid

● Drama

● Constantinople

ITALY

● Valona

● Salonika

● Kavalla

TURKEY

● Chanak

GREECE

Aegean Sea

| | 0 | 100 | |
| Miles |

Occupied by Germany, Austria-Hungary and Bulgaria in 1917

The Allied armies of France, Britain, Italy, Serbia and Greece, forming the "Salonika Front" since July 1916

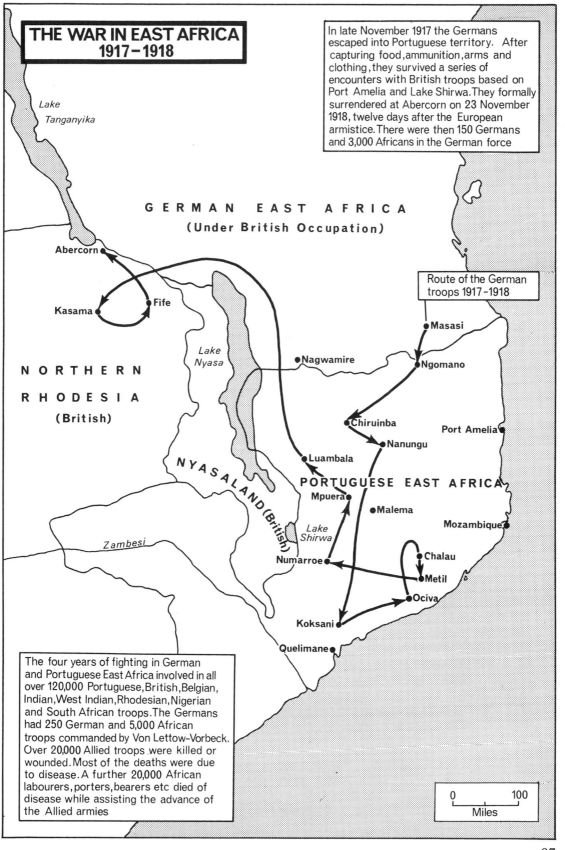

THE WAR IN EAST AFRICA
1917–1918

In late November 1917 the Germans escaped into Portuguese territory. After capturing food, ammunition, arms and clothing, they survived a series of encounters with British troops based on Port Amelia and Lake Shirwa. They formally surrendered at Abercorn on 23 November 1918, twelve days after the European armistice. There were then 150 Germans and 3,000 Africans in the German force

Lake Tanganyika

G E R M A N   E A S T   A F R I C A
(Under British Occupation)

Abercorn

Kasama ● Fife

Route of the German troops 1917–1918

● Masasi

N O R T H E R N

R H O D E S I A
(British)

Lake Nyasa

● Nagwamire ● Ngomano

● Chiruinba ● Port Amelia

● Nanungu

N Y A S A L A N D (British)

● Luambala

P O R T U G U E S E   E A S T   A F R I C A

● Mpuera

● Malema

● Mozambique

Zambesi

Lake Shirwa

● Chalau

Numarroe ● ● Metil

● Ociva

Koksani ●

Quelimane ●

The four years of fighting in German and Portuguese East Africa involved in all over 120,000 Portuguese, British, Belgian, Indian, West Indian, Rhodesian, Nigerian and South African troops. The Germans had 250 German and 5,000 African troops commanded by Von Lettow-Vorbeck. Over 20,000 Allied troops were killed or wounded. Most of the deaths were due to disease. A further 20,000 African labourers, porters, bearers etc died of disease while assisting the advance of the Allied armies

0   100
Miles

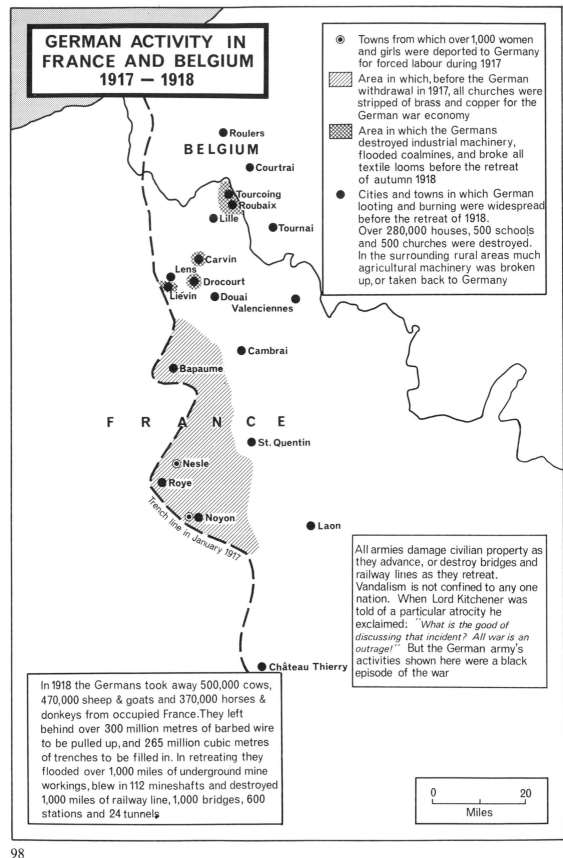

GERMAN ACTIVITY IN FRANCE AND BELGIUM 1917 — 1918

◉ Towns from which over 1,000 women and girls were deported to Germany for forced labour during 1917

▨ Area in which, before the German withdrawal in 1917, all churches were stripped of brass and copper for the German war economy

▩ Area in which the Germans destroyed industrial machinery, flooded coalmines, and broke all textile looms before the retreat of autumn 1918

● Cities and towns in which German looting and burning were widespread before the retreat of 1918. Over 280,000 houses, 500 schools and 500 churches were destroyed. In the surrounding rural areas much agricultural machinery was broken up, or taken back to Germany

BELGIUM

● Roulers
● Courtrai
● Tourcoing
● Roubaix
● Lille
● Tournai
● Carvin
● Lens
● Drocourt
● Liévin
● Douai
Valenciennes

F R A N C E

● Cambrai
● Bapaume
● St. Quentin
◉ Nesle
● Roye
◉ Noyon
● Laon

Trench line in January 1917

● Château Thierry

All armies damage civilian property as they advance, or destroy bridges and railway lines as they retreat. Vandalism is not confined to any one nation. When Lord Kitchener was told of a particular atrocity he exclaimed: *"What is the good of discussing that incident? All war is an outrage!"* But the German army's activities shown here were a black episode of the war

In 1918 the Germans took away 500,000 cows, 470,000 sheep & goats and 370,000 horses & donkeys from occupied France. They left behind over 300 million metres of barbed wire to be pulled up, and 265 million cubic metres of trenches to be filled in. In retreating they flooded over 1,000 miles of underground mine workings, blew in 112 mineshafts and destroyed 1,000 miles of railway line, 1,000 bridges, 600 stations and 24 tunnels

0   20
Miles

GERMAN SOCIAL UNREST 1917–1918

North Sea

Baltic Sea

SCHLESWIG-HOLSTEIN

●Kiel

◉●Hamburg

●Bremen

Danzig●

P R U S S I A

◉●Berlin

◉●Magdeburg

Duisberg
● ●
Essen

RHINELAND

Halle●
◉●Leipzig

S A X O N Y   ●Dresden

Chemnitz●

●Nuremburg

B A V A R I A

●Munich

Throughout 1917 there was growing industrial unrest in Germany. The Allied blockade forced the German Government to introduce increasingly severe food rationing. Early in 1918 "meatless weeks" were decreed. These heightened the discontent, and led to growing hatred of the rich, who could still afford contraband food. Added to social unrest was a mounting war-weariness, stimulated by the Russian Bolshevik decision in November 1917, to leave the war altogether. Bolshevik ideas and propaganda inside Germany were also gaining significant successes

◉ Strikes in April 1917, against reduction in the bread ration.
● Strikes in January 1918, against the continuation of the war

0 ——— 90
Miles

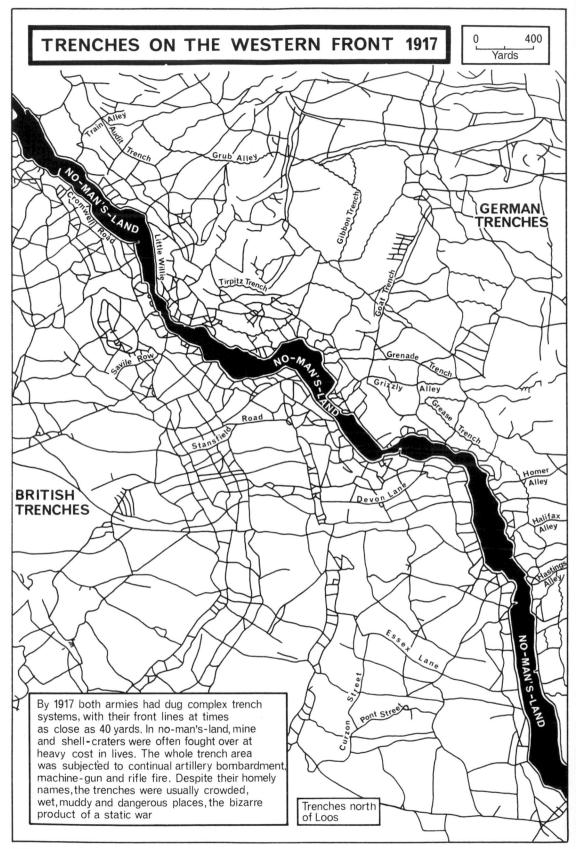

TRENCHES ON THE WESTERN FRONT 1917

0   400
Yards

Train Alley

Audit Trench

Grub Alley

GERMAN TRENCHES

Gibbon Trench

NO-MAN'S-LAND

Cromwell Road

Little Willie

Tirpitz Trench

Goat Trench

Savile Row

NO-MAN'S-LAND

Grenade Trench

Grizzly Alley

Grease Trench

Road

Stansfield Road

Devon Lane

Homer Alley

BRITISH TRENCHES

Halifax Alley

Hastings Alley

Essex Lane

NO-MAN'S-LAND

Curzon Street

Pont Street

By 1917 both armies had dug complex trench systems, with their front lines at times as close as 40 yards. In no-man's-land, mine and shell-craters were often fought over at heavy cost in lives. The whole trench area was subjected to continual artillery bombardment, machine-gun and rifle fire. Despite their homely names, the trenches were usually crowded, wet, muddy and dangerous places, the bizarre product of a static war

Trenches north of Loos

100

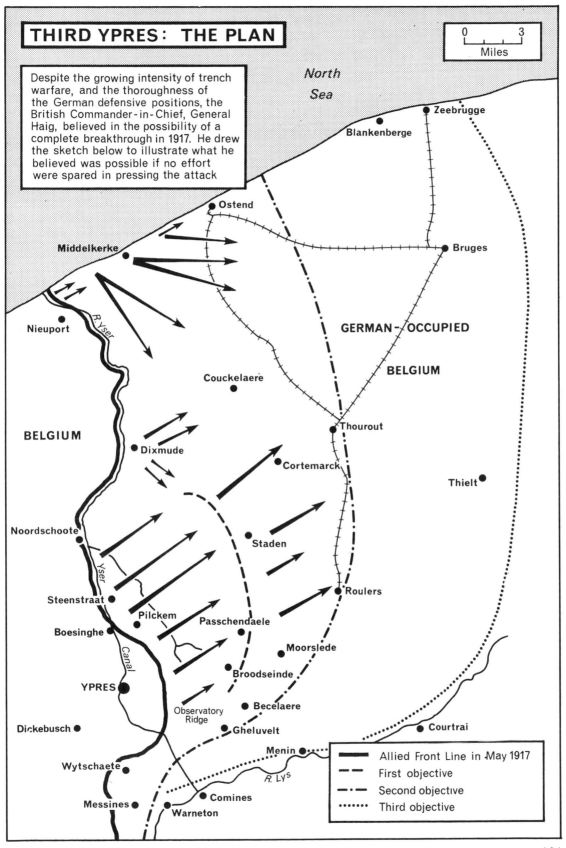

THIRD YPRES: THE PLAN

Despite the growing intensity of trench warfare, and the thoroughness of the German defensive positions, the British Commander-in-Chief, General Haig, believed in the possibility of a complete breakthrough in 1917. He drew the sketch below to illustrate what he believed was possible if no effort were spared in pressing the attack

0   3
Miles

North
Sea

Zeebrugge

Blankenberge

Ostend

Middelkerke

Bruges

Nieuport

R. Yser

GERMAN-OCCUPIED

BELGIUM

Couckelaere

BELGIUM

Dixmude

Thourout

Cortemarck

Thielt

Noordschoote

Yser

Staden

Steenstraat

Roulers

Pilckem

Boesinghe

Passchendaele

Canal

Moorslede

Broodseinde

YPRES

Observatory
Ridge

Becelaere

Dickebusch

Gheluvelt

Courtrai

Menin

Allied Front Line in May 1917

Wytschaete

R. Lys

First objective

Second objective

Messines

Comines

Warneton

Third objective

101

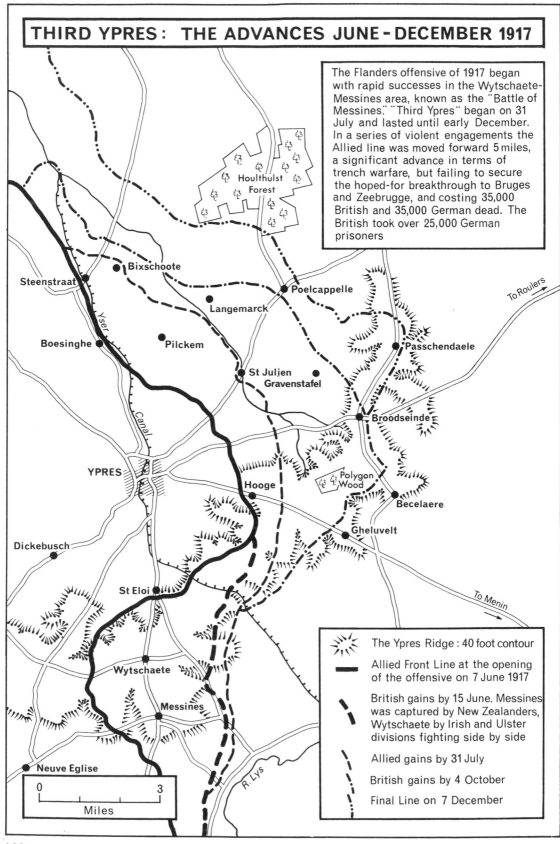

THIRD YPRES : THE ADVANCES JUNE - DECEMBER 1917

The Flanders offensive of 1917 began with rapid successes in the Wytschaete-Messines area, known as the "Battle of Messines." "Third Ypres" began on 31 July and lasted until early December. In a series of violent engagements the Allied line was moved forward 5 miles, a significant advance in terms of trench warfare, but failing to secure the hoped-for breakthrough to Bruges and Zeebrugge, and costing 35,000 British and 35,000 German dead. The British took over 25,000 German prisoners

Houlthulst Forest

Bixschoote

Steenstraat

To Roulers

Poelcappelle

Langemarck

Boesinghe

Pilckem

Passchendaele

St Julien
Gravenstafel

Broodseinde

YPRES

Hooge

Polygon Wood

Becelaere

Dickebusch

Gheluvelt

To Menin

St Eloi

Wytschaete

Messines

Neuve Eglise

R. Lys

0   3
Miles

The Ypres Ridge : 40 foot contour

Allied Front Line at the opening of the offensive on 7 June 1917

British gains by 15 June. Messines was captured by New Zealanders, Wytschaete by Irish and Ulster divisions fighting side by side

Allied gains by 31 July

British gains by 4 October

Final Line on 7 December

102

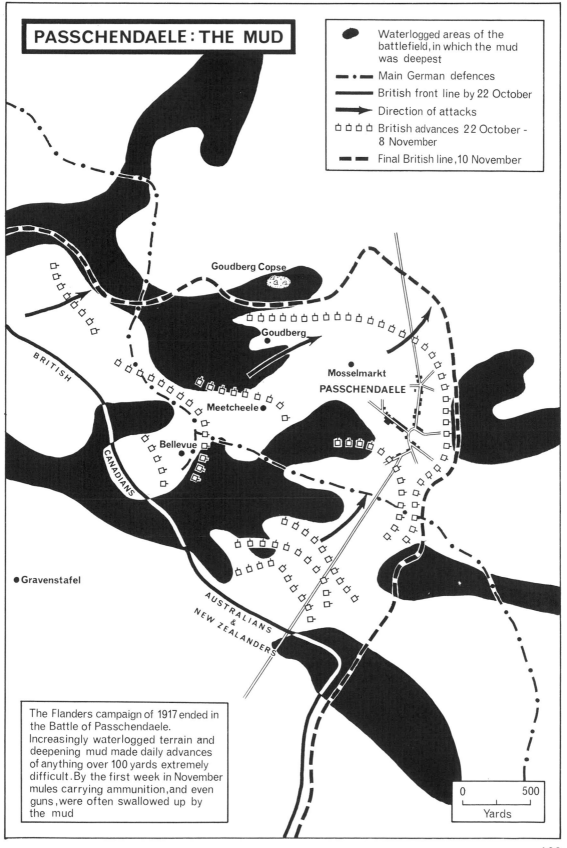

PASSCHENDAELE : THE MUD

Waterlogged areas of the battlefield, in which the mud was deepest

—·—·— Main German defences

——— British front line by 22 October

——➤ Direction of attacks

▱ ▱ ▱ ▱ British advances 22 October - 8 November

━ ━ ━ Final British line, 10 November

Goudberg Copse

Goudberg

Mosselmarkt

PASSCHENDAELE

Meetcheele

Bellevue

BRITISH

CANADIANS

Gravenstafel

AUSTRALIANS
&
NEW ZEALANDERS

The Flanders campaign of 1917 ended in the Battle of Passchendaele. Increasingly waterlogged terrain and deepening mud made daily advances of anything over 100 yards extremely difficult. By the first week in November mules carrying ammunition, and even guns, were often swallowed up by the mud

0   500

Yards

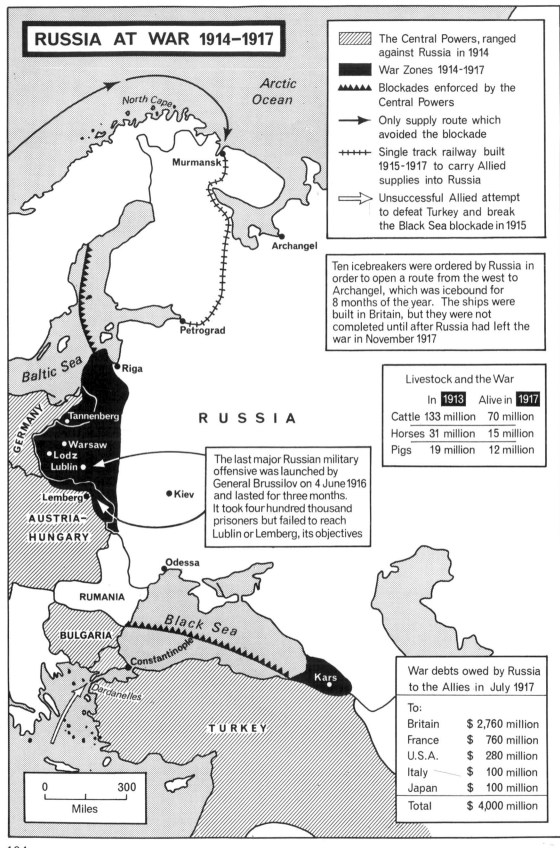

RUSSIA AT WAR 1914–1917

Arctic Ocean

North Cape

Murmansk

Archangel

Petrograd

Baltic Sea

Riga

GERMANY

R U S S I A

Tannenberg

Warsaw
Lodz
Lublin

Lemberg

Kiev

AUSTRIA–HUNGARY

Odessa

RUMANIA

Black Sea

BULGARIA

Constantinople

Dardanelles

Kars

T U R K E Y

Legend:

The Central Powers, ranged against Russia in 1914

War Zones 1914-1917

Blockades enforced by the Central Powers

Only supply route which avoided the blockade

Single track railway built 1915-1917 to carry Allied supplies into Russia

Unsuccessful Allied attempt to defeat Turkey and break the Black Sea blockade in 1915

Ten icebreakers were ordered by Russia in order to open a route from the west to Archangel, which was icebound for 8 months of the year. The ships were built in Britain, but they were not completed until after Russia had left the war in November 1917

Livestock and the War

	In 1913	Alive in 1917
Cattle	133 million	70 million
Horses	31 million	15 million
Pigs	19 million	12 million

The last major Russian military offensive was launched by General Brussilov on 4 June 1916 and lasted for three months. It took four hundred thousand prisoners but failed to reach Lublin or Lemberg, its objectives

0   300
Miles

War debts owed by Russia to the Allies in July 1917

To:	
Britain	$ 2,760 million
France	$ 760 million
U.S.A.	$ 280 million
Italy	$ 100 million
Japan	$ 100 million
Total	$ 4,000 million

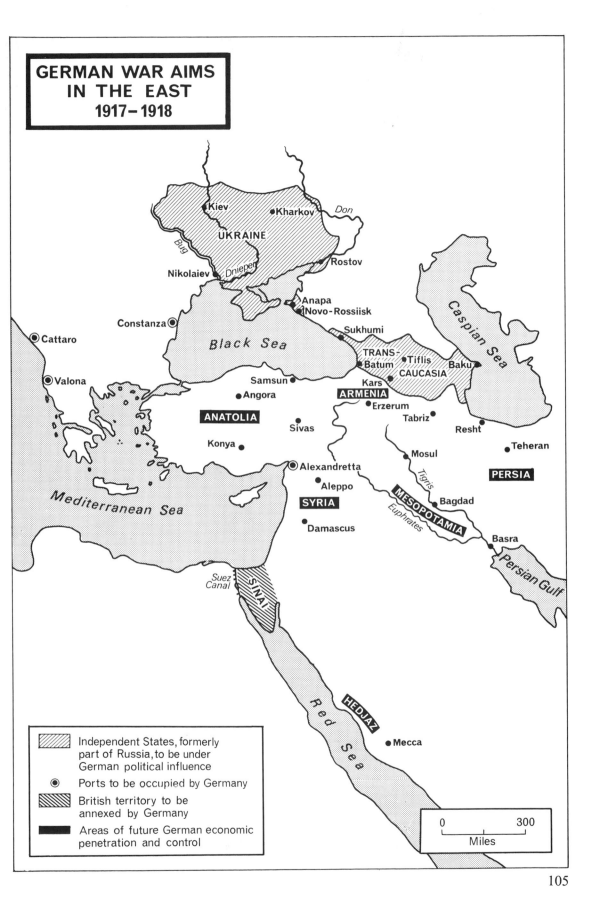

GERMAN WAR AIMS IN THE EAST 1917–1918

Kiev

Kharkov

Don

UKRAINE

Bug

Dnieper

Nikolaiev

Rostov

Anapa

Novo-Rossiisk

Constanza

Sukhumi

Black Sea

TRANS-

Tiflis

Batum

CAUCASIA

Baku

Caspian Sea

Cattaro

Samsun

Kars

ARMENIA

Valona

Angora

Erzerum

Tabriz

ANATOLIA

Resht

Sivas

Teheran

Konya

Mosul

PERSIA

Alexandretta

Tigris

Aleppo

SYRIA

MESOPOTAMIA

Bagdad

Mediterranean Sea

Euphrates

Damascus

Basra

Persian Gulf

Suez
Canal

SINAI

Red
Sea

HEDJAZ

Mecca

Independent States, formerly part of Russia, to be under German political influence

⊙ Ports to be occupied by Germany

British territory to be annexed by Germany

Areas of future German economic penetration and control

0   300

Miles

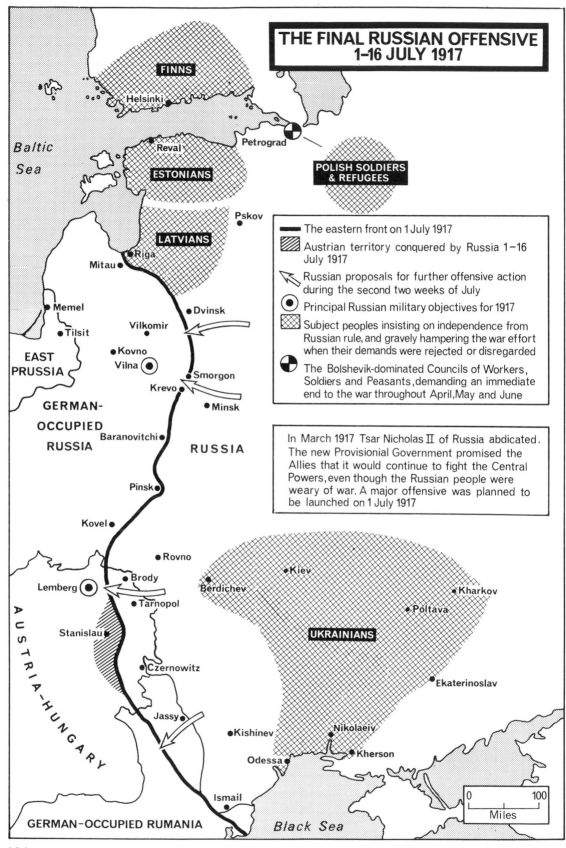

THE FINAL RUSSIAN OFFENSIVE 1–16 JULY 1917

FINNS

Helsinki

Baltic Sea

Reval

Petrograd

ESTONIANS

POLISH SOLDIERS & REFUGEES

Pskov

LATVIANS

Riga

Mitau

Memel

Dvinsk

Tilsit

Vilkomir

EAST PRUSSIA

Kovno

Vilna ⊙

Smorgon

Krevo

GERMAN-OCCUPIED RUSSIA

Minsk

Baranovitchi

RUSSIA

Pinsk

Kovel

Rovno

Lemberg ⊙

Brody

Kiev

Berdichev

Kharkov

Tarnopol

Poltava

Stanislau

UKRAINIANS

A U S T R I A - H U N G A R Y

Czernowitz

Ekaterinoslav

Jassy

Kishinev

Nikolaeiv

Odessa

Kherson

Ismail

GERMAN-OCCUPIED RUMANIA

Black Sea

Legend:

━━━ The eastern front on 1 July 1917

▨ Austrian territory conquered by Russia 1–16 July 1917

⇦ Russian proposals for further offensive action during the second two weeks of July

⊙ Principal Russian military objectives for 1917

▨ Subject peoples insisting on independence from Russian rule, and gravely hampering the war effort when their demands were rejected or disregarded

◑ The Bolshevik-dominated Councils of Workers, Soldiers and Peasants, demanding an immediate end to the war throughout April, May and June

In March 1917 Tsar Nicholas II of Russia abdicated. The new Provisionial Government promised the Allies that it would continue to fight the Central Powers, even though the Russian people were weary of war. A major offensive was planned to be launched on 1 July 1917.

0   100
Miles

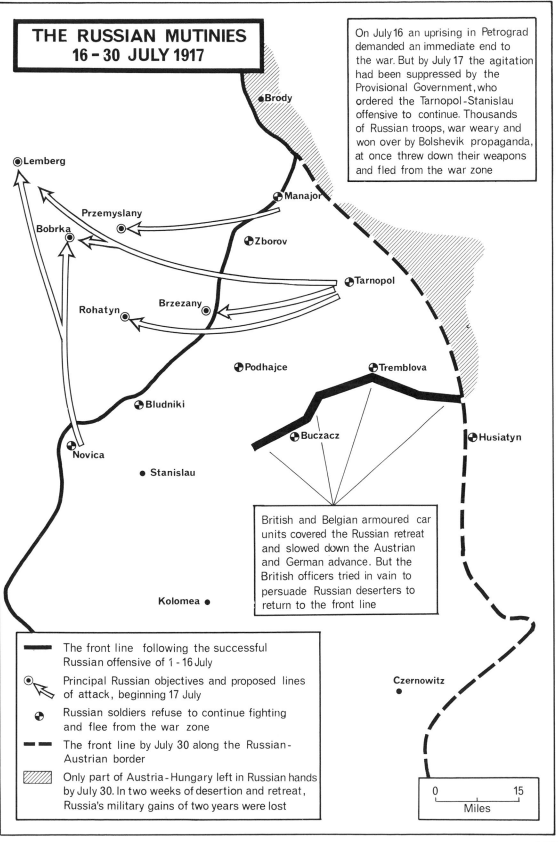

THE RUSSIAN MUTINIES 16 – 30 JULY 1917

On July 16 an uprising in Petrograd demanded an immediate end to the war. But by July 17 the agitation had been suppressed by the Provisional Government, who ordered the Tarnopol-Stanislau offensive to continue. Thousands of Russian troops, war weary and won over by Bolshevik propaganda, at once threw down their weapons and fled from the war zone

●Brody

◉Lemberg

◐Manajor

Przemyslany
◉
Bobrka
◉
◐Zborov

◐Tarnopol

Rohatyn
◉
Brzezany
◉

◐Podhajce

◐Tremblova

◐Bludniki

◐Buczacz

◐Husiatyn

Novica

● Stanislau

British and Belgian armoured car units covered the Russian retreat and slowed down the Austrian and German advance. But the British officers tried in vain to persuade Russian deserters to return to the front line

Kolomea ●

Czernowitz
●

The front line following the successful Russian offensive of 1 - 16 July

◉ Principal Russian objectives and proposed lines of attack, beginning 17 July

◐ Russian soldiers refuse to continue fighting and flee from the war zone

The front line by July 30 along the Russian-Austrian border

Only part of Austria-Hungary left in Russian hands by July 30. In two weeks of desertion and retreat, Russia's military gains of two years were lost

0   15
Miles

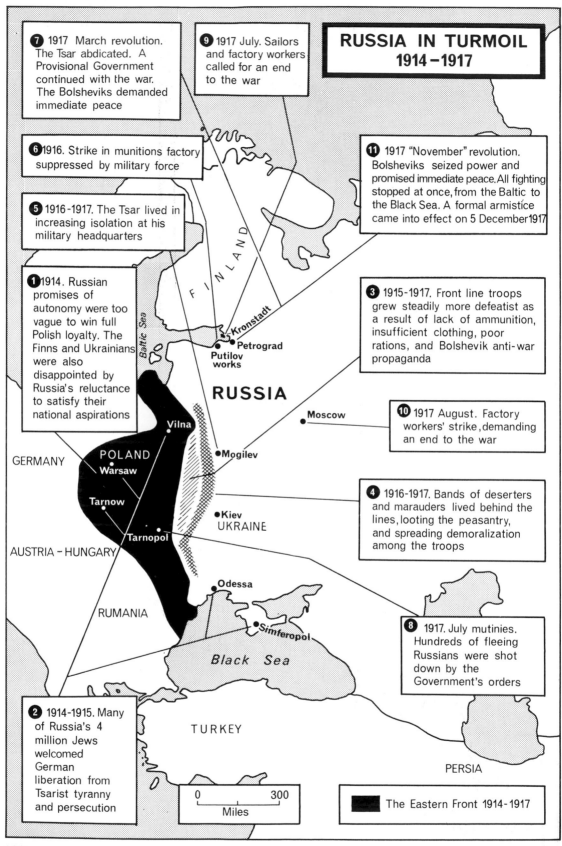

RUSSIA IN TURMOIL
1914 – 1917

7 1917 March revolution. The Tsar abdicated. A Provisional Government continued with the war. The Bolsheviks demanded immediate peace

9 1917 July. Sailors and factory workers called for an end to the war

6 1916. Strike in munitions factory suppressed by military force

5 1916-1917. The Tsar lived in increasing isolation at his military headquarters

11 1917 "November" revolution. Bolsheviks seized power and promised immediate peace. All fighting stopped at once, from the Baltic to the Black Sea. A formal armistice came into effect on 5 December 1917

1 1914. Russian promises of autonomy were too vague to win full Polish loyalty. The Finns and Ukrainians were also disappointed by Russia's reluctance to satisfy their national aspirations

3 1915-1917. Front line troops grew steadily more defeatist as a result of lack of ammunition, insufficient clothing, poor rations, and Bolshevik anti-war propaganda

10 1917 August. Factory workers' strike, demanding an end to the war

4 1916-1917. Bands of deserters and marauders lived behind the lines, looting the peasantry, and spreading demoralization among the troops

8 1917. July mutinies. Hundreds of fleeing Russians were shot down by the Government's orders

2 1914-1915. Many of Russia's 4 million Jews welcomed German liberation from Tsarist tyranny and persecution

FINLAND

Baltic Sea

Kronstadt

Petrograd

Putilov works

RUSSIA

Moscow

Vilna

•Mogilev

POLAND

Warsaw

GERMANY

Tarnow

•Kiev
UKRAINE

AUSTRIA – HUNGARY

Tarnopol

Odessa

RUMANIA

Simferopol

Black Sea

TURKEY

PERSIA

0   300
Miles

■ The Eastern Front 1914-1917

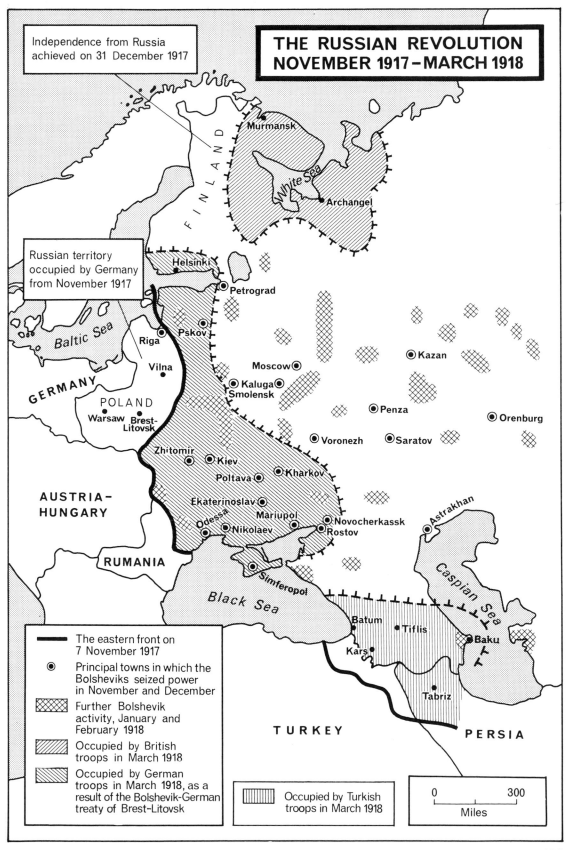

Independence from Russia
achieved on 31 December 1917

THE RUSSIAN REVOLUTION
NOVEMBER 1917 – MARCH 1918

Murmansk

White Sea

Archangel

Russian territory
occupied by Germany
from November 1917

Helsinki

Petrograd

Baltic Sea

Riga

Pskov

Vilna

Moscow

Kazan

GERMANY

POLAND

Kaluga
Smolensk

Warsaw Brest-
Litovsk

Penza

Orenburg

Zhitomir

Voronezh

Saratov

Kiev

Poltava

Kharkov

AUSTRIA-
HUNGARY

Ekaterinoslav

Odessa

Mariupol

Astrakhan

Nikolaev

Novocherkassk
Rostov

RUMANIA

Simferopol

Caspian Sea

Black Sea

Batum Tiflis

The eastern front on
7 November 1917

Baku

Kars

Principal towns in which the
Bolsheviks seized power
in November and December

Further Bolshevik
activity, January and
February 1918

Tabriz

Occupied by British
troops in March 1918

TURKEY

PERSIA

Occupied by German
troops in March 1918, as a
result of the Bolshevik-German
treaty of Brest-Litovsk

Occupied by Turkish
troops in March 1918

0   300

Miles

109

Section Eight

1918

. . . You smug-faced crowds with kindling eye
Who cheer when soldier lads march by,
Sneak home and pray you'll never know
The hell where youth and laughter go.

SIEGFRIED SASSOON
"SUICIDE IN THE TRENCHES"

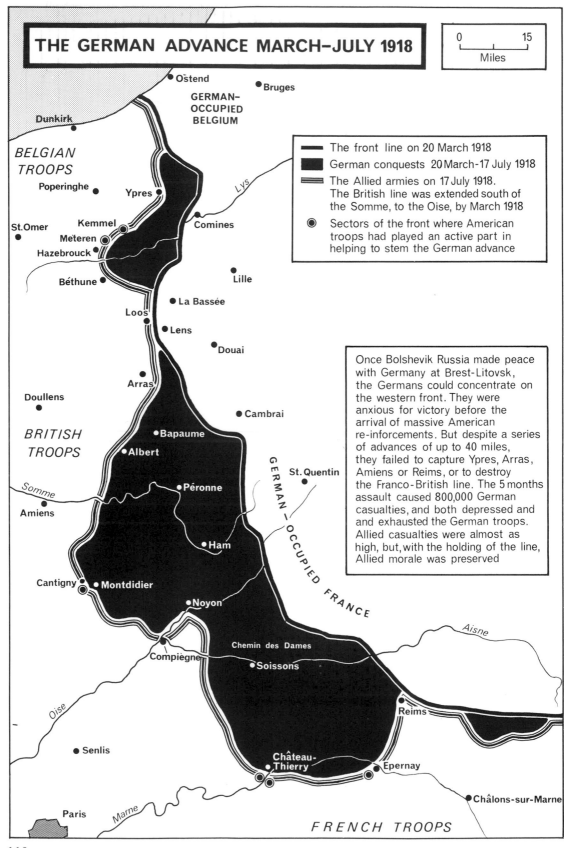

THE GERMAN ADVANCE MARCH–JULY 1918

0   15
Miles

Ostend ● ● Bruges

GERMAN–
OCCUPIED
BELGIUM

Dunkirk ●

BELGIAN
TROOPS

— The front line on 20 March 1918
■ German conquests 20 March–17 July 1918
≡ The Allied armies on 17 July 1918.
   The British line was extended south of
   the Somme, to the Oise, by March 1918
◉ Sectors of the front where American
   troops had played an active part in
   helping to stem the German advance

Poperinghe ●
Ypres ●
St.Omer ●
Kemmel ●
Meteren ●
Hazebrouck ●
Comines ●
Lys

Lille ●

Béthune ●
La Bassée ●
Loos ●
Lens ●
Douai ●

Arras ●

Doullens ●

BRITISH
TROOPS

Cambrai ●

Bapaume ●
Albert ●

Once Bolshevik Russia made peace
with Germany at Brest-Litovsk,
the Germans could concentrate on
the western front. They were
anxious for victory before the
arrival of massive American
re-inforcements. But despite a series
of advances of up to 40 miles,
they failed to capture Ypres, Arras,
Amiens or Reims, or to destroy
the Franco-British line. The 5 months
assault caused 800,000 German
casualties, and both depressed and
and exhausted the German troops.
Allied casualties were almost as
high, but, with the holding of the line,
Allied morale was preserved

St. Quentin ●

GERMAN – OCCUPIED FRANCE

Péronne ●

Somme
Amiens

Ham ●

Cantigny ◉ ● Montdidier
Noyon ●

Aisne

Compiègne
Chemin des Dames
Soissons ●

Oise

Reims ●

Senlis ●

Château-
Thierry ◉
● Epernay

● Châlons-sur-Marne

Paris
Marne

FRENCH TROOPS

110

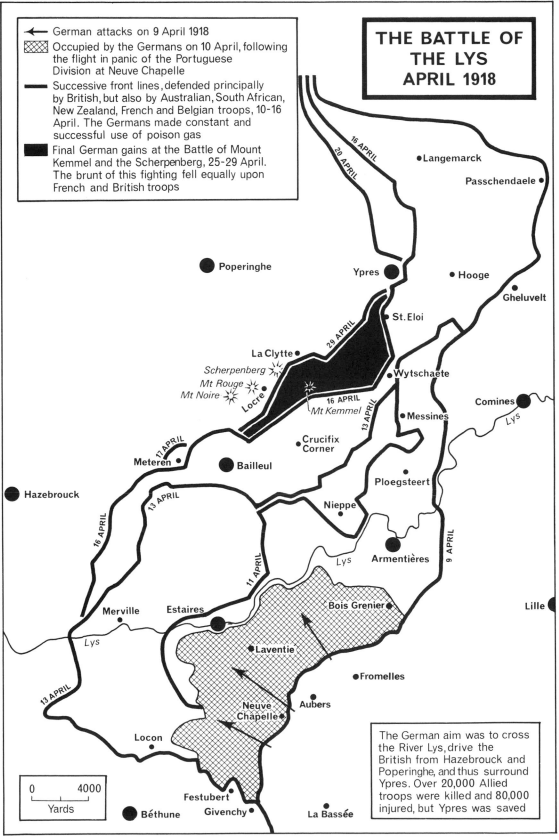

THE BATTLE OF THE LYS APRIL 1918

Legend:
- German attacks on 9 April 1918
- Occupied by the Germans on 10 April, following the flight in panic of the Portuguese Division at Neuve Chapelle
- Successive front lines, defended principally by British, but also by Australian, South African, New Zealand, French and Belgian troops, 10-16 April. The Germans made constant and successful use of poison gas
- Final German gains at the Battle of Mount Kemmel and the Scherpenberg, 25-29 April. The brunt of this fighting fell equally upon French and British troops

Places: Langemarck, Passchendaele, Poperinghe, Ypres, Hooge, Gheluvelt, St. Eloi, La Clytte, Scherpenberg, Mt Rouge, Mt Noire, Locre, Mt Kemmel, Wytschaete, Comines, Messines, Crucifix Corner, Meteren, Bailleul, Ploegsteert, Hazebrouck, Nieppe, Armentières, Lille, Merville, Estaires, Bois Grenier, Laventie, Fromelles, Neuve Chapelle, Aubers, Locon, Festubert, Givenchy, La Bassée, Béthune

Dates on front lines: 16 APRIL, 20 APRIL, 29 APRIL, 16 APRIL, 13 APRIL, 17 APRIL, 13 APRIL, 16 APRIL, 11 APRIL, 9 APRIL, 13 APRIL

Lys (river, labelled in several places)

Scale: 0 — 4000 Yards

The German aim was to cross the River Lys, drive the British from Hazebrouck and Poperinghe, and thus surround Ypres. Over 20,000 Allied troops were killed and 80,000 injured, but Ypres was saved

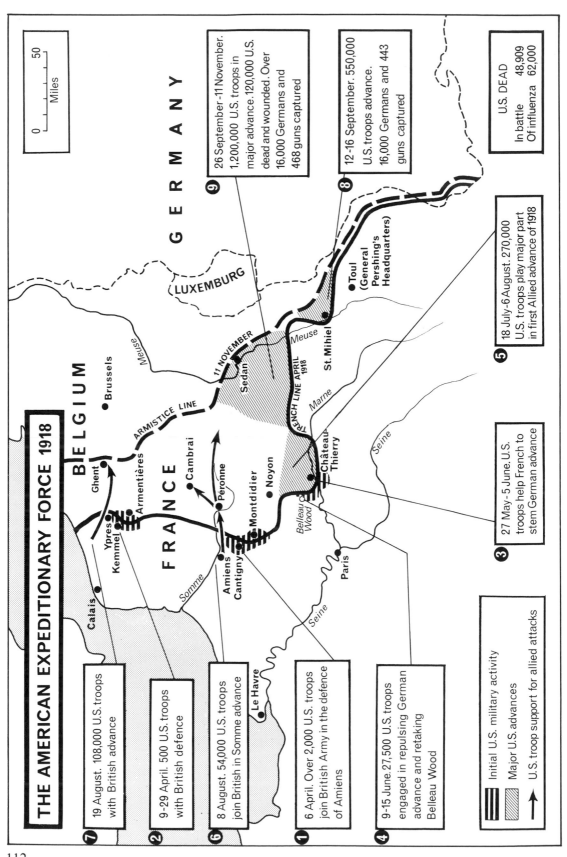

THE AMERICAN EXPEDITIONARY FORCE 1918

Miles 0 50

GERMANY

LUXEMBURG

BELGIUM

Brussels

FRANCE

Calais

Ypres
Kemmel
Armentières
Ghent

Cambrai
Péronne
Montdidier
Noyon

Amiens
Cantigny

Belleau
Wood

Château-Thierry

Sedan
ARMISTICE LINE
11 NOVEMBER

FRENCH LINE APRIL 1918

St. Mihiel

Toul
(General Pershing's Headquarters)

Meuse
Meuse
Marne
Seine
Seine
Somme

Le Havre
Paris

❾ 26 September -11 November. 1,200,000 U.S. troops in major advance.120,000 U.S. dead and wounded. Over 16,000 Germans and 468 guns captured

❽ 12-16 September. 550,000 U.S. troops advance. 16,000 Germans and 443 guns captured

U.S. DEAD
In battle   48,909
Of influenza   62,000

❺ 18 July-6 August. 270,000 U.S. troops play major part in first Allied advance of 1918

❸ 27 May- 5 June. U.S. troops help French to stem German advance

❼ 19 August. 108,000 U.S. troops with British advance

❷ 9-29 April. 500 U.S. troops with British defence

❻ 8 August. 54,000 U.S. troops join British in Somme advance

❶ 6 April. Over 2,000 U.S. troops join British Army in the defence of Amiens

❹ 9-15 June. 27,500 U.S. troops engaged in repulsing German advance and retaking Belleau Wood

▦ Initial U.S. military activity

▨ Major U.S. advances

↑ U.S. troop support for allied attacks

112

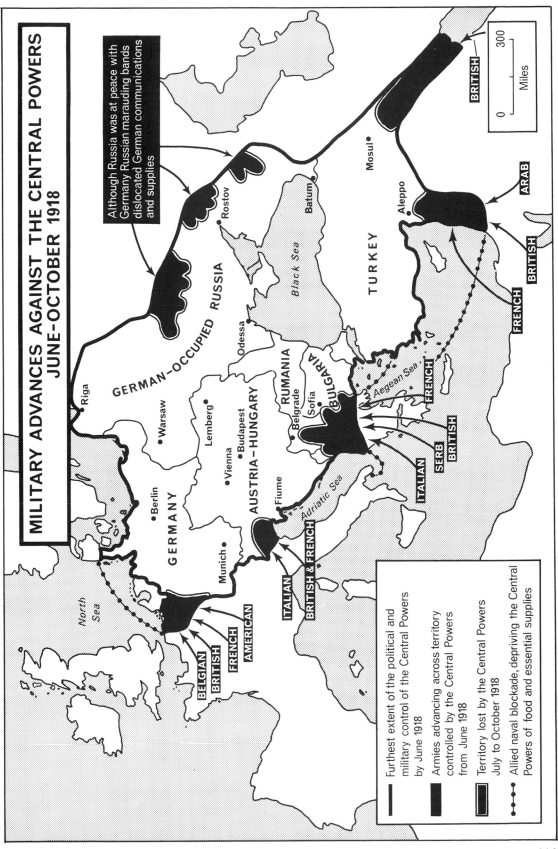

MILITARY ADVANCES AGAINST THE CENTRAL POWERS JUNE–OCTOBER 1918

Although Russia was at peace with Germany Russian marauding bands dislocated German communications and supplies

GERMAN-OCCUPIED RUSSIA

Riga

Rostov

Black Sea

Batum

Mosul●

TURKEY

Aleppo●

BRITISH

ARAB

BRITISH

FRENCH

Odessa●

●Warsaw

Lemberg●

●Budapest

RUMANIA

Belgrade●

Sofia●

BULGARIA

Aegean Sea

FRENCH

SERB

BRITISH

ITALIAN

●Vienna

AUSTRIA–HUNGARY

Fiume●

Adriatic Sea

●Berlin

GERMANY

Munich●

ITALIAN

BRITISH & FRENCH

BELGIAN

BRITISH

FRENCH

AMERICAN

North Sea

Furthest extent of the political and military control of the Central Powers by June 1918

Armies advancing across territory controlled by the Central Powers from June 1918

Territory lost by the Central Powers July to October 1918

Allied naval blockade, depriving the Central Powers of food and essential supplies

0   300

Miles

113

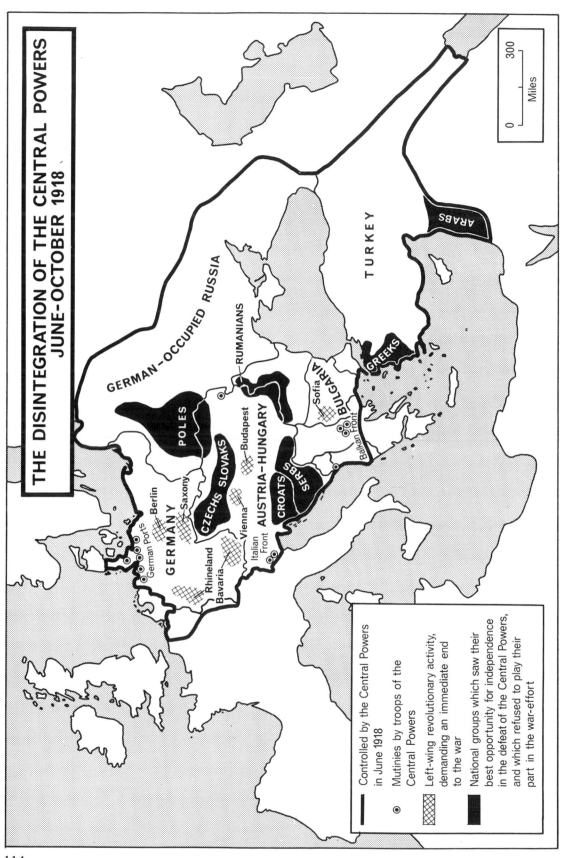

THE DISINTEGRATION OF THE CENTRAL POWERS
JUNE–OCTOBER 1918

GERMAN-OCCUPIED RUSSIA

TURKEY

ARABS

GREEKS

RUMANIANS

POLES

BULGARIA

Sofia

Balkan Front

CZECHS

SLOVAKS

Budapest

AUSTRIA-HUNGARY

CROATS

SERBS

Saxony

GERMANY

Berlin

German Ports

Vienna

Rhineland

Bavaria

Italian Front

Miles

0   300

Controlled by the Central Powers
in June 1918

Mutinies by troops of the
Central Powers

Left-wing revolutionary activity,
demanding an immediate end
to the war

National groups which saw their
best opportunity for independence
in the defeat of the Central Powers,
and which refused to play their
part in the war-effort

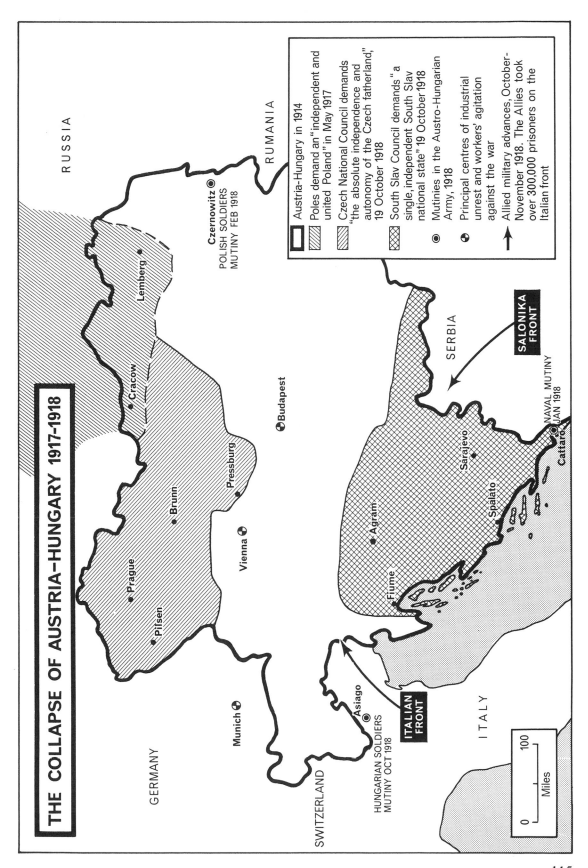

THE COLLAPSE OF AUSTRIA–HUNGARY 1917–1918

RUSSIA

RUMANIA

GERMANY

SWITZERLAND

ITALY

SERBIA

Czernowitz ◉
POLISH SOLDIERS
MUTINY FEB 1918

Lemberg ●

Cracow ●

●Budapest

Pressburg ●

Brunn ●

Prague ●

Vienna ✪

Pilsen ●

Munich ✪

Asiago ◉
HUNGARIAN SOLDIERS
MUTINY OCT 1918

ITALIAN FRONT

SALONIKA FRONT

Agram ●

Sarajevo ●

Spalato ●

Fiume ●

NAVAL MUTINY
JAN 1918
Cattaro ◉

Austria-Hungary in 1914

Poles demand an "independent and united Poland" in May 1917

Czech National Council demands "the absolute independence and autonomy of the Czech fatherland", 19 October 1918

South Slav Council demands "a single, independent South Slav national state" 19 October 1918

◉ Mutinies in the Austro-Hungarian Army, 1918

✪ Principal centres of industrial unrest and workers' agitation against the war

→ Allied military advances, October-November 1918. The Allies took over 300,000 prisoners on the Italian front

0 — 100 Miles

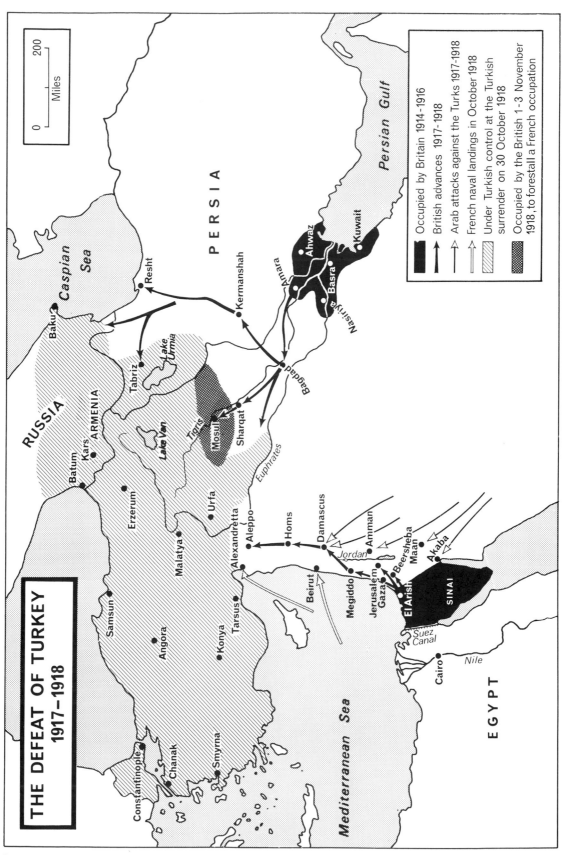

THE DEFEAT OF TURKEY 1917–1918

Legend:
- Occupied by Britain 1914–1916
- British advances 1917–1918
- Arab attacks against the Turks 1917–1918
- French naval landings in October 1918
- Under Turkish control at the Turkish surrender on 30 October 1918
- Occupied by the British 1–3 November 1918, to forestall a French occupation

Scale: 200 Miles / 0

Labels on map:

Seas and waters: Caspian Sea, Persian Gulf, Mediterranean Sea, Lake Urmia, Lake Van, Tigris, Euphrates, Jordan, Nile, Suez Canal

Regions: PERSIA, RUSSIA, ARMENIA, EGYPT, SINAI

Places: Resht, Baku, Kermanshah, Ahwaz, Kuwait, Basra, Amara, Nasiriya, Tabriz, Baghdad, Batum, Kars, Erzerum, Mosul, Sharqat, Urfa, Malatya, Samsun, Aleppo, Alexandretta, Homs, Damascus, Amman, Beersheba, Maan, Akaba, Angora, Konya, Tarsus, Beirut, Megiddo, Jerusalem, Gaza, El Arish, Constantinople, Chanak, Smyrna, Cairo

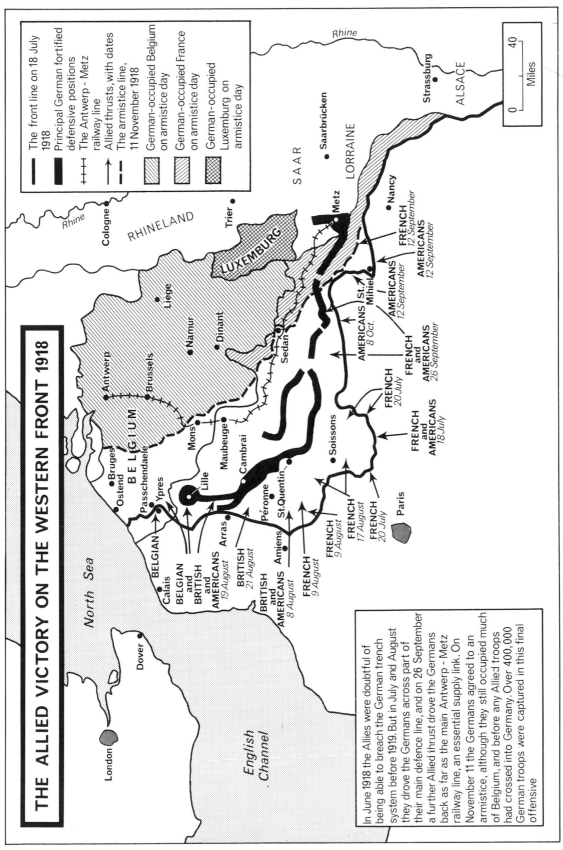

THE ALLIED VICTORY ON THE WESTERN FRONT 1918

The front line on 18 July 1918

Principal German fortified defensive positions

The Antwerp - Metz railway line

Allied thrusts, with dates

The armistice line, 11 November 1918

German-occupied Belgium on armistice day

German-occupied France on armistice day

German-occupied Luxemburg on armistice day

Rhine

Rhine

Strassburg

ALSACE

Saarbrücken

SAAR

LORRAINE

Metz

Nancy

Cologne

RHINELAND

Trier

LUXEMBURG

Liège

Namur

Dinant

Sedan

FRENCH 12 September

AMERICANS 12 September

AMERICANS 12 September

FRENCH and AMERICANS 12 September

St. Mihiel

AMERICANS 8 Oct.

FRENCH and AMERICANS 26 September

FRENCH 20 July

FRENCH and AMERICANS 18 July

Antwerp

Brussels

BELGIUM

Mons

Maubeuge

Cambrai

Soissons

Bruges

Ostend

Passchendaele

Ypres

Lille

Péronne

St.Quentin

Amiens

Arras

Calais

BELGIAN

BELGIAN and BRITISH and AMERICANS 19 August

BRITISH 21 August

BRITISH and AMERICANS 8 August

FRENCH 9 August

FRENCH 9 August

FRENCH 17 August

FRENCH 20 July

Paris

North Sea

Dover

London

English Channel

Miles
0   40

In June 1918 the Allies were doubtful of being able to breach the German trench system before 1919. But in July and August they drove the Germans across part of their main defence line, and on 26 September a further Allied thrust drove the Germans back as far as the main Antwerp - Metz railway line, an essential supply link. On November 11 the Germans agreed to an armistice, although they still occupied much of Belgium, and before any Allied troops had crossed into Germany. Over 400,000 German troops were captured in this final offensive

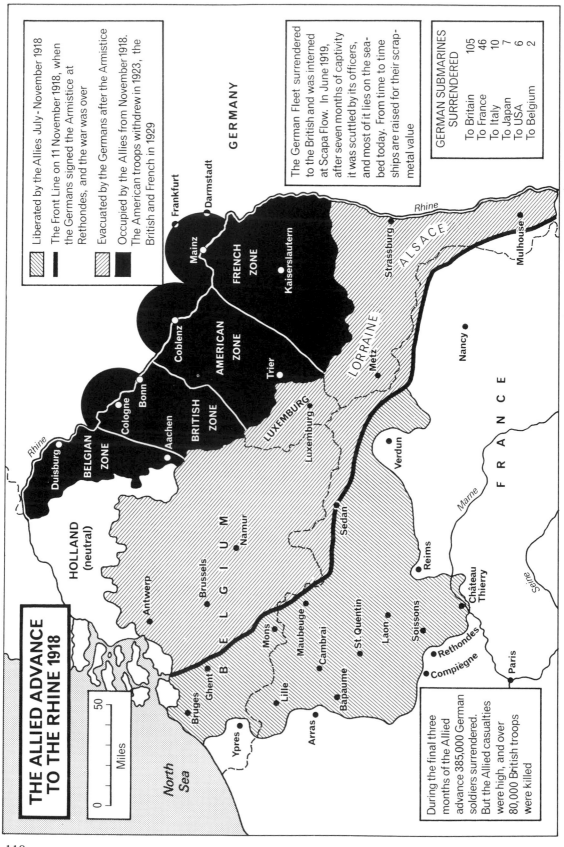

THE ALLIED ADVANCE
TO THE RHINE 1918

North Sea

HOLLAND
(neutral)

Duisburg

Rhine

BELGIAN
ZONE

Cologne

Bonn

Aachen

BRITISH
ZONE

Coblenz

AMERICAN
ZONE

Trier

LUXEMBURG

Luxemburg

Mainz

Frankfurt

Darmstadt

FRENCH
ZONE

Kaiserslautern

GERMANY

Rhine

Strassburg

A L S A C E

Mulhouse

L O R R A I N E

Metz

Nancy

Verdun

B E L G I U M

Antwerp

Brussels

Namur

Sedan

Reims

Château
Thierry

Bruges

Ghent

Mons

Maubeuge

Cambrai

St. Quentin

Laon

Soissons

Rethondes

Compiègne

Ypres

Lille

Bapaume

Arras

Marne

Seine

Paris

F R A N C E

0   50
Miles

Liberated by the Allies July - November 1918

The Front Line on 11 November 1918, when
the Germans signed the Armistice at
Rethondes, and the war was over

Evacuated by the Germans after the Armistice

Occupied by the Germans after November 1918.
The American troops withdrew in 1923, the
British and French in 1929

The German Fleet surrendered
to the British and was interned
at Scapa Flow. In June 1919,
after seven months of captivity
it was scuttled by its officers,
and most of it lies on the sea-
bed today. From time to time
ships are raised for their scrap-
metal value

GERMAN SUBMARINES
SURRENDERED

To Britain	105
To France	46
To Italy	10
To Japan	7
To USA	6
To Belgium	2

During the final three
months of the Allied
advance 385,000 German
soldiers surrendered.
But the Allied casualties
were high, and over
80,000 British troops
were killed

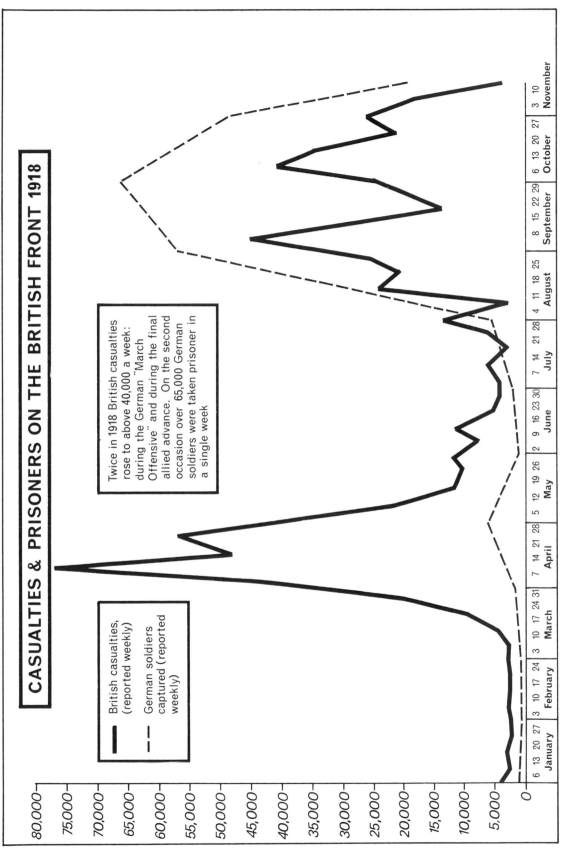

CASUALTIES & PRISONERS ON THE BRITISH FRONT 1918

Twice in 1918 British casualties rose to above 40,000 a week: during the German "March Offensive" and during the final allied advance. On the second occasion over 65,000 German soldiers were taken prisoner in a single week

British casualties, (reported weekly)

German soldiers captured (reported weekly)

80,000
75,000
70,000
65,000
60,000
55,000
50,000
45,000
40,000
35,000
30,000
25,000
20,000
15,000
10,000
5,000
0

| 6 13 20 27 | 3 10 17 24 | 3 10 17 24 31 | 7 14 21 28 | 5 12 19 26 | 2 9 16 23 30 | 7 14 21 28 | 4 11 18 25 | 8 15 22 29 | 6 13 20 27 | 3 10 |
| January | February | March | April | May | June | July | August | September | October | November |

THE WAR IN THE BALKANS SEPTEMBER – OCTOBER 1918

In 1917 the Bulgarians, having conquered Serbia Macedonia and the Dobruja, began secret negotiations with the Allies to end the war, but without success. In June 1918 Germany ended her annual 50 million francs subsidy, and stopped sending munitions. The Bulgars resented the way in which the Germans treated them increasingly as a conquered people, requisitioning food and supplies. On 20 September troop mutinies began. On 29 September Bulgaria surrendered unconditionally to the Allies

0 — 60
Miles

RUSSIA
(Under German Control)

• Vienna

• Budapest

Lake Balaton

AUSTRIA – HUNGARY

• Arad

Pécs •

• Temesvar

Zadar

Belgrade

RUMANIA
(Under German Occupation)

DOBRUJA

(Under Bulgarian Occupation)

Sarajevo •

BOSNIA   SERBIA

• Vidin

Mostar •

Nish

• Plevna

MONTENEGRO

Cattaro •

• Sofia

BULGARIA

• Skopje

MACEDONIA

• Ochrid

• Adrianople

Constantinople

ITALY

ALBANIA

Salonika •

• Chanak
Dardanelles

Allied Fleet
10 November
1918

TURKEY

GREECE

	The Allied armies on 14 September 1918
■	Liberated by the Allies, 14-29 September
▨	Serbs, Bosnians and Montenegrins rising against their Austrian overlords in the last two weeks of September
▨	Area in which 30,000 Bulgarian troops mutinied, refused to continue the war and marched on Sofia, 20-29 September
→	Allied advances 29 September to 30 October

BALKAN DEAD IN 1918	
Bulgarians	63,000
Serbs	45,000
French	20,000
British	10,000
Greeks	5,000
Italians	3,000

THE GERMAN REVOLUTION NOVEMBER 1918

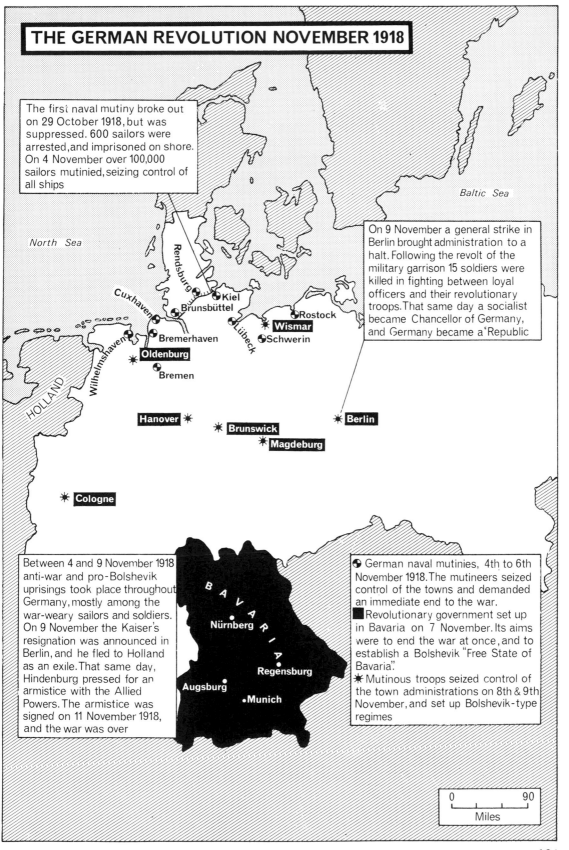

The first naval mutiny broke out on 29 October 1918, but was suppressed. 600 sailors were arrested, and imprisoned on shore. On 4 November over 100,000 sailors mutinied, seizing control of all ships

Baltic Sea

North Sea

On 9 November a general strike in Berlin brought administration to a halt. Following the revolt of the military garrison 15 soldiers were killed in fighting between loyal officers and their revolutionary troops. That same day a socialist became Chancellor of Germany, and Germany became a 'Republic'

Rendsburg

Cuxhaven

Kiel
Brunsbüttel

Rostock

Wismar

Lübeck
Schwerin

Bremerhaven

Wilhelmshaven

Oldenburg

Bremen

HOLLAND

Hanover

Brunswick

Magdeburg

Berlin

Cologne

Between 4 and 9 November 1918 anti-war and pro-Bolshevik uprisings took place throughout Germany, mostly among the war-weary sailors and soldiers. On 9 November the Kaiser's resignation was announced in Berlin, and he fled to Holland as an exile. That same day, Hindenburg pressed for an armistice with the Allied Powers. The armistice was signed on 11 November 1918, and the war was over

BAVARIA

Nürnberg

Regensburg

Augsburg

Munich

◑ German naval mutinies, 4th to 6th November 1918. The mutineers seized control of the towns and demanded an immediate end to the war.
■ Revolutionary government set up in Bavaria on 7 November. Its aims were to end the war at once, and to establish a Bolshevik "Free State of Bavaria".
✳ Mutinous troops seized control of the town administrations on 8th & 9th November, and set up Bolshevik-type regimes

0   90
Miles

121

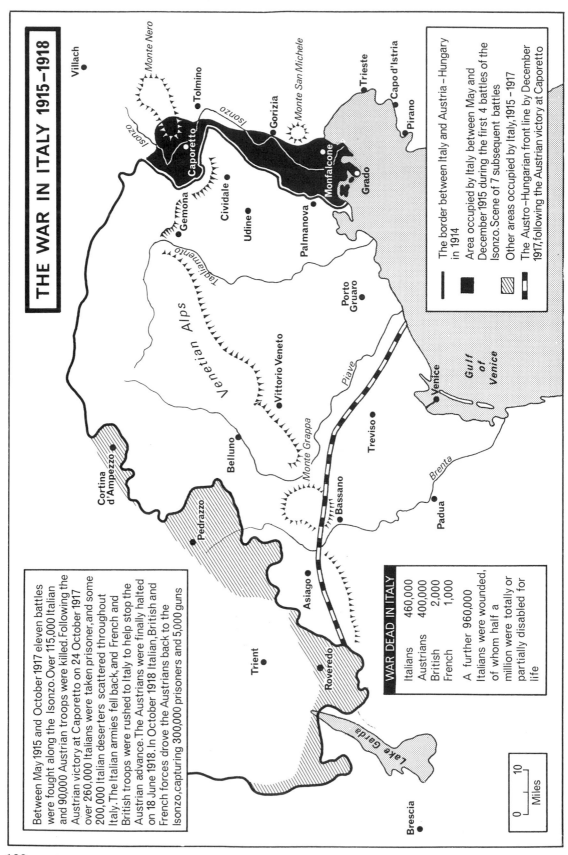

THE WAR IN ITALY 1915–1918

Villach

Monte Nero

Tolmino

Isonzo

Isonzo

Caporetto

Isonzo

Gorizia

Monte San Michele

Trieste

Capo d'Istria

Pirano

Monfalcone

Grado

Gemona

Cividale

Udine

Palmanova

Tagliamento

Porto Gruaro

Venetian Alps

Vittorio Veneto

Piave

Venice

Gulf of Venice

Monte Grappa

Belluno

Treviso

Brenta

Cortina d'Ampezzo

Pedrazzo

Bassano

Padua

Asiago

Trient

Roveredo

Lake Garda

Brescia

The border between Italy and Austria – Hungary in 1914

Area occupied by Italy between May and December 1915 during the first 4 battles of the Isonzo. Scene of 7 subsequent battles

Other areas occupied by Italy, 1915 – 1917

The Austro–Hungarian front line by December 1917, following the Austrian victory at Caporetto

Between May 1915 and October 1917 eleven battles were fought along the Isonzo. Over 115,000 Italian and 90,000 Austrian troops were killed. Following the Austrian victory at Caporetto on 24 October 1917 over 260,000 Italians were taken prisoner, and some 200,000 Italian deserters scattered throughout Italy. The Italian armies fell back, and French and British troops were rushed to Italy to help stop the Austrian advance. The Austrians were finally halted on 18 June 1918. In October 1918 Italian, British and French forces drove the Austrians back to the Isonzo, capturing 300,000 prisoners and 5,000 guns

WAR DEAD IN ITALY	
Italians	460,000
Austrians	400,000
British	2,000
French	1,000

A further 960,000 Italians were wounded, of whom half a million were totally or partially disabled for life

0   10
Miles

122

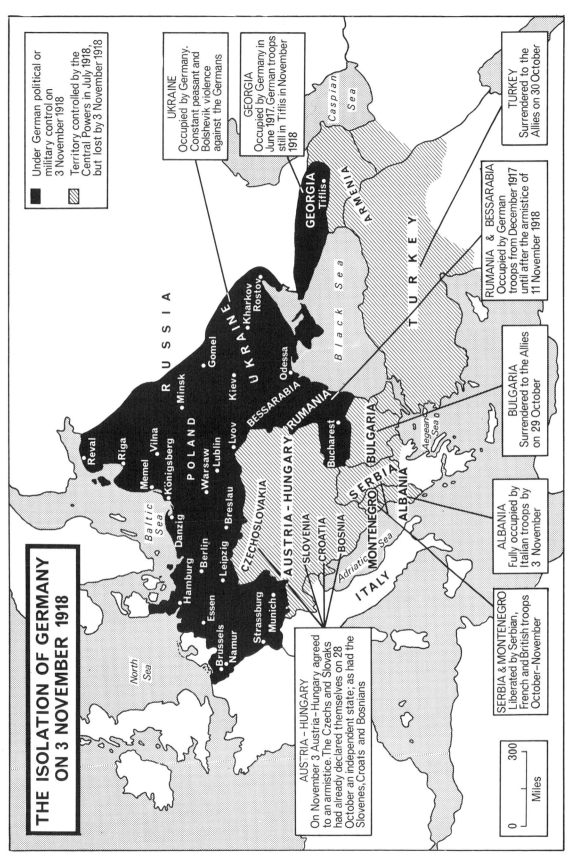

THE ISOLATION OF GERMANY ON 3 NOVEMBER 1918

Under German political or military control on 3 November 1918

Territory controlled by the Central Powers in July 1918, but lost by 3 November 1918

UKRAINE
Occupied by Germany. Constant peasant and Bolshevik violence against the Germans

GEORGIA
Occupied by Germany in June 1917. German troops still in Tiflis in November 1918

TURKEY
Surrendered to the Allies on 30 October

RUMANIA & BESSARABIA
Occupied by German troops from December 1917 until after the armistice of 11 November 1918

BULGARIA
Surrendered to the Allies on 29 October

ALBANIA
Fully occupied by Italian troops by 3 November

SERBIA & MONTENEGRO
Liberated by Serbian, French and British troops October–November

AUSTRIA–HUNGARY
On November 3 Austria-Hungary agreed to an armistice. The Czechs and Slovaks had already declared themselves on 28 October an independent state; as had the Slovenes, Croats and Bosnians

RUSSIA

GEORGIA
Tiflis

ARMENIA

Caspian Sea

TURKEY

Black Sea

Kharkov
Rostov

UKRAINE

Gomel

Minsk

Odessa

BESSARABIA

RUMANIA

Kiev

Lvov

Lublin

Warsaw

POLAND

Breslau

Bucharest

BULGARIA

SERBIA

MONTENEGRO

ALBANIA

Aegean Sea

Reval

Riga

Vilna

Memel

Königsberg

Danzig

CZECHOSLOVAKIA

AUSTRIA–HUNGARY

SLOVENIA

CROATIA

BOSNIA

Adriatic Sea

ITALY

Baltic Sea

Hamburg

Berlin

Leipzig

Essen

Brussels

Namur

Strassburg

Munich

North Sea

0   300
Miles

123

Section Nine

THE WORLD AT WAR

Oh Oh Oh it's a lovely war
Who wouldn't be a soldier, eh?
Oh it's a shame to take the pay.
As soon as reveille has gone
We feel just as heavy as lead
But we never get up till the Sergeant
Brings our breakfast up to bed.
Oh Oh Oh it's a lovely war. . . .

Who wouldn't join the army
That's what we all inquire
Don't we pity the poor civilians
Sitting beside the fire.
Oh Oh Oh it's a lovely war. . . .

POPULAR SONG

GERMAN WAR AIMS IN THE WEST 1914–1918

0   50
Miles

BRITAIN

North

Sea

Amsterdam

The Hague

Rotterdam

HOLLAND

Arnhem

Rhine

Düsseldorf

Cologne

Dover

Zeebrugge

Ostend

Bruges

Scheldt

Antwerp

GERMANY

Dunkirk

Calais

Ypres

Brussels

Boulogne

Lille

BELGIUM

Liege

Montreuil

Namur

Arras

Cambrai

LUXEMBURG

Trier

Somme

Sedan

Speyer

FRANCE

Verdun

Saarbrücken

Paris

Nancy

ALSACE – LORRAINE

Toul

Strassburg

Epinal

Mulhouse

Belfort

Territory to be annexed outright
in the event of a German victory

Future possible annexations to be
obtained at the Peace Conference

The"Tributary State" of Flanders-
Wallonia, to be under German political
and economic supervision

⊙ "Strongpoints", or fortified towns
to be under German control

Area to come within the German
Customs Union, and to subordinate its
economic life to that of Germany

— — Western boundary of German strategic
control, within which the existing French
fortresses were to be dismantled

FRENCH WAR AIMS
IN THE WEST
1914–1918

0   50
Miles

HOLLAND

Rhine

RUHR

●Düsseldorf

●Ostend   ●Antwerp   Cologne●

●Calais   Aachen●

●Ypres   ●Brussels

B E L G I U M   ●Liége

●Namur

●Arras

●Cambrai

F R A N C E   Sedan ●

LUXEMBURG

●Trier

Coblenz●

G E R M A N Y

●Soissons

—Reims

●Paris   Verdun ●   ●Metz

●Speyer

S A A R

ALSACE – LORRAINE

●Strassburg

Rhine

●Mulhouse

Belfort ●

SWITZERLAND

Belgian neutrality to be
guaranteed and secured

To be detached from the
German Customs Union
and brought into the
French economic orbit

To become part of France
(having been annexed
by Germany in 1871)

German coalfields to be
under French economic
and political control

A Rhineland-Palatinate
State, to be separated
from Germany, and under
French political influence

— — War zone, within which Germany
was to pay financial reparations
for all war damage

Principal German industrial zone,
to be occupied by France in the
event of Germany refusing to
pay reparations for war damage

125

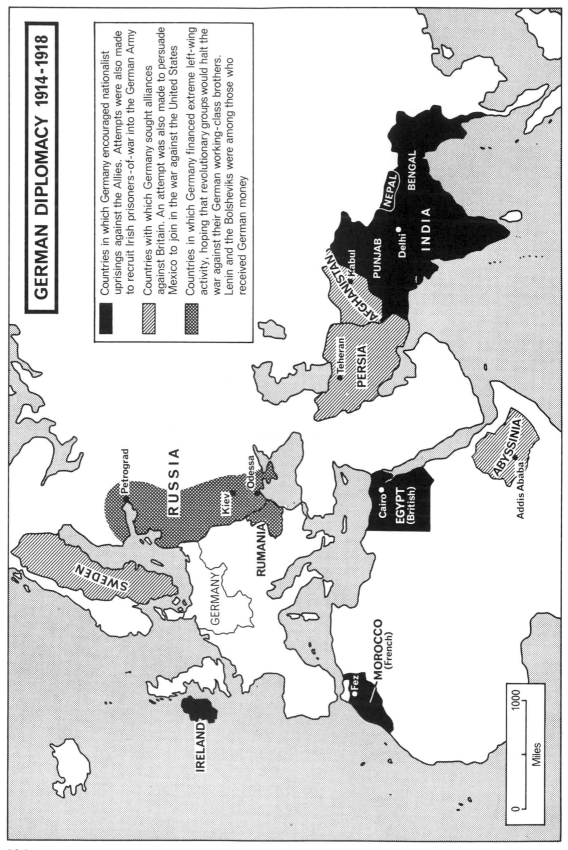

GERMAN DIPLOMACY 1914-1918

Countries in which Germany encouraged nationalist uprisings against the Allies. Attempts were also made to recruit Irish prisoners-of-war into the German Army

Countries with which Germany sought alliances against Britain. An attempt was also made to persuade Mexico to join in the war against the United States

Countries in which Germany financed extreme left-wing activity, hoping that revolutionary groups would halt the war against their German working-class brothers. Lenin and the Bolsheviks were among those who received German money

NEPAL

BENGAL

INDIA

Delhi

PUNJAB

Kabul

AFGHANISTAN

Teheran

PERSIA

ABYSSINIA

Addis Ababa

RUSSIA

Petrograd

Odessa

Kiev

Cairo

EGYPT
(British)

SWEDEN

RUMANIA

GERMANY

MOROCCO
(French)

Fez

IRELAND

1000

Miles

0

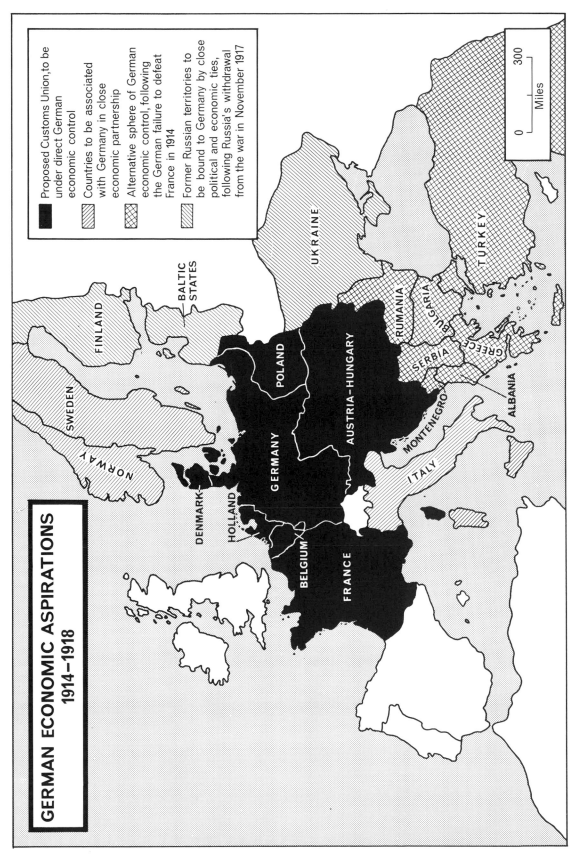

GERMAN ECONOMIC ASPIRATIONS 1914–1918

Legend:

- **Proposed Customs Union, to be under direct German economic control**
- **Countries to be associated with Germany in close economic partnership**
- **Alternative sphere of German economic control, following the German failure to defeat France in 1914**
- **Former Russian territories to be bound to Germany by close political and economic ties, following Russia's withdrawal from the war in November 1917**

0 300
Miles

FINLAND
BALTIC STATES
UKRAINE
SWEDEN
NORWAY
POLAND
AUSTRIA–HUNGARY
RUMANIA
BULGARIA
SERBIA
GREECE
TURKEY
MONTENEGRO
ALBANIA
ITALY
DENMARK
HOLLAND
GERMANY
BELGIUM
FRANCE

GERMAN WAR AIMS IN AFRICA 1916–1918

German territory in 1914

Annexations proposed in a secret draft Treaty of Peace in May 1916

Annexations proposed by the German Admiralty September-November 1916, and by the German Colonial Ministry April-May 1917

Annexations planned or speculated upon at the time of the German breakthrough on the Western Front, March-August 1918

MADEIRA
Portuguese

SINAI
British

Suez Canal
British

Red Sea

SENEGAL
French

GAMBIA
British

FRENCH
GUINEA

PORTUGUESE
GUINEA

TOGO

NIGERIA

CAMEROON

French
SOMALILAND
British

PRINCES I.
ST. THOMAS
Portuguese

Libreville
French

Pointe Noire
French

UGANDA

KENYA

British

GERMAN
EAST
AFRICA

PEMBA
ZANZIBAR

NYASALAND

NORTHERN
RHODESIA

COMORO
French

ANGOLA

Mozambique

Portuguese

MOZAMBIQUE

MADAGASCAR
French

WALVIS BAY
British

GERMAN
SOUTH-
WEST
AFRICA

0   300
Miles

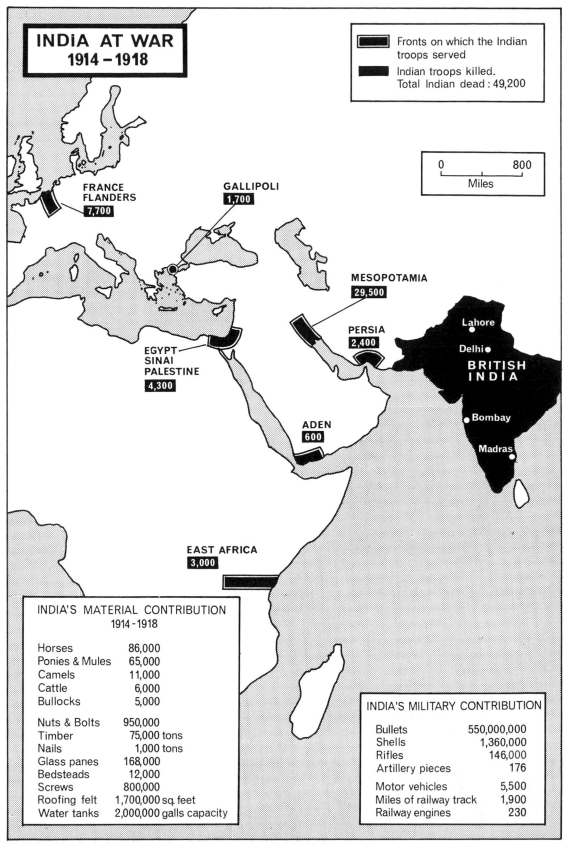

INDIA AT WAR
1914-1918

Fronts on which the Indian troops served

Indian troops killed.
Total Indian dead : 49,200

0   800
Miles

FRANCE FLANDERS
7,700

GALLIPOLI
1,700

MESOPOTAMIA
29,500

PERSIA
2,400

Lahore

Delhi

BRITISH INDIA

EGYPT SINAI PALESTINE
4,300

ADEN
600

Bombay

Madras

EAST AFRICA
3,000

INDIA'S MATERIAL CONTRIBUTION
1914-1918

Horses	86,000
Ponies & Mules	65,000
Camels	11,000
Cattle	6,000
Bullocks	5,000
Nuts & Bolts	950,000
Timber	75,000 tons
Nails	1,000 tons
Glass panes	168,000
Bedsteads	12,000
Screws	800,000
Roofing felt	1,700,000 sq. feet
Water tanks	2,000,000 galls capacity

INDIA'S MILITARY CONTRIBUTION

Bullets	550,000,000
Shells	1,360,000
Rifles	146,000
Artillery pieces	176
Motor vehicles	5,500
Miles of railway track	1,900
Railway engines	230

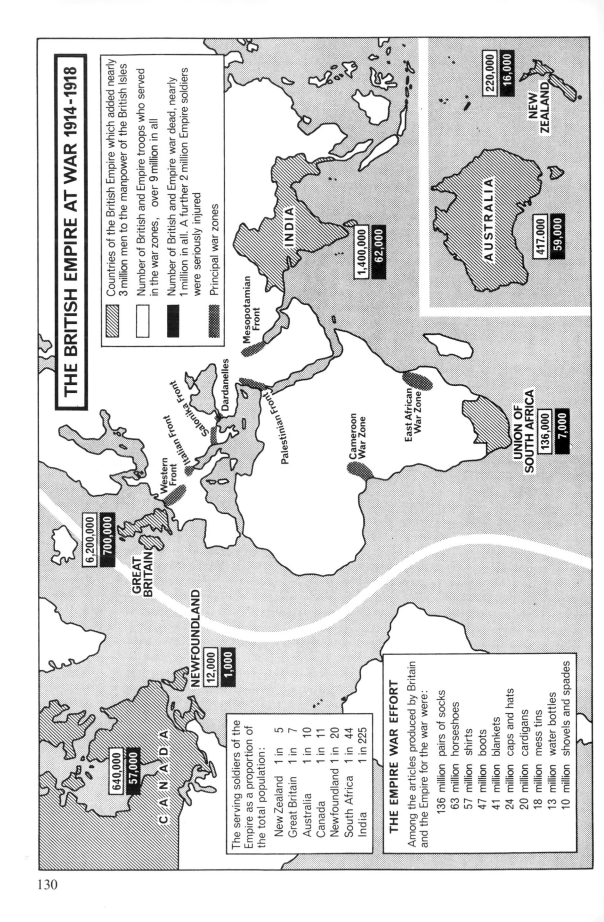

THE BRITISH EMPIRE AT WAR 1914-1918

Countries of the British Empire which added nearly 3 million men to the manpower of the British Isles

Number of British and Empire troops who served in the war zones, over 9 million in all

Number of British and Empire war dead, nearly 1 million in all. A further 2 million Empire soldiers were seriously injured

Principal war zones

NEW ZEALAND 220,000 / 16,000

AUSTRALIA 417,000 / 59,000

INDIA 1,400,000 / 62,000

Mesopotamian Front

UNION OF SOUTH AFRICA 136,000 / 7,000

East African War Zone

Cameroon War Zone

Palestinian Front

Dardanelles

Salonika Front

Italian Front

Western Front

GREAT BRITAIN 6,200,000 / 700,000

NEWFOUNDLAND 12,000 / 1,000

CANADA 640,000 / 57,000

The serving soldiers of the Empire as a proportion of the total population:

New Zealand	1 in 5
Great Britain	1 in 7
Australia	1 in 10
Canada	1 in 11
Newfoundland	1 in 20
South Africa	1 in 44
India	1 in 225

THE EMPIRE WAR EFFORT

Among the articles produced by Britain and the Empire for the war were:

136 million	pairs of socks
63 million	horseshoes
57 million	shirts
47 million	boots
41 million	blankets
24 million	caps and hats
20 million	cardigans
18 million	mess tins
13 million	water bottles
10 million	shovels and spades

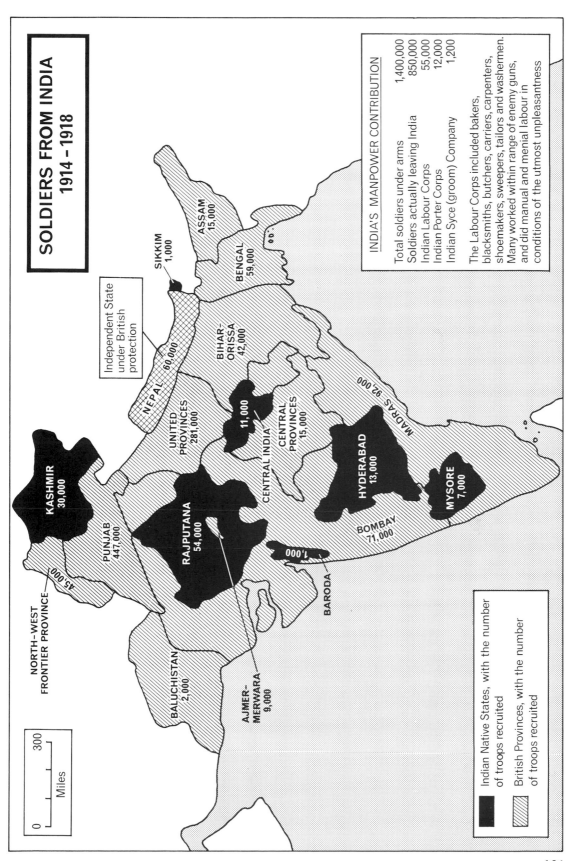

SOLDIERS FROM INDIA
1914 – 1918

INDIA'S MANPOWER CONTRIBUTION

Total soldiers under arms	1,400,000
Soldiers actually leaving India	850,000
Indian Labour Corps	55,000
Indian Porter Corps	12,000
Indian Syce (groom) Company	1,200

The Labour Corps included bakers, blacksmiths, butchers, carriers, carpenters, shoemakers, sweepers, tailors and washermen. Many worked within range of enemy guns, and did manual and menial labour in conditions of the utmost unpleasantness

Independent State under British protection

NORTH-WEST
FRONTIER PROVINCE
45,000

KASHMIR
30,000

PUNJAB
447,000

BALUCHISTAN
2,000

AJMER-
MERWARA
9,000

RAJPUTANA
54,000

UNITED
PROVINCES
281,000

NEPAL
60,000

SIKKIM
1,000

ASSAM
15,000

BENGAL
59,000

BIHAR-
ORISSA
42,000

CENTRAL INDIA
11,000

CENTRAL
PROVINCES
15,000

BARODA
1,000

MADRAS – 92,000

HYDERABAD
13,000

BOMBAY
71,000

MYSORE
7,000

Indian Native States, with the number of troops recruited

British Provinces, with the number of troops recruited

0   300
Miles

131

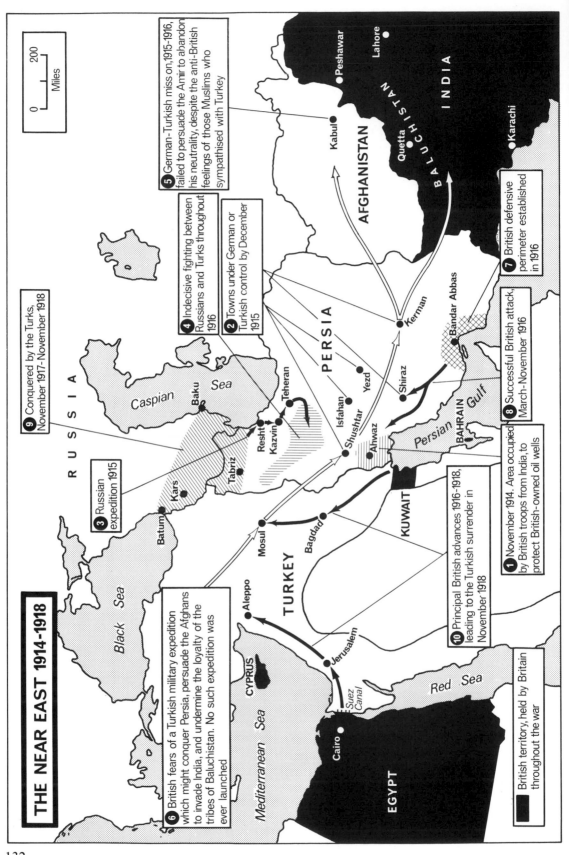

THE NEAR EAST 1914-1918

Scale: 0 — 200 Miles

5 German-Turkish miss on,1915-1916, failed to persuade the Amir to abandon his neutrality, despite the anti-British feelings of those Muslims who sympathised with Turkey

4 Indecisive fighting between Russians and Turks throughout 1916

2 Towns under German or Turkish control by December 1915

9 Conquered by the Turks, November 1917–November 1918

3 Russian expedition 1915

7 British defensive perimeter established in 1916

8 Successful British attack, March–November 1916

6 British fears of a Turkish military expedition which might conquer Persia, persuade the Afghans to invade India, and undermine the loyalty of the tribes of Baluchistan. No such expedition was ever launched

1 November 1914. Area occupied by British troops from India, to protect British-owned oil wells

10 Principal British advances 1916-1918, leading to the Turkish surrender in November 1918

British territory, held by Britain throughout the war

Labels on map: Peshawar, Lahore, Kabul, AFGHANISTAN, Quetta, BALUCHISTAN, INDIA, Karachi, Bandar Abbas, Kerman, PERSIA, Yezd, Shiraz, Isfahan, Shushtar, Ahwaz, Teheran, Resht, Kazvin, Tabriz, Baku, Caspian Sea, RUSSIA, Kars, Batum, Black Sea, Mosul, Bagdad, TURKEY, Aleppo, BAHRAIN, Persian Gulf, KUWAIT, Jerusalem, Suez Canal, CYPRUS, Mediterranean Sea, Cairo, Red Sea, EGYPT

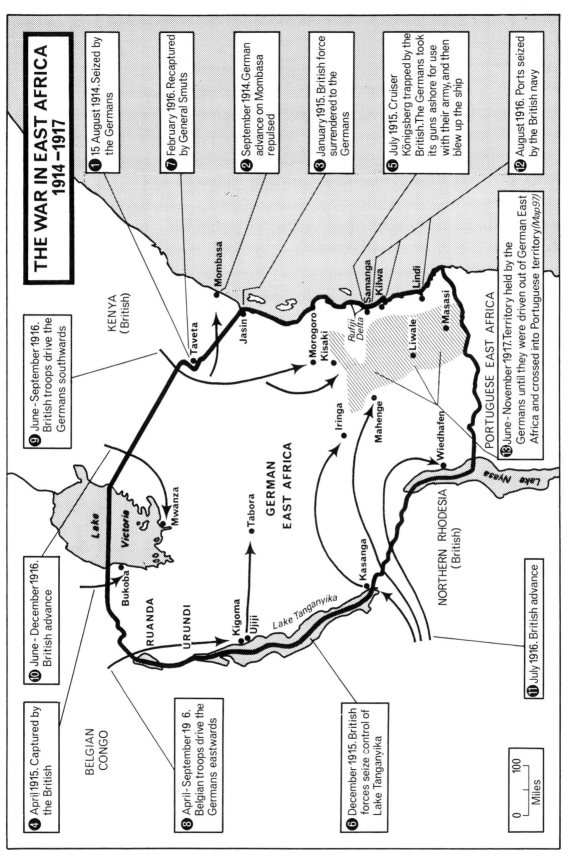

THE WAR IN EAST AFRICA 1914–1917

1 15 August 1914. Seized by the Germans

7 February 1916. Recaptured by General Smuts

2 September 1914. German advance on Mombasa repulsed

3 January 1915. British force surrendered to the Germans

5 July 1915. Cruiser Königsberg trapped by the British. The Germans took its guns ashore for use with their army, and then blew up the ship

12 August 1916. Ports seized by the British navy

9 June - September 1916. British troops drive the Germans southwards

4 April 1915. Captured by the British

8 April - September 19 6. Belgian troops drive the Germans eastwards

10 June - December 1916. British advance

6 December 1915. British forces seize control of Lake Tanganyika

11 July 1916. British advance

13 June - November 1917. Territory held by the Germans until they were driven out of German East Africa and crossed into Portuguese territory *(Map97)*

KENYA (British)

Mombasa

Taveta

Jasin

Morogoro

Kisaki

Rufiji Delta

Samanga

Kilwa

Lindi

Liwale

Masasi

Iringa

Mahenge

Wiedhafen

GERMAN EAST AFRICA

PORTUGUESE EAST AFRICA

BELGIAN CONGO

Lake Victoria

Mwanza

Bukoba

RUANDA

URUNDI

Kigoma

Ujiji

Tabora

Lake Tanganyika

Kasanga

NORTHERN RHODESIA (British)

Lake Nyasa

0   100

Miles

133

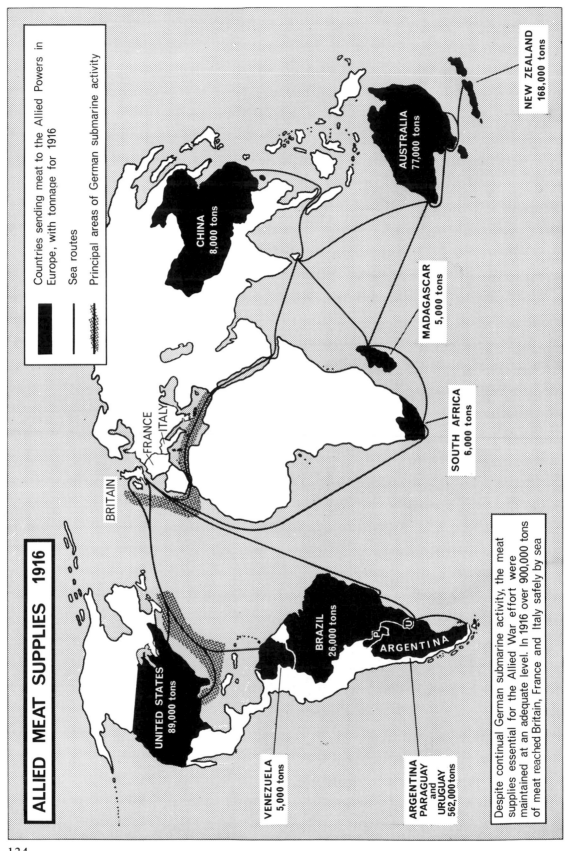

ALLIED MEAT SUPPLIES 1916

Countries sending meat to the Allied Powers in Europe, with tonnage for 1916

Sea routes

Principal areas of German submarine activity

NEW ZEALAND
168,000 tons

AUSTRALIA
77,000 tons

CHINA
8,000 tons

MADAGASCAR
5,000 tons

SOUTH AFRICA
6,000 tons

BRITAIN

FRANCE

ITALY

UNITED STATES
89,000 tons

BRAZIL
26,000 tons

ARGENTINA

VENEZUELA
5,000 tons

ARGENTINA
PARAGUAY
and
URUGUAY
562,000 tons

Despite continual German submarine activity, the meat supplies essential for the Allied War effort were maintained at an adequate level. In 1916 over 900,000 tons of meat reached Britain, France and Italy safely by sea

134

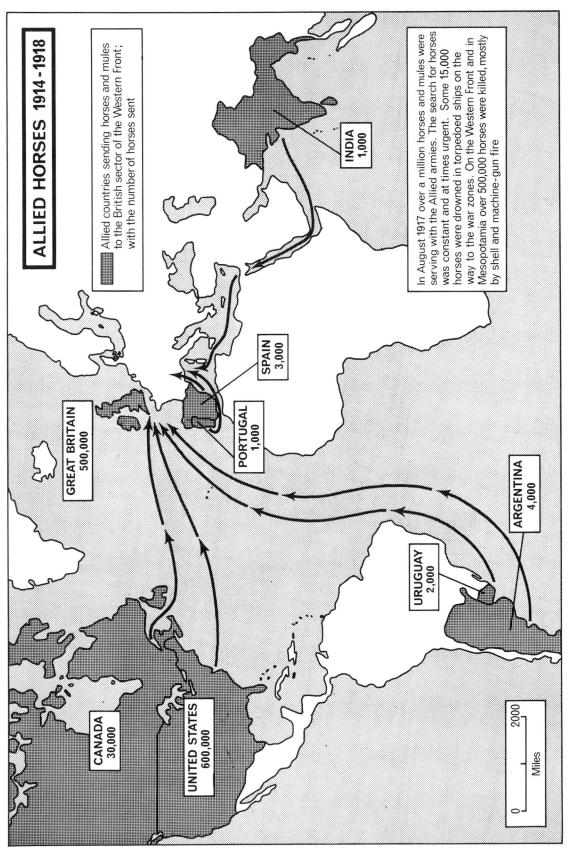

ALLIED HORSES 1914-1918

Allied countries sending horses and mules to the British sector of the Western Front ; with the number of horses sent

CANADA
30,000

UNITED STATES
600,000

GREAT BRITAIN
500,000

PORTUGAL
1,000

SPAIN
3,000

INDIA
1,000

URUGUAY
2,000

ARGENTINA
4,000

In August 1917 over a million horses and mules were serving with the Allied armies. The search for horses was constant and at times urgent. Some 15,000 horses were drowned in torpedoed ships on the way to the war zones. On the Western Front and in Mesopotamia over 500,000 horses were killed, mostly by shell and machine-gun fire

0   2000
Miles

135

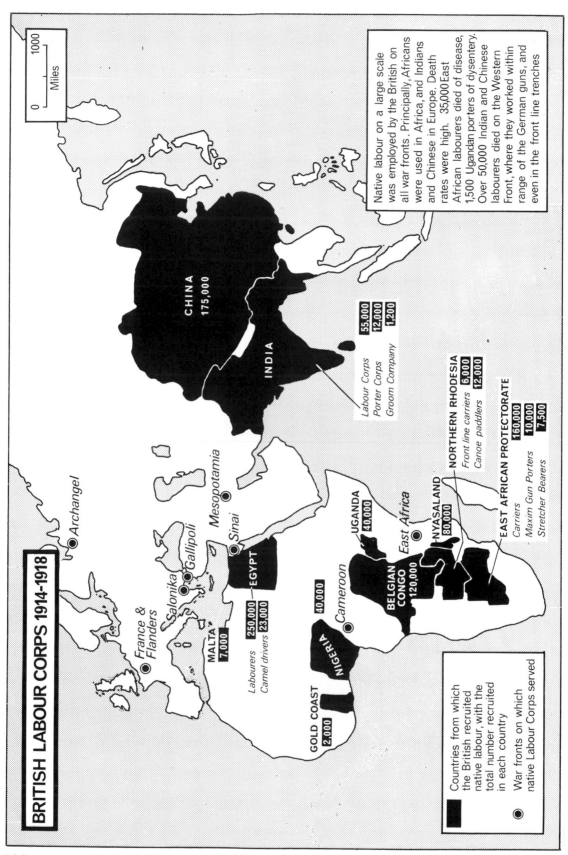

BRITISH LABOUR CORPS 1914-1918

Native labour on a large scale was employed by the British on all war fronts. Principally, Africans were used in Africa, and Indians and Chinese in Europe. Death rates were high. 35,000 East African labourers died of disease, 1,500 Ugandan porters of dysentery. Over 50,000 Indian and Chinese labourers died on the Western Front, where they worked within range of the German guns, and even in the front line trenches

CHINA
175,000

INDIA

Labour Corps	55,000
Porter Corps	12,000
Groom Company	1,200

NORTHERN RHODESIA
Front line carriers	6,000
Canoe paddlers	12,000

EAST AFRICAN PROTECTORATE
Carriers	160,000
Maxim Gun Porters	10,000
Stretcher Bearers	7,500

● Archangel

Mesopotamia
● Sinai

Gallipoli
Salonika

France & Flanders
●

MALTA
7,000

EGYPT
Labourers	250,000
Camel drivers	23,000

Cameroon ●

UGANDA
40,000

East Africa ●

NYASALAND
80,000

BELGIAN CONGO
120,000

GOLD COAST
2,000

NIGERIA
40,000

■ Countries from which the British recruited native labour, with the total number recruited in each country

● War fronts on which native Labour Corps served

136

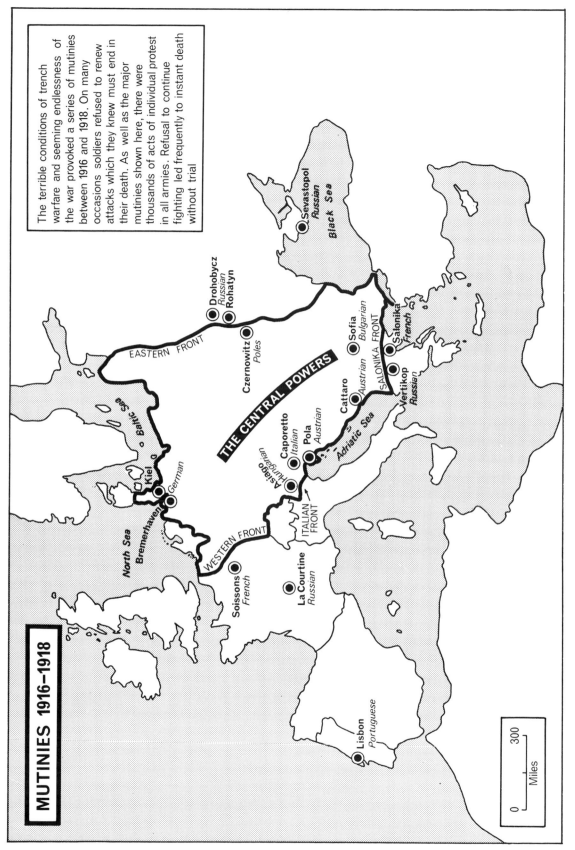

MUTINIES 1916–1918

The terrible conditions of trench warfare and seeming endlessness of the war provoked a series of mutinies between 1916 and 1918. On many occasions soldiers refused to renew attacks which they knew must end in their death. As well as the major mutinies shown here, there were thousands of acts of individual protest in all armies. Refusal to continue fighting led frequently to instant death without trial

Sevastopol
Russian

Black Sea

Drohobycz
Russian **Rohatyn**

Czernowitz
Poles

EASTERN FRONT

Sofia
Bulgarian

Salonika
French

THE CENTRAL POWERS

Cattaro
Austrian

SALONIKA FRONT

Vertikop
Russian

Adriatic Sea

Caporetto
Italian

Pola
Austrian

Asiago
Hungarian

Kiel
German

o Baltic Sea

ITALIAN
FRONT

WESTERN FRONT

North Sea
Bremerhaven

Soissons
French

La Courtine
Russian

Lisbon
Portuguese

300

0

Miles

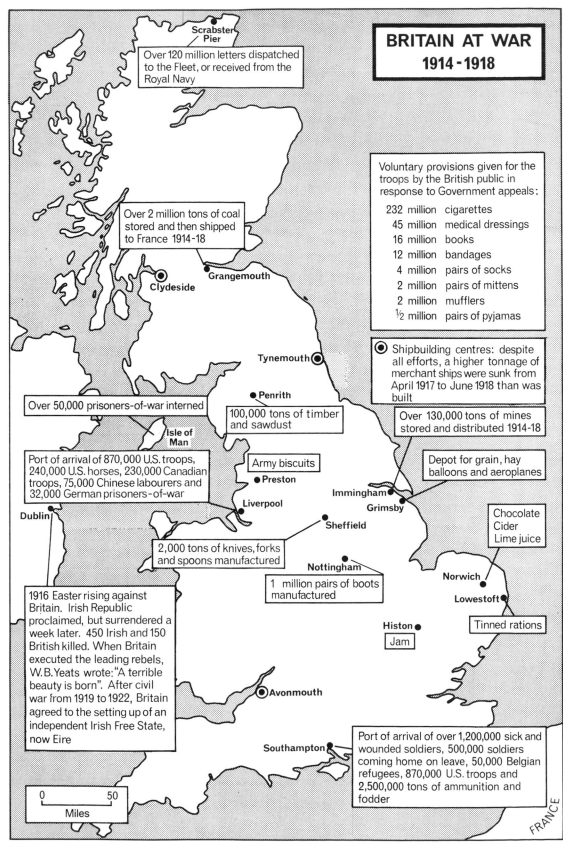

BRITAIN AT WAR 1914-1918

Scrabster Pier

Over 120 million letters dispatched to the Fleet, or received from the Royal Navy

Over 2 million tons of coal stored and then shipped to France 1914-18

Clydeside

Grangemouth

Voluntary provisions given for the troops by the British public in response to Government appeals:

232 million   cigarettes
45 million   medical dressings
16 million   books
12 million   bandages
4 million   pairs of socks
2 million   pairs of mittens
2 million   mufflers
½ million   pairs of pyjamas

⊙ Shipbuilding centres: despite all efforts, a higher tonnage of merchant ships were sunk from April 1917 to June 1918 than was built

Tynemouth

Penrith

Over 50,000 prisoners-of-war interned

100,000 tons of timber and sawdust

Over 130,000 tons of mines stored and distributed 1914-18

Isle of Man

Depot for grain, hay balloons and aeroplanes

Port of arrival of 870,000 U.S. troops, 240,000 U.S. horses, 230,000 Canadian troops, 75,000 Chinese labourers and 32,000 German prisoners-of-war

Army biscuits

Preston

Immingham

Grimsby

Liverpool

Chocolate Cider Lime juice

Dublin

Sheffield

2,000 tons of knives, forks and spoons manufactured

Nottingham

Norwich

Lowestoft

1 million pairs of boots manufactured

1916 Easter rising against Britain. Irish Republic proclaimed, but surrendered a week later. 450 Irish and 150 British killed. When Britain executed the leading rebels, W.B.Yeats wrote:"A terrible beauty is born". After civil war from 1919 to 1922, Britain agreed to the setting up of an independent Irish Free State, now Eire

Histon

Jam

Tinned rations

Avonmouth

Southampton

Port of arrival of over 1,200,000 sick and wounded soldiers, 500,000 soldiers coming home on leave, 50,000 Belgian refugees, 870,000 U.S. troops and 2,500,000 tons of ammunition and fodder

0   50
Miles

FRANCE

138

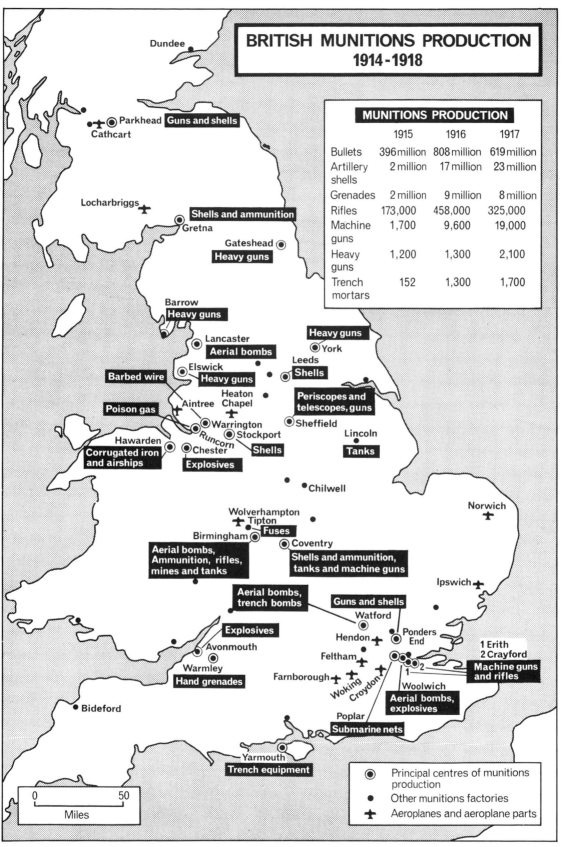

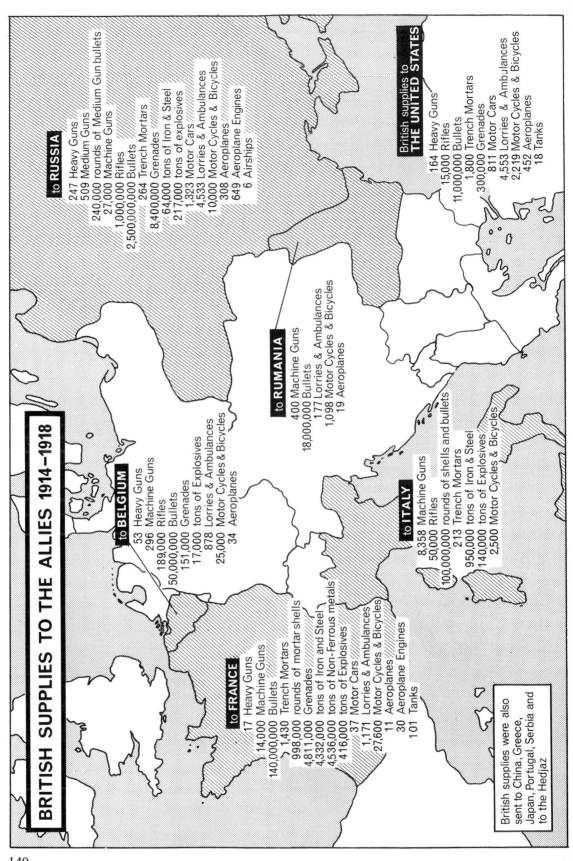

BRITISH SUPPLIES TO THE ALLIES 1914–1918

to RUSSIA
247 Heavy Guns
509 Medium Guns
240,000 rounds of Medium Gun bullets
27,000 Machine Guns
1,000,000 Rifles
2,500,000,000 Bullets
264 Trench Mortars
8,400,000 Grenades
64,000 tons of Iron & Steel
217,000 tons of explosives
1,323 Motor Cars
4,533 Lorries & Ambulances
10,000 Motor Cycles & Bicycles
308 Aeroplanes
649 Aeroplane Engines
6 Airships

British supplies to THE UNITED STATES
164 Heavy Guns
15,000 Rifles
11,000,000 Bullets
1,800 Trench Mortars
300,000 Grenades
811 Motor Cars
4,553 Lorries & Ambulances
2,219 Motor Cycles & Bicycles
452 Aeroplanes
18 Tanks

to BELGIUM
53 Heavy Guns
296 Machine Guns
189,000 Rifles
50,000,000 Bullets
151,000 Grenades
17,000 tons of Explosives
878 Lorries & Ambulances
25,000 Motor Cycles & Bicycles
34 Aeroplanes

to RUMANIA
400 Machine Guns
18,000,000 Bullets
177 Lorries & Ambulances
1,098 Motor Cycles & Bicycles
19 Aeroplanes

to ITALY
8,358 Machine Guns
50,000 Rifles
100,000,000 rounds of shells and bullets
213 Trench Mortars
950,000 tons of Iron & Steel
140,000 tons of Explosives
2,500 Motor Cycles & Bicycles

to FRANCE
17 Heavy Guns
14,000 Machine Guns
140,000,000 Bullets
1,430 Trench Mortars
998,000 rounds of mortar shells
4,811,000 Grenades
4,332,000 tons of Iron and Steel
4,536,000 tons of Non-Ferrous metals
416,000 tons of Explosives
37 Motor Cars
1,171 Lorries & Ambulances
27,600 Motor Cycles & Bicycles
11 Aeroplanes
30 Aeroplane Engines
101 Tanks

British supplies were also sent to China, Greece, Japan, Portugal, Serbia and to the Hedjaz

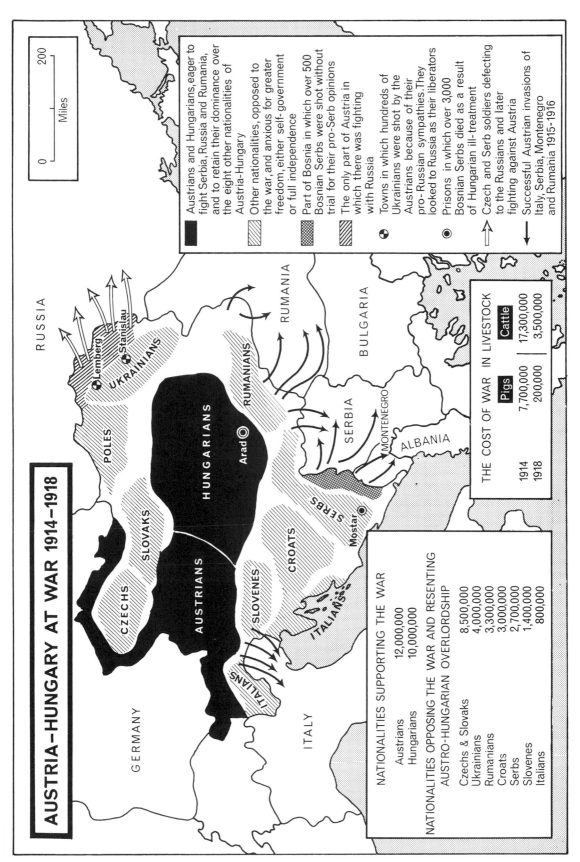

AUSTRIA–HUNGARY AT WAR 1914–1918

RUSSIA

GERMANY

POLES

Lemberg

Stanislau

UKRAINIANS

CZECHS

SLOVAKS

HUNGARIANS

Arad

RUMANIANS

RUMANIA

AUSTRIANS

SLOVENES

CROATS

SERBS

Mostar

SERBIA

MONTENEGRO

ALBANIA

BULGARIA

ITALIANS

ITALY

Austrians and Hungarians, eager to fight Serbia, Russia and Rumania, and to retain their dominance over the eight other nationalities of Austria-Hungary

Other nationalities, opposed to the war, and anxious for greater freedom, either self-government or full independence

Part of Bosnia in which over 500 Bosnian Serbs were shot without trial for their pro-Serb opinions

The only part of Austria in which there was fighting with Russia

Towns in which hundreds of Ukrainians were shot by the Austrians because of their pro-Russian sympathies. They looked to Russia as their liberators

Prisons in which over 3,000 Bosnian Serbs died as a result of Hungarian ill-treatment

Czech and Serb soldiers defecting to the Russians and later fighting against Austria

Successful Austrian invasions of Italy, Serbia, Montenegro and Rumania 1915-1916

0   200
Miles

THE COST OF WAR IN LIVESTOCK		
	Pigs	Cattle
1914	7,700,000	17,300,000
1918	200,000	3,500,000

NATIONALITIES SUPPORTING THE WAR

Austrians   12,000,000
Hungarians   10,000,000

NATIONALITIES OPPOSING THE WAR AND RESENTING
AUSTRO-HUNGARIAN OVERLORDSHIP

Czechs & Slovaks   8,500,000
Ukrainians   4,000,000
Rumanians   3,300,000
Croats   3,000,000
Serbs   2,700,000
Slovenes   1,400,000
Italians   800,000

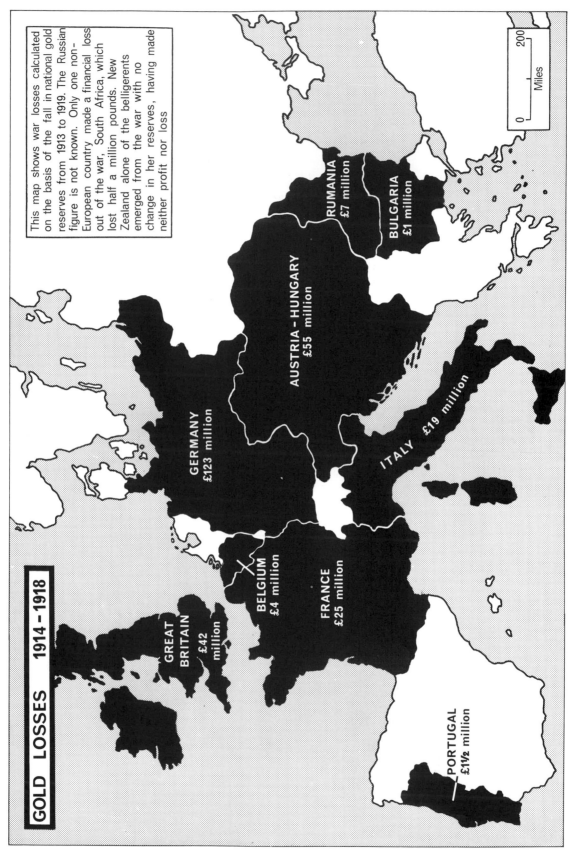

GOLD LOSSES   1914 – 1918

This map shows war losses calculated on the basis of the fall in national gold reserves from 1913 to 1919. The Russian figure is not known. Only one non-European country made a financial loss out of the war, South Africa, which lost half a million pounds. New Zealand alone of the belligerents emerged from the war with no change in her reserves, having made neither profit nor loss

0   200
Miles

RUMANIA
£7 million

BULGARIA
£1 million

AUSTRIA – HUNGARY
£55 million

GERMANY
£123 million

ITALY £19 million

BELGIUM
£4 million

FRANCE
£25 million

GREAT BRITAIN
£42 million

PORTUGAL
£1½ million

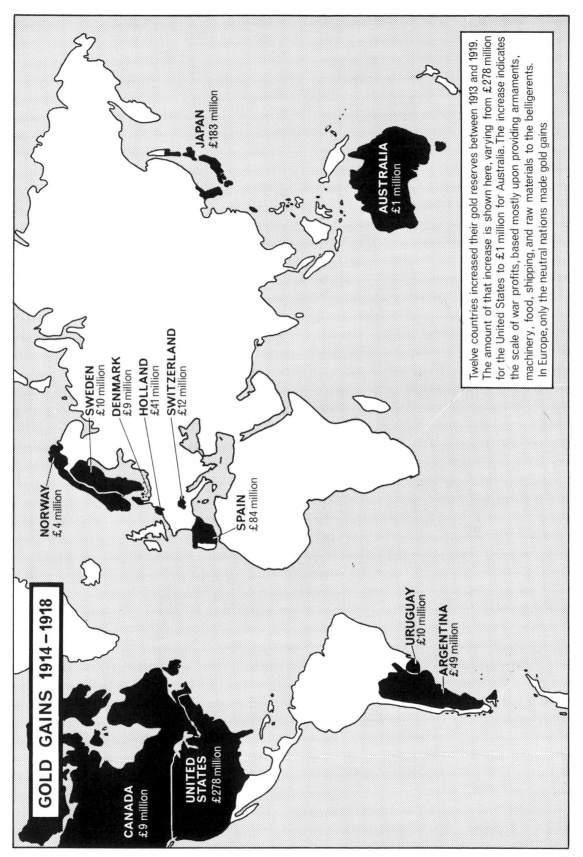

GOLD GAINS 1914–1918

CANADA
£9 million

UNITED STATES
£278 million

NORWAY
£4 million

SWEDEN
£10 million

DENMARK
£9 million

HOLLAND
£41 million

SWITZERLAND
£12 million

SPAIN
£84 million

URUGUAY
£10 million

ARGENTINA
£49 million

JAPAN
£183 million

AUSTRALIA
£1 million

Twelve countries increased their gold reserves between 1913 and 1919. The amount of that increase is shown here, varying from £278 million for the United States to £1 million for Australia. The increase indicates the scale of war profits, based mostly upon providing armaments, machinery, food, shipping, and raw materials to the belligerents. In Europe, only the neutral nations made gold gains

Section Ten

AFTERMATH

Too much blood had been spilt. Too much life-essence had been consumed. The gaps in every home were too wide and empty. The shock of an awakening and the sense of disillusion followed swiftly upon the poor rejoicings with which hundreds of millions saluted the achievement of their hearts' desire. There still remained the satisfactions of safety assured, of peace restored, of honour preserved, of the comforts of fruitful industry, of the home-coming of the soldiers; but these were in the background; and with them all there mingled the ache for those who would never come home.

WINSTON S. CHURCHILL
"THE WORLD CRISIS: THE AFTERMATH"

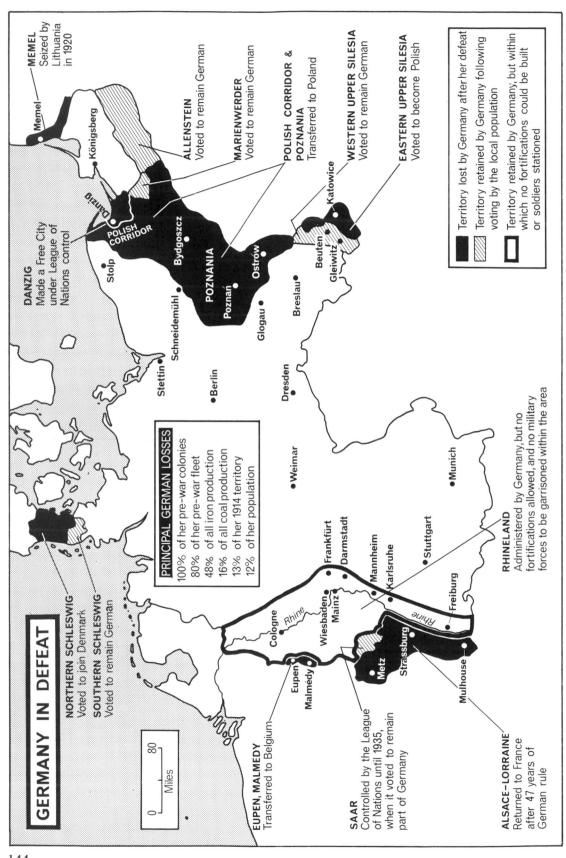

GERMANY IN DEFEAT

NORTHERN SCHLESWIG
Voted to join Denmark
SOUTHERN SCHLESWIG
Voted to remain German

MEMEL
Seized by Lithuania in 1920

ALLENSTEIN
Voted to remain German

MARIENWERDER
Voted to remain German

POLISH CORRIDOR & POZNANIA
Transferred to Poland

WESTERN UPPER SILESIA
Voted to remain German

EASTERN UPPER SILESIA
Voted to become Polish

Territory lost by Germany after her defeat

Territory retained by Germany following voting by the local population

Territory retained by Germany, but within which no fortifications could be built or soldiers stationed

DANZIG
Made a Free City under League of Nations control

POLISH CORRIDOR

POZNANIA

PRINCIPAL GERMAN LOSSES
100% of her pre-war colonies
80% of her pre-war fleet
48% of all iron production
16% of all coal production
13% of her 1914 territory
12% of her population

Memel
Königsberg
Danzig
Stolp
Bydgoszcz
Schneidemühl
Poznań
Ostrów
Glogau
Breslau
Beuten
Gleiwitz
Katowice
Stettin
Berlin
Dresden
Weimar
Munich

RHINELAND
Administered by Germany, but no fortifications allowed, and no military forces to be garrisoned within the area

Frankfürt
Darmstadt
Mannheim
Karlsruhe
Stuttgart
Freiburg
Cologne
Rhine
Wiesbaden
Mainz
Rhine
Metz
Strassburg
Mulhouse

Eupen
Malmédy

EUPEN, MALMEDY
Transferred to Belgium

SAAR
Controlled by the League of Nations until 1935, when it voted to remain part of Germany

ALSACE-LORRAINE
Returned to France after 47 years of German rule

0   80
Miles

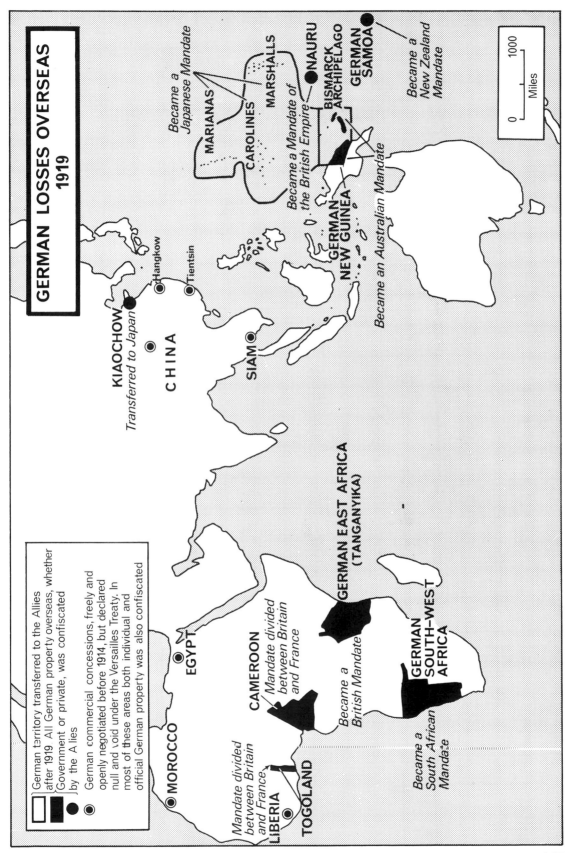

GERMAN LOSSES OVERSEAS 1919

German territory transferred to the Allies after 1919. All German property overseas, whether Government or private, was confiscated by the Allies

German commercial concessions, freely and openly negotiated before 1914, but declared null and void under the Versailles Treaty. In most of these areas both individual and official German property was also confiscated

MOROCCO

EGYPT

LIBERIA

TOGOLAND
Mandate divided between Britain and France

CAMEROON
Mandate divided between Britain and France

GERMAN EAST AFRICA (TANGANYIKA)
Became a British Mandate

GERMAN SOUTH-WEST AFRICA
Became a South African Mandate

KIAOCHOW
Transferred to Japan

CHINA

Hangkow

Tientsin

SIAM

MARIANAS

CAROLINES

MARSHALLS

Became a Japanese Mandate

NAURU
Became a Mandate of the British Empire

BISMARCK ARCHIPELAGO

GERMAN NEW GUINEA
Became an Australian Mandate

GERMAN SAMOA
Became a New Zealand Mandate

0   1000

Miles

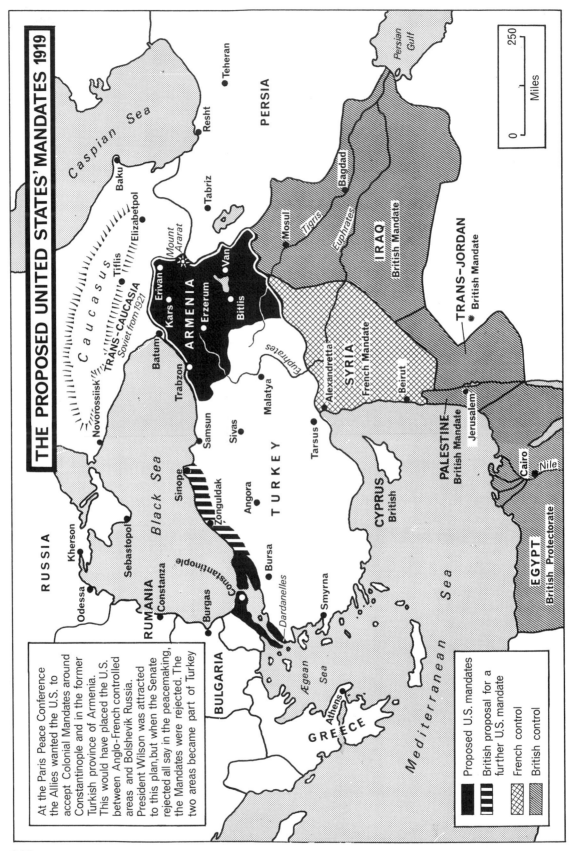

THE PROPOSED UNITED STATES' MANDATES 1919

At the Paris Peace Conference the Allies wanted the U.S. to accept Colonial Mandates around Constantinople and in the former Turkish province of Armenia. This would have placed the U.S. between Anglo-French controlled areas and Bolshevik Russia. President Wilson was attracted to this plan, but when the Senate rejected all say in the peacemaking, the Mandates were rejected. The two areas became part of Turkey.

Proposed U.S. mandates
British proposal for a further U.S. mandate
French control
British control

RUSSIA

Odessa
Kherson
Sebastopol

Black Sea

Constanza
RUMANIA
Burgas

BULGARIA

GREECE
Athens

Aegean Sea

Smyrna

Mediterranean Sea

CYPRUS
British

Caspian Sea

Teheran

PERSIA

Resht

Baku

Tabriz

Elizabetpol

Novorossiisk
Caucasus
Tiflis
TRANS-CAUCASIA
Soviet from 1921
Kars
Erivan
Mount Ararat
ARMENIA
Erzerum
Van
Bitlis

Batum
Trabzon
Samsun
Sivas
Angora
TURKEY
Bursa
Constantinople
Dardanelles
Sinope
Zonguldak

Mosul
Tigris
Euphrates
IRAQ
British Mandate

Bagdad
Persian Gulf

TRANS-JORDAN
British Mandate

Malatya
Tarsus

Alexandretta
SYRIA
French Mandate
Beirut

PALESTINE
British Mandate
Jerusalem

Cairo
Nile

EGYPT
British Protectorate

0   250
Miles

146

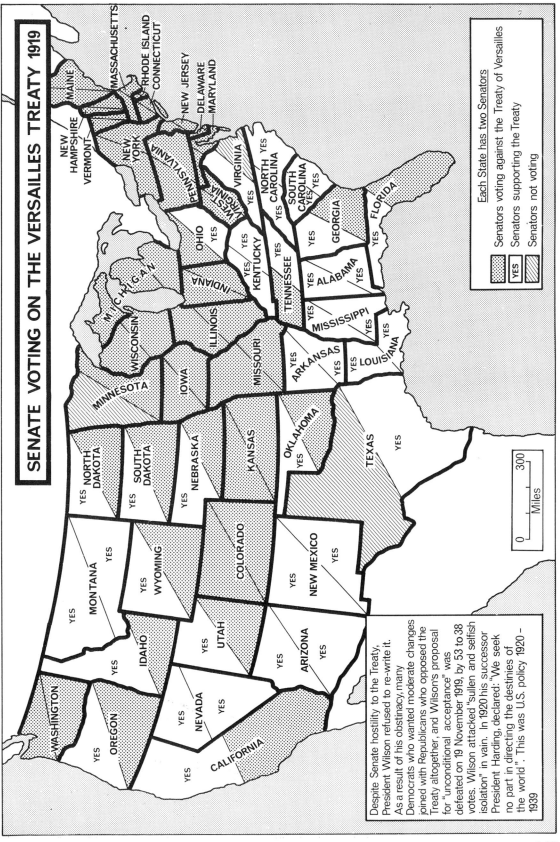

SENATE VOTING ON THE VERSAILLES TREATY 1919

MAINE
NEW HAMPSHIRE
VERMONT
MASSACHUSETTS
RHODE ISLAND
CONNECTICUT
NEW JERSEY
DELAWARE
MARYLAND
NEW YORK
PENNSYLVANIA
WEST VIRGINIA
VIRGINIA YES
NORTH CAROLINA YES
SOUTH CAROLINA YES YES
GEORGIA YES
FLORIDA YES
OHIO YES
KENTUCKY YES YES
TENNESSEE YES
ALABAMA YES YES
MISSISSIPPI YES YES
INDIANA YES
ILLINOIS
MICHIGAN
WISCONSIN
MINNESOTA
IOWA
MISSOURI
ARKANSAS YES
LOUISIANA YES YES
NORTH DAKOTA YES
SOUTH DAKOTA YES
NEBRASKA YES
KANSAS
OKLAHOMA YES
TEXAS YES
MONTANA YES
WYOMING YES
COLORADO
NEW MEXICO YES
IDAHO YES
UTAH YES
ARIZONA YES
WASHINGTON YES
OREGON YES
NEVADA YES
CALIFORNIA YES

Each State has two Senators
Senators voting against the Treaty of Versailles
Senators supporting the Treaty
Senators not voting
YES

0   300
Miles

Despite Senate hostility to the Treaty, President Wilson refused to re-write it. As a result of his obstinacy, many Democrats who wanted moderate changes joined with Republicans who opposed the Treaty altogether, and Wilson's proposal for "unconditional acceptance" was defeated on 19 November 1919, by 53 to 38 votes. Wilson attacked "sullen and selfish isolation" in vain. In 1920 his successor President Harding, declared: "We seek no part in directing the destinies of the world". This was U.S. policy 1920 – 1939

147

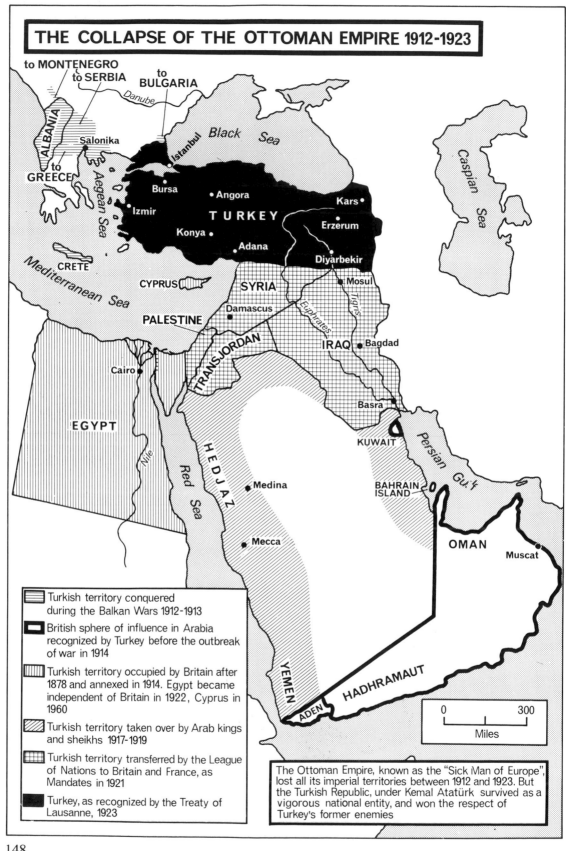

THE COLLAPSE OF THE OTTOMAN EMPIRE 1912-1923

to MONTENEGRO
to SERBIA
to BULGARIA
Danube
ALBANIA
Salonika
to GREECE
Aegean Sea
Black Sea
Istanbul
Bursa
Angora
Kars
Izmir
TURKEY
Erzerum
Konya
Adana
Diyarbekir
CRETE
CYPRUS
SYRIA
Mosul
Mediterranean Sea
PALESTINE
Damascus
Euphrates
Tigris
TRANSJORDAN
IRAQ
Bagdad
Cairo
Caspian Sea
EGYPT
Basra
KUWAIT
Persian Gulf
Nile
HEDJAZ
Medina
BAHRAIN ISLAND
Red Sea
OMAN
Muscat
Mecca
YEMEN
ADEN
HADHRAMAUT

0 ——— 300
Miles

Turkish territory conquered during the Balkan Wars 1912-1913

British sphere of influence in Arabia recognized by Turkey before the outbreak of war in 1914

Turkish territory occupied by Britain after 1878 and annexed in 1914. Egypt became independent of Britain in 1922, Cyprus in 1960

Turkish territory taken over by Arab kings and sheikhs 1917-1919

Turkish territory transferred by the League of Nations to Britain and France, as Mandates in 1921

Turkey, as recognized by the Treaty of Lausanne, 1923

The Ottoman Empire, known as the "Sick Man of Europe", lost all its imperial territories between 1912 and 1923. But the Turkish Republic, under Kemal Atatürk survived as a vigorous national entity, and won the respect of Turkey's former enemies

TURKEY, GREECE, AND BRITAIN 1919-1922

0   60
Miles

BULGARIA

Black Sea

Adrianople (Edirne)
Midia
Bosphorus
Rodosto (Tekirdağ)
Constantinople
Ismit
Dedeagatch
Keshan
Kavala
Sea of Marmora
Salonika
SAMOTHRACE
Biga
Mudania
Bandirma
Bursa
Dardanelles
Chanak
İnönü
IMBROS
Eskisehir
Kum Kale
LEMNOS

G R E E C E

MITYLENE
Aegean
Kütahya
T U R K E Y
Manisa
Dumlupiner
Afionkarahissar
Smyrna (Izmir)
Athens
Sea
Denizli

DODECANESE ISLANDS

RHODES

CRETE

	Greece in 1914
	Bulgarian territory ceded to Greece in 1919
	Turkish territory occupied by Greece in 1919 with British encouragement
---	The "Zone of the Straits" occupied by Britain 1919-1922
←	Turkish forces defeated the Greeks in August 1922. Hostilities ended at the Mudania Convention, and Greece withdrew from all Turkish territory occupied in 1919
⇐	Turkish advance towards British forces at Chanak halted on the verge of war in October 1922. Britain then agreed to evacuate the "Zone of the Straits", including Constantinople, which had been under British occupation since 1919

Occupied by Italy in 1912. Claimed by Greece 1920. Formally annexed by Italy, 1923. Transferred to Greece 1948

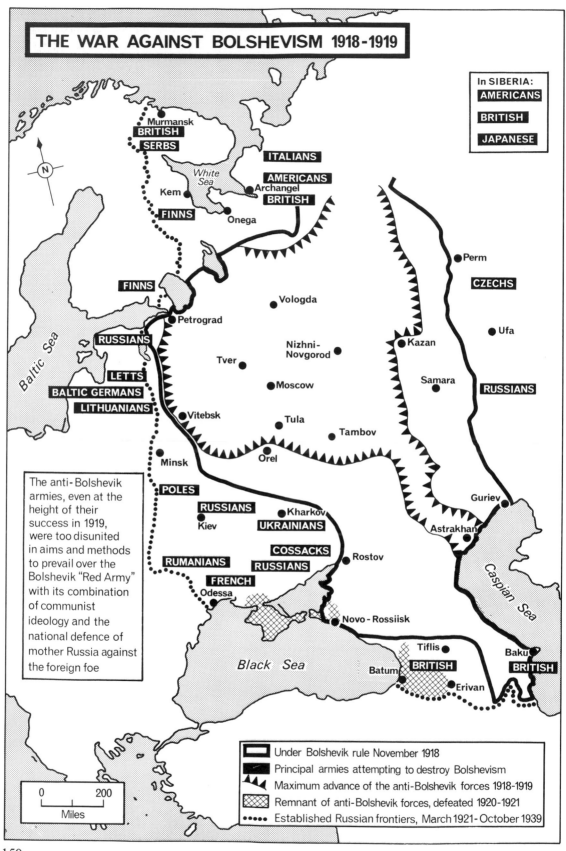

THE WAR AGAINST BOLSHEVISM 1918-1919

In SIBERIA:
AMERICANS
BRITISH
JAPANESE

Murmansk
BRITISH
SERBS

N

White Sea

ITALIANS

AMERICANS
Archangel
BRITISH

Kem

FINNS

Onega

Perm

CZECHS

FINNS

Vologda

Ufa

Petrograd

RUSSIANS

Nizhni-Novgorod

Kazan

Baltic Sea

Tver

Samara

RUSSIANS

LETTS
BALTIC GERMANS
LITHUANIANS

Moscow

Vitebsk

Tula

Tambov

Minsk

Orel

The anti-Bolshevik armies, even at the height of their success in 1919, were too disunited in aims and methods to prevail over the Bolshevik "Red Army" with its combination of communist ideology and the national defence of mother Russia against the foreign foe

POLES

RUSSIANS
Kiev

Kharkov
UKRAINIANS

Guriev

Astrakhan

COSSACKS
Rostov

RUMANIANS
RUSSIANS
FRENCH
Odessa

Caspian Sea

Novo-Rossiisk

Tiflis
BRITISH
Batum
Erivan

Baku
BRITISH

Black Sea

☐	Under Bolshevik rule November 1918
■	Principal armies attempting to destroy Bolshevism
◣◣◣	Maximum advance of the anti-Bolshevik forces 1918-1919
▦	Remnant of anti-Bolshevik forces, defeated 1920-1921
••••	Established Russian frontiers, March 1921-October 1939

0   200
Miles

150

THE RUSSO-POLISH WAR 1920

Poland's established frontiers, June 1920
The eastern extent of Polish conquests, April, May and June 1920
Russian attacks following the Polish occupation of Kiev in June 1920
Polish lines of defence, August 1920
The 'Miracle of the Vistula'. Russian armies were defeated; they retreated to Russia
Seized by Poland from Lithuania, October 1920
Annexed by Poland from Russia, Treaty of Riga, March 1921
Poland's eastern frontier from 1921 to 1939

ESTONIA

LATVIA

Baltic Sea

LITHUANIA

Vilna

RUSSIA

Minsk

DANZIG

EAST PRUSSIA

Grodno

Vistula

Bialystok

GERMANY

Plotzk

Poznan

Warsaw

Pinsk

POLAND

Radom

Lublin

GERMANY

Kholm

Kiev

Vistula

Lvov

Cracow

Kamenets Podolsk

0   100
Miles

CZECHOSLOVAKIA

HUNGARY

RUMANIA

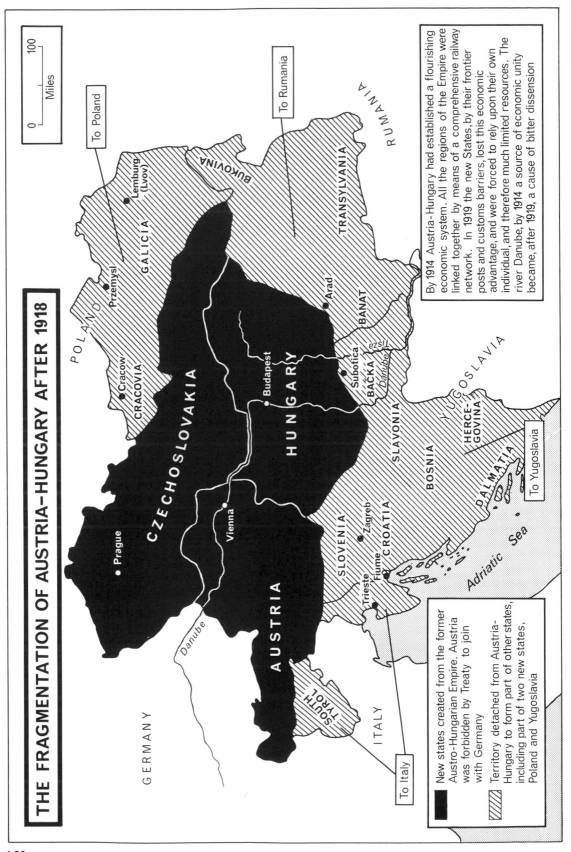

THE FRAGMENTATION OF AUSTRIA–HUNGARY AFTER 1918

By 1914 Austria-Hungary had established a flourishing economic system. All the regions of the Empire were linked together by means of a comprehensive railway network. In 1919 the new States, by their frontier posts and customs barriers, lost this economic advantage, and were forced to rely upon their own individual, and therefore much limited resources. The river Danube, by 1914 a source of economic unity became, after 1919, a cause of bitter dissension

New states created from the former Austro-Hungarian Empire. Austria was forbidden by Treaty to join with Germany

Territory detached from Austria-Hungary to form part of other states, including part of two new states, Poland and Yugoslavia

To Poland

To Rumania

To Italy

To Yugoslavia

GERMANY

POLAND

CZECHOSLOVAKIA

Prague •

Cracow

CRACOVIA

Przemysl

Lemburg
(Lvov)

GALICIA

BUKOVINA

RUMANIA

TRANSYLVANIA

Arad

BANAT

AUSTRIA

Vienna •

Danube

SOUTH
TYROL

ITALY

HUNGARY

Budapest •

Tisza
Danube

Subotica

BAČKA

YUGOSLAVIA

SLAVONIA

Zagreb

CROATIA

SLOVENIA

Trieste
Fiume

BOSNIA

HERCE-
GOVINA

DALMATIA

Adriatic Sea

Miles
0   100

152

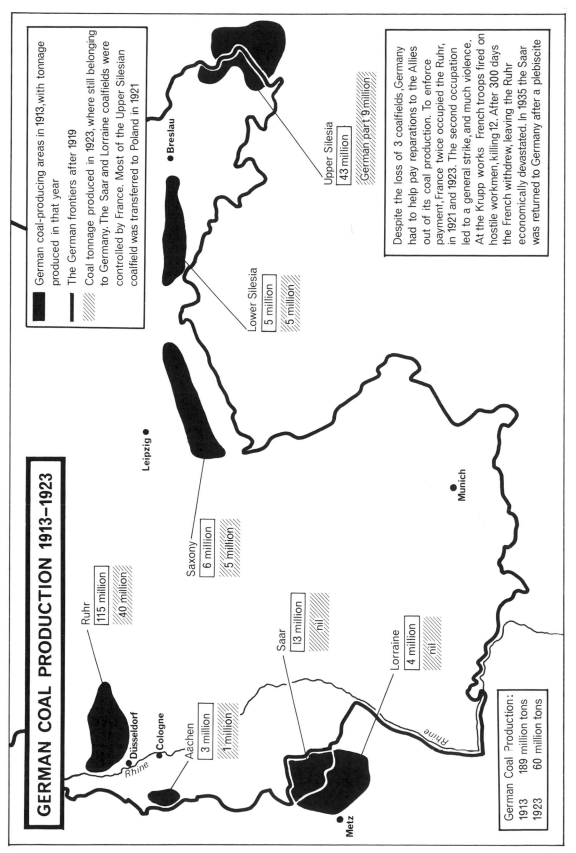

GERMAN COAL PRODUCTION 1913-1923

German coal-producing areas in 1913, with tonnage produced in that year

The German frontiers after 1919

Coal tonnage produced in 1923, where still belonging to Germany. The Saar and Lorraine coalfields were controlled by France. Most of the Upper Silesian coalfield was transferred to Poland in 1921

Breslau

Upper Silesia
43 million
German part 9 million

Lower Silesia
5 million
5 million

Leipzig

Saxony
6 million
5 million

Munich

Düsseldorf
Cologne

Ruhr
115 million
40 million

Aachen
3 million
1 million

Saar
13 million
nil

Lorraine
4 million
nil

Rhine

Metz

Despite the loss of 3 coalfields, Germany had to help pay reparations to the Allies out of its coal production. To enforce payment, France twice occupied the Ruhr, in 1921 and 1923. The second occupation led to a general strike, and much violence. At the Krupp works French troops fired on hostile workmen, killing 12. After 300 days the French withdrew, leaving the Ruhr economically devastated. In 1935 the Saar was returned to Germany after a plebiscite

German Coal Production:
1913   189 million tons
1923   60 million tons

153

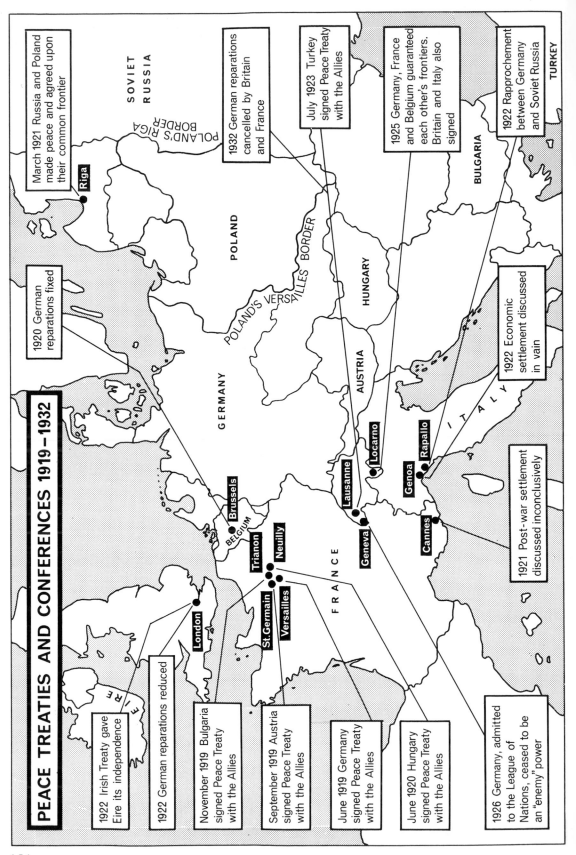

PEACE TREATIES AND CONFERENCES 1919–1932

March 1921 Russia and Poland made peace and agreed upon their common frontier

1932 German reparations cancelled by Britain and France

July 1923 Turkey signed Peace Treaty with the Allies

1925 Germany, France and Belgium guaranteed each other's frontiers. Britain and Italy also signed

1922 Rapprochement between Germany and Soviet Russia

1920 German reparations fixed

1922 Economic settlement discussed in vain

1921 Post-war settlement discussed inconclusively

1922 Irish Treaty gave Eire its independence

1922 German reparations reduced

November 1919 Bulgaria signed Peace Treaty with the Allies

September 1919 Austria signed Peace Treaty with the Allies

June 1919 Germany signed Peace Treaty with the Allies

June 1920 Hungary signed Peace Treaty with the Allies

1926 Germany, admitted to the League of Nations, ceased to be an "enemy" power

SOVIET RUSSIA

POLAND'S RIGA BORDER

POLAND

POLANDS VERSAILLES BORDER

HUNGARY

AUSTRIA

BULGARIA

TURKEY

GERMANY

BELGIUM

FRANCE

EIRE

ITALY

Riga

Brussels

Lausanne

Locarno

Genoa

Rapallo

Geneva

Cannes

Trianon

Neuilly

St.Germain

Versailles

London

THE NEW STATES OF CENTRAL EUROPE 1920

New states established by 1920 with the encouragement of the Allied powers

The remnant of Austria-Hungary, two independent and separate states established by the Allied powers

Austro-Hungarian territory added to Rumania and Serbia by the Allied powers. The enlarged Serbia became the Serb-Croat-Slovene kingdom, later known as Yugoslavia

Former Russian territory joined to Rumania

POPULATIONS IN 1920

Poland	27,000,000
Rumania	17,400,000
Czechoslovakia	14,600,000
Yugoslavia	12,000,000
Hungary	8,700,000
Austria	6,500,000
Finland	3,600,000
Lithuania	2,400,000
Latvia	1,800,000
Estonia	1,000,000
Danzig	400,000
Fiume	50,000

FINLAND

ESTONIA

LATVIA

LITHUANIA

RUSSIA

FREE CITY OF DANZIG

EAST PRUSSIA

Baltic Sea

POLAND

GERMANY

CZECHOSLOVAKIA

BESSARABIA

AUSTRIA

HUNGARY

RUMANIA

FREE CITY OF FIUME

YUGOSLAVIA

ITALY

Adriatic Sea

BULGARIA

Black Sea

ALBANIA

GREECE

TURKEY

0 — 300
Miles

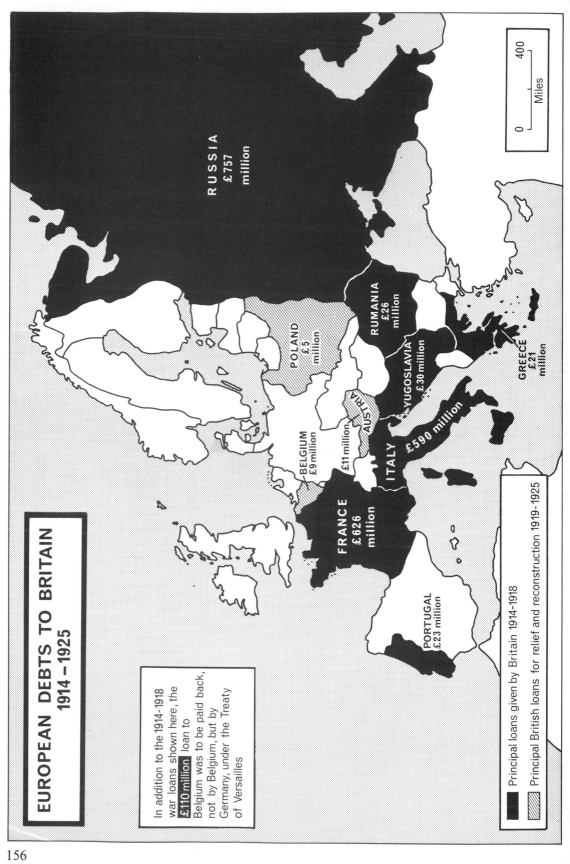

EUROPEAN DEBTS TO BRITAIN 1914 – 1925

In addition to the 1914-1918 war loans shown here, the £110 million loan to Belgium was to be paid back, not by Belgium, but by Germany, under the Treaty of Versailles

RUSSIA
£757 million

POLAND
£5 million

RUMANIA
£26 million

AUSTRIA
£11 million

YUGOSLAVIA
£30 million

GREECE
£21 million

BELGIUM
£9 million

ITALY
£590 million

FRANCE
£626 million

PORTUGAL
£23 million

0   400
Miles

■ Principal loans given by Britain 1914-1918

▨ Principal British loans for relief and reconstruction 1919-1925

156

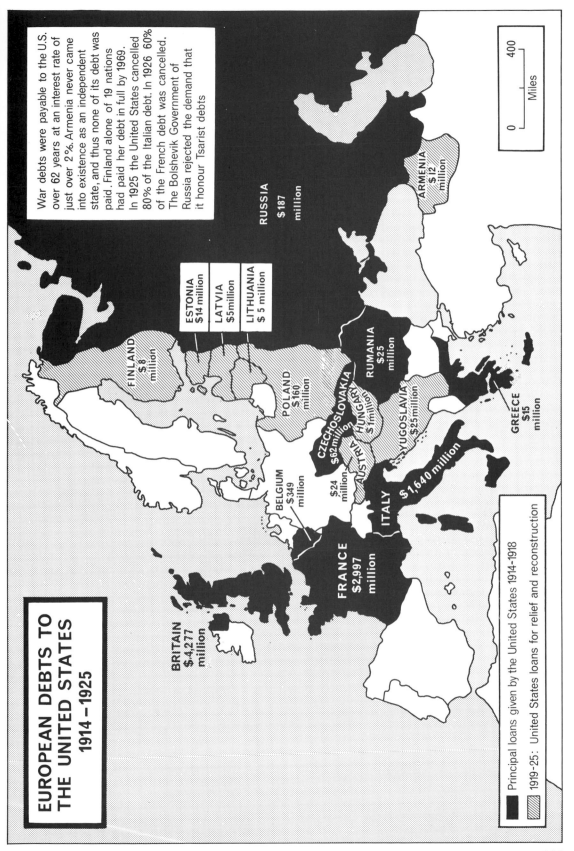

EUROPEAN DEBTS TO THE UNITED STATES 1914–1925

War debts were payable to the U.S. over 62 years at an interest rate of just over 2%. Armenia never came into existence as an independent state, and thus none of its debt was paid. Finland alone of 19 nations had paid her debt in full by 1969. In 1925 the United States cancelled 80% of the Italian debt. In 1926 60% of the French debt was cancelled. The Bolshevik Government of Russia rejected the demand that it honour Tsarist debts

0 — 400
Miles

RUSSIA $187 million

ARMENIA $12 million

ESTONIA $14 million
LATVIA $5 million
LITHUANIA $ 5 million

FINLAND $8 million

POLAND $160 million

RUMANIA $25 million

CZECHOSLOVAKIA $62 million

HUNGARY $ million

AUSTRIA $24 million

YUGOSLAVIA $25 million

GREECE $15 million

BELGIUM $349 million

ITALY $1,640 million

FRANCE $2,997 million

BRITAIN $4,277 million

■ Principal loans given by the United States 1914-1918

▨ 1919-25: United States loans for relief and reconstruction

157

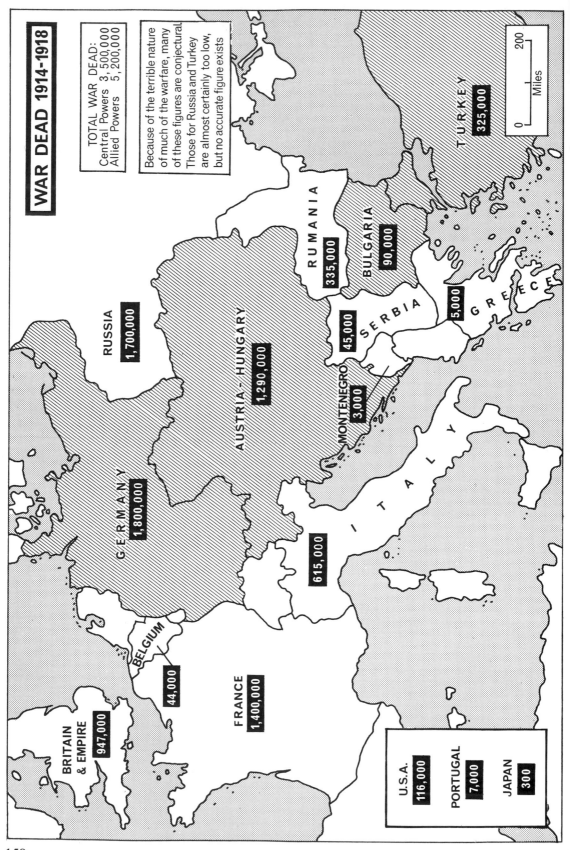

WAR DEAD 1914-1918

TOTAL WAR DEAD:
Central Powers 3,500,000
Allied Powers 5,200,000

Because of the terrible nature of much of the warfare, many of these figures are conjectural. Those for Russia and Turkey are almost certainly too low, but no accurate figure exists

0 200 Miles

TURKEY 325,000

RUMANIA 335,000

BULGARIA 90,000

RUSSIA 1,700,000

AUSTRIA-HUNGARY 1,290,000

SERBIA 45,000

5,000

GREECE

MONTENEGRO 3,000

GERMANY 1,800,000

ITALY 615,000

BELGIUM 44,000

FRANCE 1,400,000

BRITAIN & EMPIRE 947,000

U.S.A. 116,000

PORTUGAL 7,000

JAPAN 300

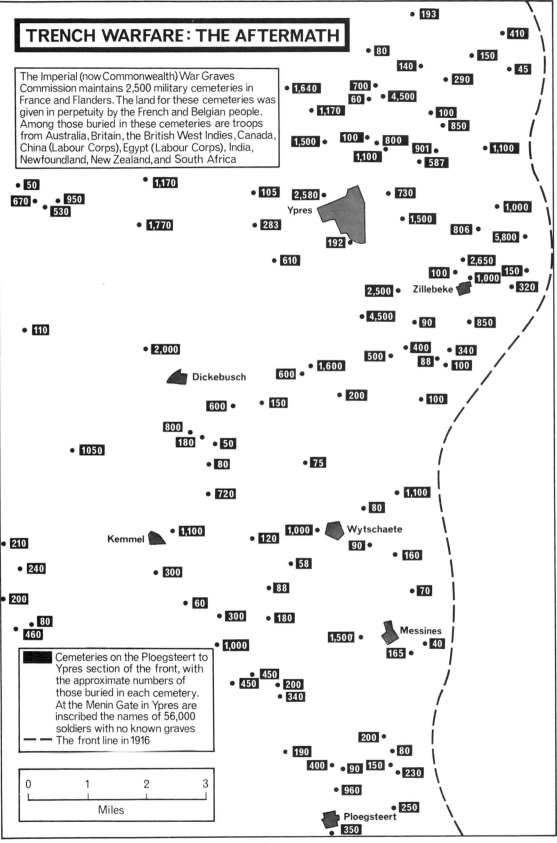

TRENCH WARFARE: THE AFTERMATH

The Imperial (now Commonwealth) War Graves Commission maintains 2,500 military cemeteries in France and Flanders. The land for these cemeteries was given in perpetuity by the French and Belgian people. Among those buried in these cemeteries are troops from Australia, Britain, the British West Indies, Canada, China (Labour Corps), Egypt (Labour Corps), India, Newfoundland, New Zealand, and South Africa

193
410
80
150
140
45
290
1,640
700
60 · 4,500
1,170
100
850
1,500 · 100 · 800
1,100 901 · 1,100
587

50
1,170
670 · 950
530
105 · 2,580 · 730
Ypres
1,770
283 · 1,500
806 ·
5,800
192
610
2,650
100 · 150
1,000
2,500 · **Zillebeke** 320

110
4,500
90 · 850
2,000
500 · 400 · 340
88 · 100
600 · 1,600
Dickebusch
600 · 150 · 200 · 100
800
180 · 50
1050
80 · 75
720
1,100
80
1,100
Kemmel 120 1,000 · **Wytschaete**
210
90 ·
240
58
160
300
200
88
70
60
80
300 · 180
460
1,000
Messines
1,500 · 40
165 ·

450
450 · 200
340
200 ·
190
80
400 · 90 150 · 230
960
250
Ploegsteert
350

■ Cemeteries on the Ploegsteert to Ypres section of the front, with the approximate numbers of those buried in each cemetery. At the Menin Gate in Ypres are inscribed the names of 56,000 soldiers with no known graves
– – The front line in 1916

0   1   2   3
Miles

159

UNITED STATES SOLDIERS, STATE BY STATE, 1917-1918

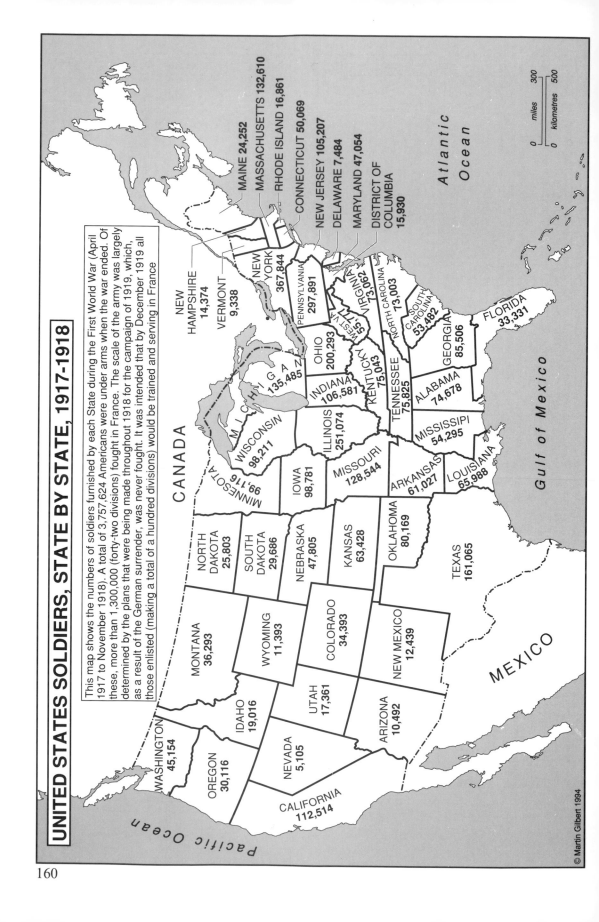

This map shows the numbers of soldiers furnished by each State during the First World War (April 1917 to November 1918). A total of 3,757,624 Americans were under arms when the war ended. Of these, more than 1,300,000 (forty-two divisions) fought in France. The scale of the army was largely determined by the plans that were being made throughout 1918 for the campaign of 1919, which, as a result of the German surrender, was never fought. It was intended that by December 1919 all those enlisted (making a total of a hundred divisions) would be trained and serving in France

Atlantic Ocean

MAINE 24,252
MASSACHUSETTS 132,610
RHODE ISLAND 16,861
CONNECTICUT 50,069
NEW JERSEY 105,207
DELAWARE 7,484
MARYLAND 47,054
DISTRICT OF COLUMBIA 15,930

NEW HAMPSHIRE 14,374
VERMONT 9,338
NEW YORK 367,844
PENNSYLVANIA 297,891
VIRGINIA 73,062
WEST VIRGINIA 55,043
NORTH CAROLINA 73,003
SOUTH CAROLINA 53,482
FLORIDA 33,331
GEORGIA 85,506
ALABAMA 74,678
TENNESSEE 75,825
KENTUCKY 75,043
MISSISSIPPI 54,295
LOUISIANA 65,988
ARKANSAS 61,027

OHIO 200,293
INDIANA 106,581
MICHIGAN 135,485
WISCONSIN 98,211
ILLINOIS 251,074
MISSOURI 128,544
IOWA 98,781
MINNESOTA 99,116

CANADA

NORTH DAKOTA 25,803
SOUTH DAKOTA 29,686
NEBRASKA 47,805
KANSAS 63,428
OKLAHOMA 80,169
TEXAS 161,065

MONTANA 36,293
WYOMING 11,393
COLORADO 34,393
NEW MEXICO 12,439

WASHINGTON 45,154
OREGON 30,116
IDAHO 19,016
NEVADA 5,105
UTAH 17,361
ARIZONA 10,492
CALIFORNIA 112,514

Gulf of Mexico

MEXICO

Pacific Ocean

miles 300
kilometres 500

© Martin Gilbert 1994

160

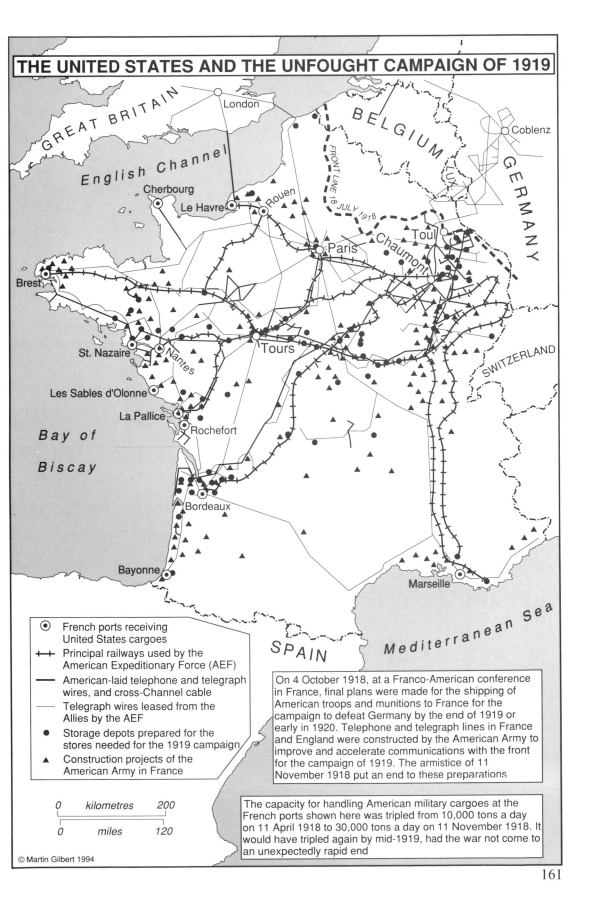

THE UNITED STATES AND THE UNFOUGHT CAMPAIGN OF 1919

GREAT BRITAIN

London

English Channel

BELGIUM

Coblenz

LUX.

GERMANY

Cherbourg

Le Havre

Rouen

FRONT LINE 18 JULY 1918

Toul

Paris

Chaumont

Brest

St. Nazaire

Nantes

Tours

SWITZERLAND

Les Sables d'Olonne

La Pallice

Rochefort

Bay of

Biscay

Bordeaux

Bayonne

Marseille

Mediterranean Sea

SPAIN

⊙ French ports receiving
    United States cargoes

╋╋ Principal railways used by the
    American Expeditionary Force (AEF)

━━ American-laid telephone and telegraph
    wires, and cross-Channel cable

── Telegraph wires leased from the
    Allies by the AEF

● Storage depots prepared for the
    stores needed for the 1919 campaign

▲ Construction projects of the
    American Army in France

On 4 October 1918, at a Franco-American conference
in France, final plans were made for the shipping of
American troops and munitions to France for the
campaign to defeat Germany by the end of 1919 or
early in 1920. Telephone and telegraph lines in France
and England were constructed by the American Army to
improve and accelerate communications with the front
for the campaign of 1919. The armistice of 11
November 1918 put an end to these preparations

0   kilometres   200

0   miles   120

The capacity for handling American military cargoes at the
French ports shown here was tripled from 10,000 tons a day
on 11 April 1918 to 30,000 tons a day on 11 November 1918. It
would have tripled again by mid-1919, had the war not come to
an unexpectedly rapid end

© Martin Gilbert 1994

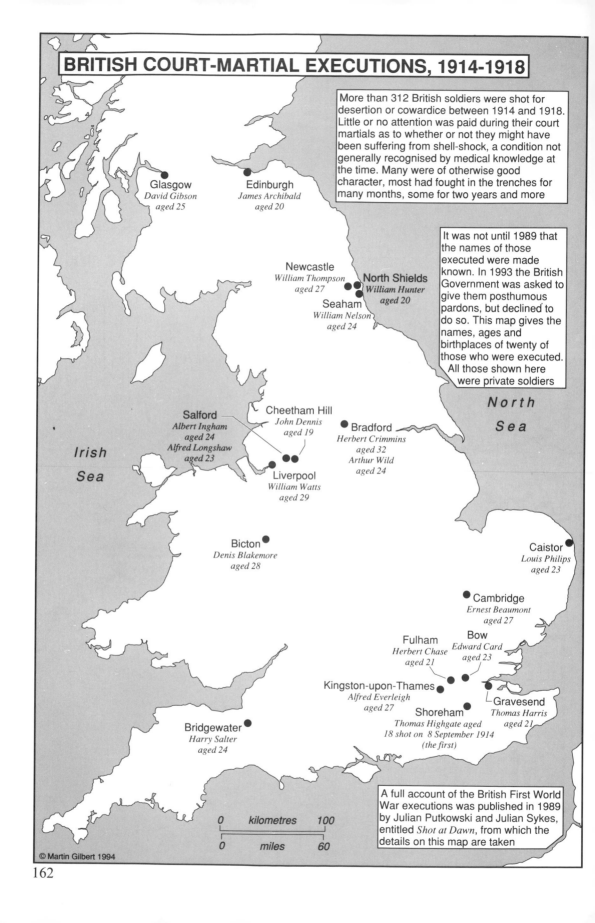

BRITISH COURT-MARTIAL EXECUTIONS, 1914-1918

More than 312 British soldiers were shot for desertion or cowardice between 1914 and 1918. Little or no attention was paid during their court martials as to whether or not they might have been suffering from shell-shock, a condition not generally recognised by medical knowledge at the time. Many were of otherwise good character, most had fought in the trenches for many months, some for two years and more

It was not until 1989 that the names of those executed were made known. In 1993 the British Government was asked to give them posthumous pardons, but declined to do so. This map gives the names, ages and birthplaces of twenty of those who were executed. All those shown here were private soldiers

Glasgow
David Gibson aged 25

Edinburgh
James Archibald aged 20

Newcastle
William Thompson aged 27

North Shields
William Hunter aged 20

Seaham
William Nelson aged 24

North Sea

Irish Sea

Salford
Albert Ingham aged 24
Alfred Longshaw aged 23

Cheetham Hill
John Dennis aged 19

Bradford
Herbert Crimmins aged 32
Arthur Wild aged 24

Liverpool
William Watts aged 29

Bicton
Denis Blakemore aged 28

Caistor
Louis Philips aged 23

Cambridge
Ernest Beaumont aged 27

Fulham
Herbert Chase aged 21

Bow
Edward Card aged 23

Kingston-upon-Thames
Alfred Everleigh aged 27

Shoreham
Thomas Highgate aged 18 shot on 8 September 1914 (the first)

Gravesend
Thomas Harris aged 21

Bridgewater
Harry Salter aged 24

A full account of the British First World War executions was published in 1989 by Julian Putkowski and Julian Sykes, entitled *Shot at Dawn*, from which the details on this map are taken

0 kilometres 100

0 miles 60

© Martin Gilbert 1994

162

THE CREATION OF YUGOSLAVIA, 1919

Acquired from Rumania

Acquired from Bulgaria

Acquired from Hungary

Former Austrian lands

Ports and islands retained by Italy

International borders, 1919-39

Yugoslavia, 1919-1941

AUSTRIA

HUNGARY

MEDJUMURJE

SLOVENIA

ITALY

ISTRIA

Fiume

CROATIA

BARANYA

BACKA

BANAT

Vrsac   Bela Crka

RUMANIA

Belgrade

ZARA

DALMATIA

BOSNIA

HERZEGOVINA

SERBIA

Caribrod

BULGARIA

Adriatic

MONTENEGRO

CHERSO   LUSSIN

Sea

ALBANIA

A
V
I
A
L
S
O
G
U
Y

MACEDONIA

Strumnica

POPULATION OF YUGOSLAVIA, 1921	
Serbs	5.5 million
Croats	3.25 million
Slovenes	1.02 miliion
Moslems	700,000
(Bosnia & Herzegovina)	
Macedonians	600,000
Germans	513,472
Hungarians	472,409
Rumanians	229,398
Albanians	441,740
Turks	90,000
Jews	64,159
Italians	12,825

ITALY

GREECE

The First World War began when Austria-Hungary declared war against Serbia in July 1914. When the war ended, and Austria-Hungary had been defeated, Serbia was one of the victor powers. But she played no part at the Peace Conference, for on 3 January 1919 an announcement from her capital, Belgrade, stated that Serbia had "completed her reorganisation" to become the "Kingdom of Serbs, Croats and Slovenes". This was known as "Yugoslavia". No mention was made of the various non-Slav minorities: Germans, Hungarians, Albanians, Italians and Greeks

Yugoslavia survived as a single State from 1919 to 1941, when the Germans and Italians conquered and divided the country, and Croatia became an independent state. A single Yugoslavia was recreated in 1945 under Communist rule, and survived until 1991, when Slovenia and Croatia declared their independence, after which Croatia and Serbia struggled to control as much as possible of Bosnia-Herzegovina

© Martin Gilbert 1994

0	miles	100
0	kilometres	150

163

THE LEIPZIG WAR CRIMES TRIALS, 1921

Atlantic Ocean

GREAT BRITAIN

North Sea

Baltic Sea

●◎ Fastnet Rock
H.M.S. Llandovery Castle
hospital ship torpedoed south-west of Fastnet 234 drowned

◎ Scilly Isles

S.S. Torrington
merchant ship sunk south-west of Scillys 34 killed

Flavy-le-Martel
prisoner-of-war camp ill treatment

● Paris

BELGIUM

Grammont
acts of cruelty to Belgian children

◎ **Herne**
coal mine ill treatment of British and Russian prisoners of war

GERMANY

● Leipzig

RUSSIA

◎ **Saarburg**
killing of French prisoners of war

FRANCE

AUSTRIA - HUNGARY

ITALY

Adriatic Sea

Tyrrehenian Sea

● Sabac

SERBIA

● Belgrade

Great bitterness was caused in Serbia when details were made known of the murder of Serb civilians by Austrian soldiers at Sabac on 12 August 1914. There were similar, authenticated cases of German atrocities against civilians in Belgium in 1914

From the opening days of the war, atrocities were committed against civilians in all the war zones. On 5 October 1918 the French Government declared that 'acts so contrary to International Law, and to the very principles of human civilisation, should not go unpunished.' When hostilities ceased on 11 November 1918 a British legal committee was set up to ensure that 'War Criminals' would be brought to justice

◎ **H.M.S. Dover Castle**
hospital ship torpedoed

On 7 February 1919 the Paris Peace Conference set up a Commission to examine the method whereby trials would be held. The trials took place in Leipzig between 23 May and 16 July 1921. Forty-five cases were tried by German judges. There were eleven prosecutions and six convictions for the crimes shown on this map, the heaviest sentence imposed being ten months in prison

Mediterranean Sea

| 0 | kilometres | 500 |
| 0 | miles | 300 |

© Martin Gilbert 1994

164

Bibliographical Note

The following bibliography is strictly selective, consisting principally of those books which I personally found most useful, both for preparing individual maps and for background knowledge about many diverse aspects of the war: its campaigns, its diplomacy, its men and its moods. It ranges from the multi-volume official histories replete with documents and maps, to much briefer narratives of particular events. Put together, I hope that these books provide a useful and varied introductory survey of the war.

GENERAL WORKS

As an introductory guide I have frequently consulted several contemporary works of reference and encyclopaedias, of which three were of particular value: *The Annual Register,* 5 vols, covering the years 1914 to 1919 (London, 1915–1920); *The Times History of the War,* 21 vols, covering 1914 to 1920 (London, 1914–1920), which contains, for example, the fullest account I have seen of America's shipbuilding crusade (map 87), and has informative articles on every theatre of war, and every aspect of the conflict, social, political, medical, the role of women, etc; and the *Encyclopaedia Britannica,* the thirteenth edition of which contains three extra volumes, numbers 29, 30 and 31, which deal with the war years and immediate post-war period (London and New York, 1926).

THE PRELUDE TO WAR

A stimulating survey of the long-term and immediate origins of the war, together with a full bibliography, is A. J. P. Taylor, *The Struggle for Mastery in Europe* (Oxford, 1954). Also of importance are Luigi Albertini, *The Origins of the War of 1914,* 3 vols (Oxford, 1952–1957) and F. H. Hinsley, *Power and the Pursuit of Peace* (Cambridge, 1963).

For diplomatic activity in Berlin on the eve of war, as well as a reflective view of events leading up to war, Sir Horace Rumbold, *The War Crisis in Berlin July to August 1914* (London, 1940) is of interest. A recent German view of responsibility is Gerhard Georg B. Ritter, *The Schlieffen Plan: Critique of a Myth* (London, 1958). For an account of the final steps to war, there is R. W. Seton-Watson, *Sarajevo: A Study in the Origin of the Great War* (London, 1926).

THE WAR IN OUTLINE

Of the many general histories of the war, three of the most readable are A. J. P. Taylor, *The First World War, An Illustrated History* (London, 1963) which has the added merit of excellent pictures; C. R. M. F. Cruttwell, *A History of the Great War, 1914 to 1918* (Oxford, 1934); and Vincent J. Esposito (ed), *A Concise History of World War One* (London, 1964). Despite its British, and at times personal bias, Winston S. Churchill, *The World Crisis,* 6 vols (London, 1923–1931) has a superb first chapter on the coming of war, and many insights into different phases of the war itself; its penultimate volume, *The Aftermath,* deals with the peace treaties and other post-war problems.

THE WAR IN THE AIR

A good general survey is R. H. Kiernan, *The First War in the Air* (London, 1934). The Official British History, extremely rich in maps, is Walter Raleigh and H. A. Jones, *The War in the Air,* 6 vols text (including many maps), 2 vols maps (Oxford, 1922–1937). The German story is told in Georg Paul Neumann, *The German Airforce in the Great War* (London, 1921); and the effect of German activity in Joseph Morris, *The German Air Raids on Great Britain 1914–1918* (London, 1926) and Kenneth Poolman, *Zeppelins Over England* (London, 1960).

Two recent books of interest are Douglas H. Robinson, *The Zeppelin in Combat* (London, 1962) and Arch Whitehouse, *The Zeppelin Fighters* (London, 1968). An important study of the most serious phase of the aerial war is Raymond H. Fredette, *The First Battle of Britain 1917–1918 and the Birth of the Royal Air Force* (London, 1966). Early methods of dealing with this new method of warfare are described in E. B. Ashmore, *Air Defence* (London, 1929).

THE WAR AT SEA

A useful introduction is Thomas G. Frothingham, *The Naval History of the World War,* 3 vols (Cambridge Mass., 1924, 1925, 1926). The British story was first told, with copious documentation and excellent maps, in Sir Julian S. Corbett and Henry Newbolt, *Naval Operations,* 5 vols text plus 5 vols maps (London, 1920–1931). A work of high scholarship which combines this material with the results of much patient research into British and German naval archives is Arthur J. Marder, *From the Dreadnought to Scapa Flow,* 5 vols (London, 1961–1970).

The story of merchant shipping and oceanic trade routes is as full of interest and drama as that of the fighting navies, and can be read in C. Ernest Fayle, *Seaborne Trade,* 4 vols (London, 1920, 1920 (maps), 1923, 1924) and Archibald Hurd, *The Merchant Navy,* 3 vols (London, 1921, 1924, 1929).

The literature is as voluminous for underwater activity as for that on the surface. Two interesting introductory books on this aspect of the war are R. H. Gibson and Maurice Prendergast, *The German Submarine War* 1914–1918 (London, 1931) and Robert M. Grant, *U-Boats Destroyed* (London, 1964).

Specific topics covered in this Atlas can be explored further in Richard Hough, *The Pursuit of Admiral von Spee* (London, 1969) and Edwin P. Hoyt, *The Last Cruise of the Emden* (London, 1967). A member of the Imperial Royal Family who was on the *Emden* has also told his story: Prince Franz Joseph of Hohenzollern, *Emden* (London, 1928). For the naval and diplomatic aspects of the war in the Italian and Adriatic zones I have consulted Archibald Hurd, *Italian Sea-Power and the Great War* (London, 1918) and P. H. Michel, *La Question de l'Adriatique 1914–1918* (Paris, 1938).

One of the most significant aspects of the war at sea was the Allied naval blockade of Germany. This can be studied in detail in H. W. C. Davis, *A History of the Blockade* (London, 1920), M. W. W. P. Consett, *The Triumph of Unarmed Force* (London, 1928), A. C. Bell, *The Blockade of Germany* (London, 1937) and Marion C. Siney, *The Allied Blockade of Germany 1914–1916* (Ann Arbor, 1957). A lesser known aspect of the blockade is given detailed study by S. L. Bane and R. H. Lutz (eds), *The Blockade of Germany After the Armistice* (Stanford, 1942).

METHODS OF WAR

There are many interesting volumes on the different methods employed during the war by the opposing armies. Their attempts to burrow underneath each other are well described in W. Grant Grieve and Bernard Newman, *Tunnellers* (London, 1936) and Alexander Barrie, *War Underground* (London, 1962). The attempt to break through the barbed-wire by mechanical means is told by J. F. C. Fuller, *Tanks in the Great War 1914–1918* (London, 1920) and B. H. Liddell Hart, *The Tanks* (London, 1959).

Some idea of the extent of the dependence of the belligerents on transport and communications can be seen in the Official British History, A. M. Henniker, *Transportation on the Western Front 1914–1918* (London, 1937) and W. J. K. Davies, *Light Railways of the First World War* (London, 1967).

BRITAIN

A good introductory history of British policy during the war is Sir Llewellyn Woodward, *Great Britain and the War of 1914–1918* (London, 1967). A voluminous compendium of statistics among which the curious reader could spend many hours is the War Office publication, printed by His Majesty's Stationery Office, *Statistics of the Military Effort of the British Empire During the Great War 1914–1920* (London, 1922). Among the many fascinating regimental histories is one of particular interest because of its author, who lost his son in the war: Rudyard Kipling, *The Irish Guards in the Great War* (London, 1923). "The only wonder to the compiler of these records," wrote Kipling in his introduction, "is that any sure fact whatever should be retrieved out of the whirlpools of war."

The munitions story, one of the most fascinating of the domestic issues of the war, can be followed in detail in the Ministry of Munitions publication, *The History of the Ministry of Munitions,* 12 vols (London, 1920–1924). A more personal aspect of the munitions struggle, together with an account of his two years as Prime Minister, is in the *War Memoirs of David Lloyd George,* 6 vols (London, 1933–1936).

Lloyd George's predecessor also left memoirs which deal with war policy: H. H. Asquith, *Memories and Reflections,* 2 vols (London, 1928). Two contemporary diarists with close contacts at the centre of events are Christopher Addison, *Politics from Within* (London, 1924), and *Lord Riddell's War Diary* (London, 1933). A graphic political narrative of this period is in Lord Beaverbrook's two volumes, *Politicians and the War 1914–1916*, 2 vols (London, 1928, 1932) and *Men and Power 1917–1918* (London, 1956). A scholarly examination of Britain's decision for war, and the nine succeeding months in British politics is Cameron Hazlehurst *Politicians at War* (London, 1971). British strategy is examined critically by Paul Guinn, *British Strategy and Politics 1914–1918* (Oxford, 1965). Both Hazlehurst and Guinn have excellent bibliographies.

Social and domestic scenes from the war are presented in a fascinating volume, Mrs C. S. Peel, *How We Lived Then 1914–1918* (London, 1929).

THE BRITISH EMPIRE

The Imperial aspects of the war are told in outline by Sir Charles Lucas (ed), *The Empire at War,* 5 vols (Oxford, 1921–1926). The Australian story has been told in detail, and with some passion, by C. E. W. Bean and others, *Official History of Australia in the War of 1914–1918*, 12 vols (Canberra, 1921–1934). A rich fund of statistics is the Government of India's official publication, *India's Contribution to the Great War* (Calcutta, 1923). A future Lord Chancellor was co-author of the well-mapped official volume, J. W. B. Merewether and Sir Frederick Smith, *The Indian Corps in France* (London, 1917). The first volume of the official story of the Canadian Expeditionary Force is a small but fascinating volume by the future Lord Beaverbrook: Sir Max Aitken, *Canada in Flanders* (London, 1916).

Two British Official Histories which cover aspects of the war in Africa are C.

Hordern, *Military Operations, East Africa* (London, 1941) and F. J. Moberly, *Military Operations, Togoland and the Cameroons 1914–1916* (London, 1931). Other useful Imperial war histories are H. T. B. Drew (ed) *The War Effort of New Zealand* (Auckland, 1924), G. W. L. Nicholson, *Official History of the Canadian Army* (Ottawa, 1962) and John Buchan, *The History of the South African Forces in France* (London, 1920).

FRANCE, BELGIUM AND THE WESTERN FRONT

A compelling account of the opening phase of the war is Major-General Sir Edward Spears, *Liaison 1914* (London, 1930). The story of the German advance has been told by its commander, Alexander von Kluck, *The March on Paris and the Battle of the Marne 1914* (London, 1920). One of the most interesting of the French military memoirs is Maréchal Foch, *Memoires Pour Servir A L'Histoire De La Guerre De 1914–1918* (Paris, 1931). A useful supplement and addition to these memoirs is Liddell Hart, *Foch* (London, 1931). Clemenceau has given his own account both of the war and post-war period in Georges Clemenceau, *Grandeur and Misery of Victory* (London, 1930). A more humble, but highly entertaining picture of the war by a young French painter serving in the British army is Paul Maze, *A Frenchman in Khaki* (London, 1934).

One of the most terrible of all the battles of the war is described in Alistair Horne, *The Price of Glory: Verdun 1916* (London, 1962). The French mutinies have been the subject of frequent accounts, of which the following two are among the more recent and more useful: Richard M. Watt, *Dare Call It Treason* (London, 1953) and John Williams, *Mutiny 1917* (London, 1962). The destructiveness of the war on the western front is shown in Charles Gide (ed), *Effects of the War Upon French Economic Life* (Oxford, 1923), and something of the efforts to restore the damage by William MacDonald, *Reconstruction in France* (London, 1922).

The rapid conquest of Belgium is told in a short Belgian publication, *Military Operations of Belgium* (London, 1915). Something of the nature of the German occupation was described at the time by two books by Jean Massart, *Belgians Under the German Eagle* (London, 1916) and *The Secret Press in Belgium* (London, 1918). There is also some disturbing evidence in Arnold J. Toynbee, *The German Terror in Belgium* (London, 1917).

British military operations on the western front are treated exhaustively and copiously mapped, by J. E. Edmonds (and others), *France and Belgium*, with several volumes of text and maps for each year of the war (London, 1922–1947). It would be invidious to select books on individual campaigns, of which there are several thousand; nor is there a good select bibliography dealing with the more recent of these. An introduction to this enormous literature can be made through two particular studies of merit, A. H. Farrar-Hockley, *The Somme* (London, 1964) and Major-General Sir Edward Spears, *Prelude to Victory* (London, 1939), which deals with the French offensive of 1917. A stimulating critique of the German, British and French naval and military commanders is Corelli Barnett, *The Swordbearers* (London, 1963).

THE FIGHTING MEN

It was the experiences of the ordinary soldiers, rather than the decisions of their commanders, which ensured that the First World War influenced men long after the Armistice. A varied and moving idea of these experiences can be gained from: Bruce Bairnsfather, *Bullets & Billets* (London, 1917) and *From Mud to Mufti* (London, 1919); Philip Gibbs, *Realities of War* (London, 1920); Edmund Blunden, *Undertones of War* (London, 1930): Brian Gardner (ed), *Up The Line To Death: The War Poets 1914–*

1918 (London, 1964); Robert Graves, *Goodbye To All That* (London, 1929); Erich Maria Remarque, *All Quiet on the Western Front* (London, 1929); Siegfried Sassoon, *Counterattack* (London, 1917), some of the most bitter poems of the war; and Siegfried Sassoon, *Memoirs of an Infantry Officer* (London, 1930).

The songs of the war with their terrifying progress from the gay to the grotesque can be heard on the Decca recording *Oh What A Lovely War* (London, 1963; mono LK 4542). Another moving record of contemporary poetry and letters is provided on *Wilfred Owen (1893–1918)* (London, 1968) published by the Argo Record Company on mono RG 593.

For a poignant survey of the British cemeteries whose ground was presented to the British people in perpetuity by the Governments of Belgium and France, and as an indispensable handbook for any visit to the western front, there is a publication by the Imperial (now Commonwealth) War Graves Commission, Sidney C. Hurst, *The Silent Cities* (London, 1929).

ITALY AND THE ITALIAN FRONT

A useful general introduction is Thomas Nelson Page, *Italy and the World War* (London, 1921). For the military story there is a fascinating account by an Italian historian who served on the Army Staff, Luigi Villari, *The War on the Italian Front* (London, 1932). A British historian who also wrote an interesting account of the Italian front, where he was serving in an ambulance unit, is G. M. Trevelyan, *Scenes From Italy's War* (London, 1919).

The British military operations in Italy are described in detail by Sir James E. Edmonds and H. R. Davies, *Military Operations, Italy 1915–1919* (London, 1949). There is an interesting eye-witness account by a future Chancellor of the Exchequer, Hugh Dalton, *With British Guns in Italy* (London, 1919). Among the most famous of all the literary works of the First World War is one which is set on the Italian front, Ernest Hemingway, *A Farewell to Arms* (New York and London, 1929).

For the broader aspects of Italian war policy, there is a useful account in M. H. H. Macartney and P. Cremona, *Italy's Foreign and Colonial Policy 1914–1937* (New York, 1938). An Italian Prime Minister's record is in Giovanni Giolitti, *Memoirs of My Life* (London, 1923).

THE SALONIKA FRONT

One of the most recent and most readable accounts, which also contains a comprehensive bibliography, is Alan Palmer, *The Gardeners of Salonika* (London, 1965). The Italian representative with the Allied forces, who has left a vivid account of this zone of war, was Luigi Villari, *The Macedonian Campaign* (London, 1922). As so often the British Official History combines detailed research with a lively style and copious maps, C. Falls, *Military Operations, Macedonia,* 2 vols (London, 1933, 1935).

RUSSIA AND THE EASTERN FRONT

A good general introduction to the period is to be found in Sir Bernard Pares, *The Fall of the Russian Monarchy* (London, 1939). The Russian defeat in East Prussia is described in detail, and with an excellent series of maps, in Sir Edmund Ironside, *Tannenberg* (Edinburgh and London, 1925). The most successful of all the Russian Generals has left his own account, A. A. Brussilov, *A Soldier's Note-Book 1914–1918* (London, 1930). Another General whose memoirs are extremely informative is General N. M. Golovin, *The Russian Army in the World War* (London, 1931). A British Officer attached to the Russian Army, who has left his own vivid account, is General Sir A. Knox, *With the Russian Army 1914–1917,* 2 vols (London, 1921).

A useful survey of Russian policy and foreign aspirations from the outbreak of war to the Revolution is to be found in C. Jay Smith, *The Russian Struggle For Power 1914–1917* (Athens, Georgia, 1956). For the Revolution itself, and the ensuing civil war and Allied intervention, the most useful account is still W. H. Chamberlin, *The Russian Revolution,* 2 vols (New York, 1935). A recent and enthralling description of the February Revolution is George Katkov, *Russia 1917* (London, 1967).

The treaty signed between the Bolsheviks and the Germans, to Russia's inevitable and enormous disadvantage, is described in detail by John W. Wheeler-Bennett, *Brest-Litovsk* (London, 1938). For British policy towards Russia after the Revolution, and a documentary account of the Allied attempt to crush the new Bolshevik state, see Richard H. Ullman, *Intervention and the War* (Princeton and London, 1961). Two earlier volumes of much value are George F. Kennan, *Russia Leaves the War* (London, 1956) and *Decision to Intervene* (London, 1956).

GERMANY

A penetrating account of German war aims during the war is Fritz Fischer, *Germany's Aims in the First World War* (London, 1967). The documentary background to the disintegration of Germany during the war is to be found in Ralph Haswell Lutz (ed), *Fall of the German Empire 1914–1918,* 2 vols (Stanford, 1932). A recent study of internal German affairs based upon much further detailed research is Gerald D. Feldman, *Army, Industry and Labor in Germany 1914–1918* (Princeton, 1966).

Among contemporaries who left accounts of their activities was General Ludendorff, *My War Memories 1914–1918,* 2 vols (London, 1933). Also of interest for the German view are Th. Von Bethmann Hollweg, *Reflections on the World War* (London, 1920) and Prince von Bülow, *Memoirs of Prince von Bülow* (Boston, 1932); volume 3, "The World War and Germany's Collapse," covers the years 1909 to 1919. Hindenburg's story has been told most effectively in J. W. Wheeler-Bennett, *Hindenburg: The Wooden Titan* (London, 1936).

One of the most stimulating of all recent historical works, based upon a careful study of the newly-opened British archives, is Wm. Roger Louis, *Great Britain and Germany's Lost Colonies 1914–1919* (Oxford, 1967). Dr Louis records that E. S. Montagu, when Secretary of State for India, declared that it would be difficult to find "some convincing argument for not annexing *all* the territories in the world". His book is both an essential introduction to British imperial policy and a model of historical research.

RUMANIA

The best introductory study is R. W. Seton-Watson, *A History of the Roumanians* (Cambridge, 1934).

Two pro-Rumanian accounts produced during the First World War are R. W. Seton-Watson, *Roumania and the Great War* (London, 1915) and D. Mitrany, *Greater Rumania: A Study in National Ideals* (London, 1917). Rumania's war effort and diplomacy is examined in detail by Pamfil Seicaru, *La Roumanie dans la Grande Guerre* (Paris, 1968).

The Rumanian Foreign Minister, Take Jonescu, published his memoirs immediately after the war as *Souvenirs* (Paris, 1919).

TURKEY, MESOPOTAMIA AND THE MIDDLE EAST

There is a discussion of German pre-war influence over Turkey in Morris Jastrow, *The War and the Bagdad Railway* (Philadelphia, 1918). The leading Turkish Minister to have left a record of political and military affairs is Djemal Pasha, *Memories of a Turkish Statesman 1913–1919* (London, 1922).

The Mesopotamian campaign is extremely well documented; and a recent general work, with much fascinating detail, is A. J. Barker, *The Neglected War: Mesopotamia 1914–1918* (London, 1967). The Official British History is once again a model of detail and exposition, F. J. Moberly, *The Campaign in Mesopotamia 1914–1918*, 4 vols (London, 1923–1927).

For the war in Arabia and Palestine, T. E. Lawrence, *The Revolt in the Desert* (London, 1927) is a graphic personal account. The defeat of Turkey in Palestine is dealt with in a short volume, Cyril Falls, *Armageddon 1918* (London, 1964). Cyril Falls was also one of the authors of the longer Official History of this campaign, Sir G. Macmunn and C. Falls, *Egypt and Palestine*, 3 vols and 2 vols maps (London, 1928–1930).

There is a good biography of the Turkish national leader by Lord Kinross, *Atatürk* (London, 1964). For a discussion of some of the plans to defeat the Turkish Empire, an early but informative work is H. N. Howard, *The Partition of Turkey 1913–1923* (Norman, Oklahoma, 1931); but this subject still awaits its historian. The best general work on British policy in the Middle East is Elizabeth Monroe, *Britain's Moment in the Middle East 1914–1956* (London, 1963). The Palestine question is best followed in Leonard Stein, *The Balfour Declaration* (London, 1961) and Christopher Sykes *Cross Roads to Israel* (London, 1965).

THE DARDANELLES AND GALLIPOLI

The attempt to defeat Turkey by an attack on Constantinople lasted for only ten months, but has been responsible for more literature than any other campaign of the war. Two good introductory works are Robert Rhodes James, *Gallipoli* (London, 1965) and John North, *Gallipoli: The Fading Vision* (London, 1936). The Official British History is the most readable and most critical of all those produced after the war, C. F. Aspinall-Oglander, *Military Operations, Gallipoli*, 2 vols (London, 1929, 1932). There is much pungent comment also in C. E. W. Bean's Australian Official History already cited.

The naval campaign is described in the Official British Naval History cited above and in Admiral of the Fleet Lord Wester-Wemyss, *The Navy in the Dardanelles Campaign* (London, 1924). There is a useful French account in A. Thomazi, *La Guerre Navale aux Dardanelles* (Paris, 1926). There is also an interesting German record by a German General, Hans Kannengiesser Pasha, *The Campaign in Gallipoli* (London, 1927).

A moving account of the campaign as seen from the trenches is A. P. Herbert's novel, *The Secret Battle* (London, 1919), of which Winston Churchill wrote: "It was one of those cries of pain wrung from the fighting troops by the prolonged and measureless torment through which they passed; and like the poems of Siegfried Sassoon should be read in each generation, so that men and women may rest under no illusion about what the war means."

AUSTRIA-HUNGARY

The best general surveys are A. J. P. Taylor, *The Habsburg Monarchy 1815–1918* (London, 1949) and A. J. May, *The Habsburg Monarchy 1867–1914* (Cambridge Mass., 1951). There is a full account of Britain's attitude towards the Habsburg monarchy in an excellent recent study, which has the added merit of a comprehensive bibliography, Harry Hanak, *Great Britain and Austria–Hungary During the First*

World War (London, 1962). The memoirs of the Austrian Foreign Minister are also of interest, Count Ottokar Czernin, *In the World War* (London, 1919); but of greater historical importance is the superb account of the final decade of Habsburg foreign policy, A. F. Pribram, *Austrian Foreign Policy 1908–1918* (London, 1923).

For the disintegration of the Empire two standard works are Oskar Jászi, *The Dissolution of the Habsburg Monarchy* (Chicago, 1929) and J. Andrássy, *The Collapse of the Austro–Hungarian Empire* (London, 1930). A recent scholarly account, which supersedes these in many ways, is Z. A. B. Zeman, *The Break-up of the Habsburg Empire 1914–1918* (London, 1961).

EASTERN EUROPE AND THE BALKANS

The best general survey, covering both world wars, and with an excellent bibliography, is C. A. Macartney and A. W. Palmer, *Independent Eastern Europe* (London, 1962). An interesting account of American policy towards central Europe can be found in V. S. Mamatey, *The United States and East Central Europe 1914–1918* (Oxford, 1958).

A wartime appraisal of the national potential of eastern Europe by a British diplomatic historian is G. P. Gooch, *The Races of Austria–Hungary* (London, 1917). For the Balkans, R. W. Seton-Watson, *The Rise of Nationality in the Balkans* (London, 1917) is a plea in favour of Balkan nationalism, particularly of the Serb variety; while M. E. Durham, *Twenty Years of Balkan Tangle* (London, 1920) is less impressed with the Serb case.

The story of the war in Montenegro can be read in Alexander Devine, *Montenegro* (London, 1918). A somewhat obscure corner of the Balkans is dealt with in detail by Edith P. Stickney, *Southern Albania or Northern Epirus in International Affairs 1912–1923* (Stanford, 1926)

SERBIA AND YUGOSLAVIA

For Serbia's war effort a useful general survey is W. H. Crawfurd Price, *Serbia's Part in the War* (London, 1918). Two British ladies have left eye-witness accounts of the débâcle: Lady Ralph Paget, *With Our Serbian Allies,* 2 vols (London, 1915, 1916), and Caroline Matthews *Experiences of A Woman Doctor in Serbia* (London, 1918). The Cambridge historian G. M. Trevelyan contributed to the pro-Serbian polemic in a pamphlet *The Serbians and Austrians* (London, 1915).

The Jugoslav Committee in London produced a series of pamphlets and appeals in favour of a South Slav state, the first of which was *Appeal to the British Nation and Parliament* (London, 1915). The best account of the formation of Yugoslavia is Henry Baerlein, *The Birth of Yugoslavia,* 2 vols (London, 1922).

GREECE

Two books written from opposing view-points give a glimpse of the complexities and antagonisms of Greek politics during the First World War: P. N. Ure, *Venizelos and his Fellow-Countrymen* (London, 1917) and George M. Melas, *Ex-King Constantine and the War* (London, 1920). There is a perceptive study of Graeco–Turkish national problems by A. J. Toynbee, *The Western Question in Greece and Turkey* (London, 1922).

CZECHOSLOVAKIA

Two wartime pleas for statehood by two future Presidents are T. G. Masaryk, *Austrian Terrorism in Bohemia* (London, 1916) and E. Benes, *Bohemia's Case for*

Independence (London, 1917). A future distinguished British historian who entered into the argument in favour of the small nations was L. B. Namier in two booklets, *The Czecho-Slovaks, an Oppressed Nationality* (London, 1917) and *The Case for Bohemia* (London, 1917).

Somewhat more reflective accounts by the Czechoslovak statesmen themselves are T. G. Masaryk, *The Making of A State* (London, 1927) and E. Beneš, *My War Memoirs* (London, 1928). The fullest general history is R. W. Seton-Watson, *History of the Czechs and Slovaks* (London, 1943).

BULGARIA

An attempt to win British support for the Bulgarian case was made by Stojan Protić, *The Aspirations of Bulgaria* (London, 1915). A more general survey of Bulgarian history and claims, intended to influence Bulgaria's position as an enemy power at the Paris peace conference, was published by D. Mishew, *The Bulgarians in the Past* (Lausanne, 1919). There is a useful recent atlas of Bulgarian history compiled by D. Kosev and others, *Atlas po Bulgarska Istoria* (Sophia, 1963).

POLAND

Two wartime pamphlets seeking to enlist British support for Poland are Arnold J. Toynbee, *The Destruction of Poland* (London, 1916) and H. N. Brailsford, *Poland and the League of Nations* (London, 1917). The fullest account of Poland's emergence to nationhood as a result of the war can be found in T. Komarnicki, *The Rebirth of the Polish Republic* (London, 1957). A most useful recent historical atlas is W. Czaplinśky and T. Ladogórski, *Atlas Historyczny Polski* (Warsaw, 1968).

THE UNITED STATES OF AMERICA

A useful introductory survey is John Bach McMaster, *The United States in the World War 1914–1918* (New York and London, 1927). There is an interesting chapter on the First World War in George F. Kennan, *American Diplomacy 1900–1950* (London, 1952). The German attempt to persuade Mexico to declare war on the United States is described in Barbara Tuchman, *The Zimmerman Telegram* (London, 1957). Woodrow Wilson's policy can best be followed in his as yet uncompleted five-volume biography, Arthur S. Link, *Wilson* (Princeton, 1960–   ). A useful general study is E. R. May, *The World War and American Isolation* (Cambridge, 1959). For diplomatic aspects of the war, and of the peacemaking, the Department of State has published, as a supplement to *Papers Relating to the Foreign Relations of the United States,* two comprehensive documentary volumes, *The World War* (Washington, 1933) and *Papers Relating to the Foreign Relations of the United States: The Paris Peace Conference 1919,* 13 vols (Washington, 1942–1947). The most detailed account of America at war is in F. H. Simonds, *History of the World War,* 5 vols (New York, 1917–1920).

The American Ambassador in London has left an interesting account of the wartime period which forms a part of Burton J. Hendrick, *The Life and Letters of Walter H. Page,* 3 vols (London, 1925). The American Ambassador in Berlin likewise left an account of his experiences, James W. Gerard, *My Four Years in Germany* (London, 1917), as did his colleague in Constantinople, Henry Morgenthau, *Secrets of the Bosphorus* (London, 1918). The German Ambassador in Washington also wrote his story, Johann H. Von Bernstorff, *My Three Years in America,* (New York, 1920).

The Peace negotiations dominate American writings on the war. Three useful volumes covering this aspect are Robert Lansing, *The Big Four and Others of the Peace Conference* (Boston, 1921), and *The Peace Negotiations: A Personal Narrative* (Boston, 1921); and J. T. Shotwell, *At the Paris Peace Conference* (New York, 1937).

TREATIES AND REPARATIONS

The wartime secret treaties were made public by the Bolsheviks immediately they seized power, and were first published in English by F. S. Cocks, *The Secret Treaties and Agreements* (London, 1918). There is a recent scholarly study of both the Constantinople agreements and the Treaty of London by W. Gottlieb, *Studies in Secret Diplomacy* (London, 1957). For the Peace Treaties themselves the most comprehensive account is still Sir H. W. V. Temperley (ed), *A History of the Peace Conference of Paris,* 6 vols (London, 1920–1924). This contains a superb essay by L. B. Namier on the disintegration of the Habsburg monarchy.

For specific treaties I have consulted F. Deak, *Hungary at the Paris Peace Conference* (New York, 1942); R. H. Lutz and G. Almond, *The Treaty of Saint Germain* (Stanford, 1935); I. F. D. Morrow, *The Peace Settlement in the German–Polish Borderlands* (Oxford, 1936); Sherman David Spector, *Rumania at the Peace Conference* (New York, 1962); and George Louis Beer, *African Questions at the Paris Peace Conference* (New York, 1923). The complexities of Italian policy during the peace negotiations are unravelled by R. Albrecht-Carrié, *Italy at the Paris Peace Conference* (New York, 1938).

A literary masterpiece, which also includes some contemporary diary material, is Harold Nicolson, *Peacemaking 1919* (London, 1933). The British Prime Minister defended and explained his policy with characteristic vigour in David Lloyd George, *The Truth About the Peace Treaties,* 2 vols (London, 1938). A recent study of the evolution of the controversial war guilt clause, and of the part which the Treaty played in influencing the British policy of appeasement between the wars is to be found in Martin Gilbert, *The Roots of Appeasement* (London, 1966). The Treaty of Versailles itself can be read in a small and useful edition of primary material, Arthur Berriedale Keith (ed), *Speeches and Documents on International Affairs 1918–1937* (London, 1938).

The story of reparations has not yet been given a full scholarly study. The British Prime Minister put his case in David Lloyd George, *The Truth about Reparations and War Debts* (London, 1932). A British Treasury official who had taken part in the negotiations in Paris was responsible for the most outspoken and most influential criticism of reparations, J. M. Keynes, *The Economic Consequences of the Peace* (London, 1919). This was answered by Etienne Mantoux, *The Carthaginian Peace* (London, 1952). The American view was given by one of the American architects of the settlement, Bernard M. Baruch, *The Making of Reparations and the Economic Sections of the Treaty* (New York, 1920).

Index

compiled by the author